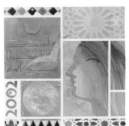

THE ARAB HUMAN DEVELOPMENT REPORT 2002

Creating Opportunities for Future Generations

UN
D P

SPONSORED BY THE REGIONAL BUREAU
FOR ARAB STATES / UNDP

ARAB FUND FOR ECONOMIC AND
SOCIAL DEVELOPMENT

D1254080

Available through:
United Nations Publications
Room DC2-853
New York, NY 10017
USA

Telephone: 212 963 8302 and 800 253 9646 (From the United States)
Email: Publications@un.org
Web: www.un.org/Publications
Web: www.undp.org/rbas

Cover design: Khaled Samar
Layout and Production: SYNTAX, Amman, Jordan
Printed at: National Press, Amman, Jordan

ISBN: 92-1-126147-3

Printed in the Hashemite Kingdom of Jordan

Foreword By the Administrator, UNDP

The United Nations Development Programme has issued annual Human Development Reports (HDRs) since 1990. Building on the work of Nobel Prize-winner Amartya Sen and others, the first HDR was a groundbreaking effort to assess the state of global development from a people-centered perspective that puts the expansion of human capabilities, choices and opportunities at the centre of the development process. The pioneering Human Development Index (HDI) also provided a powerful new way of assessing a country's success in meeting the needs of its citizens that looked beyond simple measures of wealth creation.

Successive HDRs have followed that path and fleshed out new approaches to strengthening human development and human security, in the process helping to catalyze a broader revolution in the policies and programmes of development agencies and many developing countries themselves. That process has been stimulated and accelerated in recent years by the production of a growing number of regional, sub-regional and national HDRs that have proven to be powerful tools for advocacy and national policy development.

To date, UNDP has helped prepare 35 national and sub-national HDRs for 17 Arab States. As the region as whole seeks to confront a growing range of political, social and economic challenges from unemployment and poverty reduction to peace and enhanced human security, we believe the time is right for a study that assesses the current state of human development across the region and offers some concrete suggestions on how to accelerate progress in the future. In light of recent events and tragedies, it seems important to ask how the region is doing in allowing political voice to its citizens and in meeting the economic and social aspirations of all the men and women of the region. Is economic and social reform keeping pace with demographic growth and demands for a better life?

This report, the first regional HDR for the Arab States, is the result, covering a total of 22 countries from the Maghreb to the Gulf. The report has some encouraging findings. Overall, it shows that Arab states have made substantial progress in human development over the past three decades. Life expectancy has increased by about 15 years; mortality rates for children under five years of age have fallen by about two thirds; adult literacy has almost doubled—and women's literacy has trebled—reflecting very large increases in gross educational enrollments, including those of girls. Daily caloric intake and access to safe water are higher, and the incidence of dire poverty is lower than in any other developing region.

But the report also makes it clear how much still needs to be done to provide current and future generations with the political voice, social choices and economic opportunities they need to build a better future for themselves and their families. It notes that quantitative improvements in health and education have not yet reached all citizens, and finds that too often expansion of services has not been matched by needed qualitative improvements in their delivery. It underlines how far the Arab states still need to go in order to join the global information society and economy as full partners, and to tackle the human and economic scourge of joblessness, which afflicts Arab countries as a group more seriously than any other developing region. And it clearly outlines the challenges for Arab states in terms of strengthening personal freedoms and boosting broad-based citizen participation in political and economic affairs.

The report was prepared by a team of

Arab scholars, with the advice of a distinguished panel of policymakers in the region. As with all Human Development Reports, the conclusions are not in any way a statement of UNDP policy. The disclaimer is particularly important on this occasion, as it is independent experts from the region rather than UNDP who have placed their societies under a sympathetic but critical examination and have exposed strengths, weaknesses, opportunities and threats about themselves in a way that perhaps only Arabs should.

So this is not the grandstanding of outsiders but an honest, if controversial, view through the mirror. As such, it is aimed at stimulating discussion and debate by policymakers, practitioners and the general public alike on how best to tackle the most pressing challenges to improving human development across the region. In that context, we hope its real contribution will be to help Arab countries to continue to advance the fundamental purpose of development—helping their citizens build richer, more fulfilling lives for themselves and their children.

Mark Malloch Brown.
Administrator, UNDP

Foreword by the Director General and Chairman of the Board of Directors, Arab Fund for Economic and Social Development

I am honoured to join hands with UNDP in sponsoring this report, which examines important issues and essential facets of human development in the Arab countries. The report covers critical challenges in health, education, science and technology and the environment, as well as prospects for job creation and Arab cooperation, highlighting development and progress in all these fields. The report further sheds light on the provision of opportunities and incentives for coming generations. In doing so, it looks at reforming education, stimulating research and development, securing appropriate health and environmental requirements, revitalizing economic growth, creating suitable mechanisms for the fair distribution of wealth, developing and activating institutional structures to manage the economy and promoting civil society.

The world is experiencing massive transformations driven by unprecedented and rapid technological progress in production, distribution and information and communications technologies. These world developments are linked to more openness, liberalization, transnational production integration and financial synergy on the one hand and to a trend for nations to merge into megaeconomic blocs on the other. In this context, the role of technology and know-how in creating value added has become crucial. Central to these huge developments in any society are the capabilities of people and the extent of scientific and cultural progress. All development starts with human development. This in turn emphasizes the importance of ensuring basic human rights and enhancing people's creative potential and talents as fundamental factors in the progress of any nation. Furthermore, all these elements constitute the core of international efforts in the political, economic and social fields.

Arab countries have undoubtedly seen remarkable economic and social achievements during the past three decades. But with the advent of the twenty-first century, they have started to face deep and complex economic and social problems that negatively affect their present and future. These problems comprise, inter alia, high illiteracy rates, the deterioration of education, the slow-down of scientific research and technological development, poor production bases and competitive capacity, rampant poverty and mounting unemployment rates. All these conditions compel Arab countries to adopt a balanced package of reforms so as to promote the well being of the community at large. This can be realized through reconsidering the content and goals of education and scientific research; developing institutional structures and cadres; enhancing production and services in quantitative and qualitative terms; and promoting joint and integrated initiatives among the Arab countries. Human well being is not limited to material or purely economic dimensions. It also denotes freedom, justice and partnership, which are indivisible aspects of a decent human life.

Consequently, the Arab Fund for Economic and Social Development gives due attention to the broader developmental priorities of Arab countries. The Fund has financed a wide range of social development projects and programmes. These have included rural development projects, credit schemes, social safety nets for the poor and unemployed, as well as development management, training and institutional support programmes. These efforts have targeted the social dimension of development and supported the endeavours of Arab countries to administer justice and secure a decent life for their citizens, especially in rural, poor and remote areas.

A pause is essential to take stock of the present state of, and means for achieving human development in the Arab region. The goal is to enhance human dignity and rights in Arab societies and improve levels of welfare for the whole Arab community. This is difficult to achieve without a free, educated human being fully aware of his or her role in building the future. Such conditions, in turn, require the creation of a favourable environment for these orientations to bear fruit.

The Arab Fund for Economic and Social Development and UNDP seek, through their modest efforts, to help the Arab people and countries to develop a more solid understanding of their problems and assets, deficiencies and opportunities. This constructive scrutiny of challenges to Arab human development is designed to enrich knowledge and cast light on ways and means of enhancing the essential components of human well being and human betterment. We are fully confident that Arab countries enjoy, in ample measure, the assets and resources needed to achieve these ends once serious and appropriate programmes are developed and implemented.

Abdel Latif Youssef El Hamed
Director General/ Chairman of the Board of
Directors, Arab Fund for Economic and
Social Development

Foreword by the Regional Director, UNDP/Regional Bureau for Arab States

The focus of this Report is the people of the Arab world, the citizens of the 22 member states of the Arab League. Although the countries constituting the Arab region vary significantly, in area, in population size, in physical and ecological features, and in levels of human well being, they are unified by unbreakable ties. Foremost among these is a common language and a vibrant cultural heritage that today still lives potently in a common cultural context that unites these peoples even when they, at times, go separate ways.

At the heart of this large mass of humanity, spread over a vast landscape, stand the Arab children, who constitute the 'coming generations' of the sub-title. Indeed, the Report team is especially mindful of the children of marginalized and oppressed Arabs, not excluding the Palestinian children, who, deprived of a homeland and fundamental human rights, have lost their lives in defence of freedom and national independence.

No generation of young Arabs has been as large as that of today. The Report sees, in each one of those young people, the makings of tomorrow's champions of human development in Arab countries. For that reason, the Report team has dedicated this first issue in a new series of Arab Human Development Reports to "coming generations". Its messages are, first and foremost, about building better opportunities for them.

The chapters that follow show that Arab countries have made significant strides in more than one area of human development in the last three decades. Nevertheless, the predominant characteristic of the current Arab reality seems to be the existence of deeply rooted shortcomings in Arab institutional structures. These shortcomings pose serious obstacles to human development and are summarised as the three deficits relating to free-dom, empowerment of women, and knowledge. They constitute weighty constraints on human capability that must be lifted.

From a positive perspective, the realization of human development in the Arab world requires transcending current shortcomings and transforming them into their opposites, that is, into advantages enjoyed by all Arabs and assets all Arab countries can be proud of in the Third Millennium.

Specifically, the Report concludes that Arab countries need to embark on rebuilding their societies on the basis of:
* Full respect for human rights and human freedoms as the cornerstones of good governance, leading to human development
* The complete empowerment of Arab women, taking advantage of all opportunities to build their capabilities and to enable them to exercise those capabilities to the full.
* The consolidation of knowledge acquisition and its effective utilisation. As a key driver of progress, knowledge must be brought to bear efficiently and productively in all aspects of society, with the goal of enhancing human well being across the region.

These priorities form the essence of the necessary transcendence required to overcome the crisis of human development in the Arab region. They are however by no means the ultimate target. The transcendence of current Arab shortcomings requires building Arab productive capabilities in the face of the rentier nature of Arab economies and societies. To achieve human development requires not only reforming governance regimes at the national and pan-Arab levels on a solid foundation of freedoms and economic dynamism, but also the strengthening of Arab co-operation in order to maximize the benefits of globalisation and avoid its perils.

Lagging human development constitutes a

major obstacle that prevents the Arab region from confronting the challenges of globalization. It clearly strips the region of any comparative advantage as it prepares to enter the 21st century. Indeed, it can be argued that building human development in Arab countries has become an absolute necessity for survival in the age of globalization.

The most important resource, however, for the realization of the vision outlined in this Report is unleashing the innovative energies of all Arabs, in the context of an enabling social contract. In the end, bold thinking holds the key to realizing, as opposed to only conceiving of, grand visions for the future. Great goals require great acts. Short-run "fixes" may be easier to adopt but cannot return the large results now required.

An accurate diagnosis of a problem is an important part of the solution. It is precisely for this reason that the Regional Bureau for Arab States has commissioned a group of distinguished Arab intellectuals to prepare this Report. The wealth of unbiased, objective analysis it contains is part of our contribution to Arab peoples and policy-makers in the search for a brighter future.

Naturally, not everyone will agree with every point made in this Report. Yet I think most will recognize that the endeavour is rigorous and well grounded and that the commitment to a brighter Arab future shines through on every page.

ACKNOWLEDGEMENTS

I want to thank lead author Nader Fergany for his sustained creative contributions and the entire editorial team for their tireless endeavours. I am especially grateful for the support of the Arab Fund for Economic and Social Development, the co-sponsors of this Report and our closest collaborators in its preparation. My thanks also go to the independent Advisory Board for providing quality guidance throughout the process and to Mark Malloch Brown, Administrator of UNDP, and many colleagues for their advice and support.

Dr. Rima Khalaf Hunaidi
Assistant Secretary General and Assistant Administrator, Regional Director,
Regional Bureau for Arab States United Nations Development Programme

AEUC	Arab Economic Unity Council
AFESD	Arab Fund for Economic and Social Development
AFTA	Arab Free Trade Area
AHDI	alternative human development index
AHDR	Arab Human Development Report
ALECSO	Arab League Educational, Cultural and Scientific Organization
AMF	Arab Monetary Fund
APEC	Asia-Pacific Economic Cooperation
BTU	British thermal unit
CAUS	Centre for Arab Unity Studies
CDE	carbon dioxide emissions per capita
CEDAW	Convention on the Elimination of All Forms of Discrimination against Women
CEDO	consulting and engineering development organization
CIS	Commonwealth of Independent States
CSO	civil-society organization
DALE	disability-adjusted expectation of life at birth
DARPA	Defense Advanced Research Projects Agency
EA	educational attainment
EAP	East Asia and the Pacific
ECA	Economic Commission for Africa
ESCWA	Economic and Social Commission for Western Asia
FAO	Food and Agriculture Organization of the United Nations
FCND	Food Consumption and Nutrition Division
FDI	foreign direct investment
FS	freedom score
GATT	General Agreement on Tariffs and Trade
GCC	Gulf Cooperation Council
GDP	gross domestic product
GEM	gender empowerment measure
GNP	gross national product
HDI	human development index
HDR	Human Development Report
HHW	high human welfare
HPI	human poverty index
HW-F	human welfare--freedoms and institutions
HW-T	human welfare--transparency
ICT	information and communication technology
IFPRI	International Food Policy Research Institute
IH	Internet hosts per capita
ILO	International Labour Organization
IMF	International Monetary Fund
IMR	infant mortality rate

IPPF	International Planned Parenthood Federation
LAC	Latin America and the Caribbean
LE	life expectancy at birth
LHW	low human welfare
LLP	local loop
MENA	Middle East and North Africa
MHW	medium human welfare
MMR	maternal mortality rate
NAFTA	North America Free Trade Agreement
NGO	non-governmental organization
NHDR	national human development report
OECD	Organisation for Economic Co-operation and Development
PAPCHILD	Pan Arab Project for Child Development
PPP	purchasing power parity
R&D	research and technological development
RBAS	Regional Bureau for Arab States
S&T	science and technology
SA	South Asia
SSA	sub-Saharan Africa
TACC	Technology Access Communication Centre
TAI	technology achievement index
TFR	total fertility rate
UNDP	United Nations Development Programme
UNEP	United Nations Environment Programme
UNESCO	United Nations Educational, Scientific and Cultural Organization
UNFPA	United Nations Population Fund
UNICEF	United Nations Children's Fund
UNIDO	United Nations Industrial Development Organization
UNOPS	United Nations Office for Project Services
WHO	World Health Organization
WRI	World Research Institute
WTO	World Trade Organization

Contents

Foreword By the Administrator, UNDP
Foreword by the Director General and Chairman of the Board of Directors, Arab Fund for Economic and Social Development
Foreword by the Regional Director, UNDP/Regional Bureau for Arab States

CHAPTER 6

CHAPTER 7

CHAPTER 8

List of boxes

List of figures

List of tables

In the text

In the Statistical Annex

(Tables 1-37 listed separately in statistical annex)

The analysis and policy recommendation of this Report do not necessarily reflect the views of the United Nations Development Programme, its Executive Board or its Member States. The Report is the work of an independent team of authors sponsored by the Regional Bureau for Arab States.

A future for all

From the Atlantic to the Gulf, people--women, men and children--are the real wealth and hope of Arab countries. Policies for development and growth in the Arab region must focus on freeing people from deprivation, in all its forms, and expanding their choices. Over the last five decades, remarkable progress has been achieved in advancing human development and reducing poverty. However, much still needs to be done to address the backlog of deprivation and imbalance.

Looking forward, much also needs to be done in order to empower the people of the Arab region to participate fully in the world of the twenty-first century. Globalization and accelerating technological advances have opened doors to unprecedented opportunities, but they have also posed a new risk: that of being left behind as the rate of change accelerates, often outpacing state capacity. Development is being reinvented by new markets (e.g., foreign exchange and capital markets), new tools (e.g., the Internet and cellular phones), new actors (e.g., non-governmental organizations, the European Union and World Trade Organization) and new rules (e.g., multilateral agreements on trade, services and intellectual property).

CHALLENGES

Entering the new millennium, people in Arab countries face two intertwined sets of challenges to peace and to development. The first set has been made ever more conspicuous and pressing after the tragic events of 11 September 2001. These are the challenges to the pursuit of freedom from fear. Regional and external factors intersect in this realm of peace and security. The second set of challenges is equally important if not more critical.

It encompasses challenges to the achievement of freedom from want. These are the challenges faced by people and governments, states and societies as they attempt to advance human development. These challenges are fundamental, not only for their instrumental significance to development and growth but also for their intrinsic value. Equity, knowledge and the freedom and human rights integral to good governance matter for their own sake as well as for their critical role as enablers of development. They are both means and ends. They are central to both the process and the state of human development. Some key aspects of both sets of challenges are highlighted below.

OCCUPATION STIFLES PROGRESS

Israel's illegal occupation of Arab lands is one of the most pervasive obstacles to security and progress in the region geographically (since it affects the entire region), temporally (extending over decades) and developmentally (impacting nearly all aspects of human development and human security, directly for millions and indirectly for others). The human cost extends beyond the considerable loss of lives and livelihoods of direct victims. If human development is the process of enlarging choices, if it implies that people must influence the processes that shape their lives, and if it means the full enjoyment of human rights, then nothing stifles that noble vision of development more than subjecting a people to foreign occupation.

Firstly, for Palestinians, occupation and the policies that support it, stunt their ability to grow in every conceivable way. The confiscation of Palestinian land, constraining their access to their water and other natural resources, the imposition of obstacles to the free

From the Atlantic to the Gulf, people--women, men and children--are the real wealth and hope of Arab countries.

movement of people and goods, and structural impediments to employment and economic self-management all combine to thwart the emergence of a viable economy and a secure independent state. Moreover, the expansion of illegal settlements, the frequent use of excessive force against Palestinians and the denial of their most basic human rights further circumscribe their potential to build human development. The plight of Palestinian refugees living in other countries is a further manifestation of development disfigured by occupation.

Secondly, occupation casts a pall across the political and economic life of the entire region. Among neighbouring countries, some continue to suffer themselves from Israeli occupation of parts of their lands, subjecting those people directly affected to tremendous suffering, and imposing development challenges on the rest. In most Arab states, occupation dominates national policy priorities, creates large humanitarian challenges for those receiving refugees and motivates the diversion of public investment in human development towards military spending. By symbolizing a felt and constant external threat, occupation has damaging side effects: it provides both a cause and an excuse for distorting the development agenda, disrupting national priorities and retarding political development. At certain junctures it can serve to solidify the public against an outside aggressor and justify curbing dissent at a time when democratic transition requires greater pluralism in society and more public debate on national development policies. In all these ways, occupation freezes growth, prosperity and freedom in the Arab world.

CONFLICTS, SANCTIONS AND INSTABILITY PREVENT DEVELOPMENT

Political upheavals, military conflicts, sanctions and embargoes have affected many economies of the region, causing declines in productivity and disrupting markets. Some countries struggling to recover from the ravages of war have emerged with substantial debts, limiting options for public expenditure. All affected countries have emerged with compounded socio-political problems that have

retarded progressive moves towards liberalization and democratization.

The direct impact of wars is registered in slowed growth, damaged infrastructure, social fragmentation and public-sector stagnation. Some countries have experienced hyperinflation, severe currency devaluations and curtailed foreign-currency earnings. Others have seen their standing in the international community collapse. Most affected countries have lost important human and capital resources critical for the renewal of stability and competitiveness.

ASPIRATIONS FOR FREEDOM AND DEMOCRACY REMAIN UNFULFILLED

There is a substantial lag between Arab countries and other regions in terms of participatory governance. The wave of democracy that transformed governance in most of Latin America and East Asia in the 1980s and Eastern Europe and much of Central Asia in the late 1980s and early 1990s has barely reached the Arab States. This freedom deficit undermines human development and is one of the most painful manifestations of lagging political development. While de jure acceptance of democracy and human rights is enshrined in constitutions, legal codes and government pronouncements, de facto implementation is often neglected and, in some cases, deliberately disregarded.

In most cases, the governance pattern is characterized by a powerful executive branch that exerts significant control over all other branches of the state, being in some cases free from institutional checks and balances. Representative democracy is not always genuine and sometimes absent. Freedoms of expression and association are frequently curtailed. Obsolete norms of legitimacy prevail.

DEVELOPMENT NOT ENGENDERED IS ENDANGERED

Gender inequality is the most pervasive manifestation of inequity of all kinds in any society because it typically affects half the population. There have been important quantitative improvements with respect to building women's capabilities in recent years. For example, Arab countries have shown the fastest improvements in female education of any region. Women's literacy rates have expanded three-fold since 1970; female primary and secondary enrolment rates have more than doubled. However, these achievements have not succeeded in countering gender-based social attitudes and norms that exclusively stress women's reproductive role and reinforce the gender-based asymmetry of unpaid care. As a consequence, more than half of Arab women are still illiterate. The region's maternal mortality rate is double that of Latin America and the Caribbean, and four times that of East Asia.

Women also suffer from unequal citizenship and legal entitlements, often evident in voting rights and legal codes. The utilization of Arab women's capabilities through political and economic participation remains the lowest in the world in quantitative terms, as evidenced by the very low share of women in parliaments, cabinets, and the work force and in the trend towards the feminization of unemployment. Qualitatively, women suffer from inequality of opportunity, evident in employment status, wages and gender-based occupational segregation. Society as a whole suffers when a huge proportion of its productive potential is stifled, resulting in lower family incomes and standards of living.

BRIDLED MINDS, SHACKLED POTENTIAL

About 65 million adult Arabs are illiterate, two thirds of them women. Illiteracy rates are much higher than in much poorer countries. This challenge is unlikely to disappear quickly. Ten million children between 6 and 15 years of age are currently out of school; if current trends persist, this number will increase by 40 per cent by 2015. The challenge is far more than overcoming the under-supply of knowledge to people. Equally important is overcoming the under-supply of knowledgeable people, a problem exacerbated by the low quality of education together with the lack of mechanisms for intellectual capital development and use.

A major mismatch exists between the output of educational systems and labour-market needs. The mismatch is compounded by the increasingly rapid change in these needs brought about by globalization and the needs of accelerating technology.

Arab countries' access to and use of cutting edge technology, exemplified by information and communication technology (ICT), is very limited. Only 0.6 per cent of the population uses the Internet and the personal computer penetration rate is only 1.2 per cent. More generally, investment in research and development does not exceed 0.5 per cent of gross national product, well below the world average. Moreover, while the production of scientific papers in the Arab region is within the range of leading third-world countries, the use of national scientific expertise is at much lower levels.

Addressing the knowledge challenge matters critically, both because knowledgeable people and a knowledge society are worthy objectives in themselves and because education and knowledge, as aspects of human capability and as proxies for increased human choice, are intrinsically linked to growth and equity. Failure to address capability deficits holds back human development in the larger sense of the concept. While the human development index (HDI) of the United Nations Development Programme (UNDP) measures some aspects of capability, it does not embrace other, wider variables such as freedom and human rights (or others such as knowledge acquisition, the institutional context and environmental responsibility). Yet the relationship between human development and human rights is of fundamental importance. It is a mutually reinforcing relationship where the common denominator is human freedom. Human development, by enhancing human capabilities, creates the ability to exercise freedom, and human rights, by providing the necessary framework, create the opportunities to exercise it. Freedom is the guarantor and the goal of both human development and human rights.

The utilization of Arab women's capabilities through political and economic participation remains the lowest in the world.

Failure to address capability deficits holds back human development in the larger sense of the concept.

Improving economic governance, including management of development, is a primary challenge for Arab countries. Despite largely successful stabilization in the 1990s, evident in modest subsequent levels of inflation and budget deficits, growth continues to stagnate and to be overly vulnerable to fluctuations in oil prices. The quality of public institutions, as measured by poor cost-effectiveness and heavy regulatory burdens, is low. Critical macro variables are still under-performing, including employment, savings, productivity and non-oil exports. At about 15 per cent, average unemployment across Arab countries is among the highest rates in the developing world. Unemployment is a human-development tragedy as well as a drag on economic progress. Restoring growth will be critical to attacking it, but the economies in the region would have to grow at a minimum annual rate of five per cent to absorb the currently unemployed and provide jobs for new labour-market entrants.

Trade performance has remained sluggish and the region is still relatively closed. In some countries, tariffs are high and non-tariff barriers remain important. Throughout the 1990s, exports from the region (over 70 per cent of which are accounted for by oil and oil-related products) grew at 1.5 per cent per year, far below the global rate of six per cent. Manufacturing exports have remained stagnant and private-capital flows have lagged behind those of other regions. Arab governments are taking steps to improve this state of affairs through policy initiatives to promote trade expansion as an engine of economic (including technological) development. The creation of the Arab Free Trade Area, expanding accession to the World Trade Organization and association with the European Union are formal expressions of policies that promote trade and move towards greater integration with the global economy.

Governments have had considerable success in providing growth-supporting physical infrastructure. On the other hand, the state's role in promoting, complementing and regulating markets for goods, services and factors

of production has been both constrained and constraining. Partly as a consequence, the formal private sector's contribution to development has often been hesitant and certainly below expectations. While the share of the private sector in total investment has increased, its performance with respect to job creation and exports remains unduly limited. Markets remain incomplete. Uncorrected market failures result in inefficient outcomes.

Both growth and equity considerations make promoting dynamic private-sector development a critical priority of economic governance in Arab countries. Most countries in the region formerly adopted, and some long adhered to, now discredited statist, inward-looking development models. These models may have been appropriate in early post-independence years, but they now serve neither governments (which need rapid economic growth in order to achieve policy objectives, including human-development objectives with respect to, e.g., health care, education and provision of social safety nets) nor people (who seek more good jobs with decent wages and working conditions).

Governments in many countries have taken important steps to liberate the private sector, but a large unfinished agenda remains. Sound macroeconomic policies need to be maintained; adequate economic space needs to be provided for private initiative; central banks, banking systems in general, and financial services need to be strengthened; bureaucracy needs to be streamlined and red tape minimized. In addition, a transparent rule of law, a visibly fair and appropriately swift legal system, and an efficient and professional judiciary need to become universal; and public-sector reform needs to be designed in terms of providing incentive structures to encourage private-sector investment and growth.

At the same time, beneficial regulation-- for example, measures to curb monopoly, whether in the public or the private sector-- needs be strengthened and enforced; graft and cronyism need to be firmly and comprehensively addressed. These and other distortions of incentive systems have human-development as well as economic-development costs in terms of denying merit its appropriate reward and discouraging human initiative.

Markets remain incomplete. Uncorrected market failures result in inefficient outcomes.

Another area for exploration is greater regional economic cooperation. Domestic markets in many Arab economies are too small to provide the basis for dynamic, diversified and sustainable growth based on vibrant private manufacturing and services sectors. The Arab Free Trade Area is a step in the right direction, provided it lives up to its promise. However, countries may need to consider deeper integration both among themselves via moving towards a customs union or a common market and with external partners through, for example, the association agreements with the European Union that several countries have already signed. These two trends can be mutually reinforcing; the returns from association agreements can be multiplied if regional integration arrangements are in place. Finally in this connection, regional associations that address economic cooperation or shared infrastructure development need to be revitalized and supported.

The capacity of the state has fallen short of the requirement to foster rapid growth, just as it has fallen short of the demands of human development in key areas such as health and education. Financial resources have not been the binding constraint: government spending as a percentage of gross domestic product is higher than in other developing regions. While policy changes, supported by inter- and intra-sectoral reallocation of public spending, would certainly enhance effectiveness, institutional arrangements and human resources are more binding constraints. They are evident in lack of accountability, transparency and integrity, along with ineffectiveness, inefficiency and unresponsiveness to the demands of peoples and of development.

The challenge of addressing these impediments and achieving better governance increases with the strains imposed on institutional structures and mechanisms by the combination of the expectations of a better-informed and more knowledgeable public at home together with external forces such as globalization and increasingly rapid technological progress. These changes have transformed the role of the state and its relationship with markets and civil society. Governments have only begun to adapt: state-NGO relationships, for example, are often managed as a zero-sum game.

The technological revolution has also changed key determinants of production and growth, placing more emphasis on the acquisition of knowledge and its application to social and development goals. At a time when the development prospects of Arab countries are increasingly linked to the capabilities of their work forces and the quality of their intellectual capital, addressing the knowledge gap is a critical challenge.

THE CURSE OF POVERTY: DENYING CHOICES AND OPPORTUNITIES, DEGRADING LIVES

Meeting the challenge of achieving more equitable societies, polities and economies requires a determined effort to attack poverty. While the Arab countries have the lowest level of dire poverty in the world, it remains the case that one out of every five people lives on less than $2 per day, according to World Bank estimates for the Middle East and North Africa. Moreover, income poverty is only part of the story. Poor or unavailable health care or opportunities for a quality education, a degraded habitat--whether a polluted urban slum or a rural livelihood eked out on exhausted soil--scant or non-existent social safety nets: all form part of the nexus of poverty and are widely prevalent in Arab countries.

Inequality of capabilities and of opportunities is actually more pronounced than income poverty and economic inequality. Deprivation in terms of basic human-development parameters is about 32.4 per cent as measured by the human poverty index (HPI), which defines deprivation in terms of short lives, illiteracy and lack of basic services.

It is now well established that economic growth is not a sufficient condition for eliminating income poverty but that it is certainly a necessary one. The same applies to capability poverty, which leads to inadequate human development. However it is defined, poverty retards growth prospects. Income poverty acts as a dead weight on an economy; human-development poverty limits people's and countries' capacity to make the best use of their resources, both human and material. The fact that income poverty is relatively low in Arab countries should be no cause for complacency

At a time when the development prospects of Arab countries are increasingly linked to the capabilities of their work forces and the quality of their intellectual capital, addressing the knowledge gap is a critical challenge.

when other dimensions of poverty remain substantial.

STRATEGY

The core peace and development challenges facing the Arab people are interlinked. While issues of occupation and conflict are beyond the purview of this Report, the subsections that follow synthesize aspects of a strategy for enhancing human development.

Given the importance of capturing broader challenges to human development in its fullest sense, challenges related to increasing freedom, gender equality, knowledge acquisition and environmental choice, the Report poses the question: is it not now time to look beyond the limited measurement of human development, as reflected in the HDI? In a personal contribution to the Report, its lead author explores the parameters, methodology and impact of an alternative index that could be the starting point for further research into a more insightful approach to measuring human development.

The Arab region is living in a time of accelerating change against a backdrop of increased globalization. Success in meeting today's challenges will depend on the ability to shape, and adapt to, the demands of the new economics and the new politics. Enhanced knowledge development, broadly defined, and advances in human freedom, exemplified by political and economic participation, along with a proper appreciation of the role of culture and values, could together form the foundation of a human-development path for the Arab region that responds creatively to people's aspirations for a better life and effectively taps the forces shaping the twenty-first century.

TOWARDS A KNOWLEDGE SOCIETY

Knowledge is a cornerstone of development, and its importance is increasing in an age of accelerating technological change and globalization. It is a public good that underpins economies, polities and societies, permeating all aspects of human activity. This Report suggests that Arab countries face a significant knowledge gap. Overcoming it will not be easy because knowledge, broadly defined, is a moving target; its frontiers are constantly expanding. To address the knowledge gap, it will be necessary to take simultaneous action in three linked and potentially synergistic areas: knowledge absorption, acquisition and communication.

The value of knowledge for development depends on its effective application. Therefore, working towards a knowledge society requires multisectoral strategies that integrate absorption, acquisition and communication -- for example, through links among education systems, training systems and public- and private-sector labour-market demand. Similarly, innovators, researchers and policy analysts need to be connected with producers and policy-makers. Knowledge-development strategies need to be seen as being the concern of society as a whole and of socioeconomic actors across the board -- government agencies, the private sector and civil society, particularly in local communities -- thus promoting better alignment of the structure, inputs and outputs of education, training and research systems with the requirements of production, human welfare and the development process as a whole.

Knowledge absorption involves providing people with the capacity to use knowledge via education. Despite the problems noted earlier, Arab countries have made major progress in expanding education and literacy over the years. By 1995, over 90 per cent of males and 75 per cent of females were enrolled in primary schooling, and nearly 60 per cent of males and nearly 50 per cent of females were enrolled in secondary education. At the tertiary level, Arab countries outperformed all developing regions except for Latin America and the Caribbean in terms of enrolment levels for both males and females. Total enrolment for all levels rose from 31 million in 1980 to approximately 56 million in 1995. Literacy rates improved by nearly 50 per cent between 1980 and the mid-1990s. Female literacy rates have trebled since 1970.

These achievements reflect Arab governments' long-term commitment to building education systems that respond to the needs of new generations. Taken as a group, Arab countries spend a higher percentage of GDP

Success in meeting today's challenges will depend on the ability to shape, and adapt to, the demands of the new economics and the new politics.

on education than any other developing region, registering a 50 per cent increase (at current prices) between 1980 and 1995. Per capita spending on education is substantially higher than the developing-country average. Several countries in the region are undertaking major programmes of education-system reform.

Nevertheless, much remains to be done. Priorities include, inter alia, securing universal, high-quality basic education, especially for girls and other currently under-served groups; strengthening tertiary education, particularly in science and engineering; and eliminating illiteracy at one end of the education spectrum while also providing opportunities for lifetime learning for education-system graduates at the other. Lifetime learning is not a luxury; it is critical for knowledge absorption in a world of exploding new knowledge, rapid technological change and intense international competition.

Education is a basic human right and an end in itself; through its impact on productivity and other dimensions of life such as health, it is also a critical means of enhancing human well-being. In the economic sphere, research has underscored the benefits of the formation of human capital. A study of 192 countries concludes that human and social capital explain no less than 64 per cent of growth performance. By contrast, physical capital--machinery, buildings and infrastructure-- explains only 16 per cent of growth. The remainder is explained by natural capital. More specifically, global estimates show that a one percentage-point increase in the share of the labour force with secondary education is associated with a 6 to 15 percentage-point increase in the share of income received by the poorest 40 per cent. Thus, education serves both growth and equity. While the costs of improving education systems may be substantial, the costs of perpetuating ignorance are incalculably greater.

Investment in physical resources for education needs to be complemented by enhanced attention to quality, e.g., by emphasizing standards, by improving curricula and assessment, and by better training, managing and motivating teachers. It can also be complemented by cross-fertilization of ideas, experience, technologies and methodologies among Arab countries, backed by policy analysis and dissemination of relevant information, which are also critical for building and sustaining consensus on education and training reforms at the national level.

Effective *knowledge-acquisition strategies* may need to begin with attitudinal change, involving across-the-board commitment at all levels of society, from respect for science and knowledge, to encouraging creativity and innovation, to applying new discoveries to raise productivity and income and enhance human welfare. Attitudinal change can be supported by policies that provide incentives for enhancing both the social status and the opportunities for profit of workers in the fields of science, knowledge and innovation. Public policy also has a key role in fostering potentially productive research and development (R & D) and in supporting an environment that enables the private sector to apply new knowledge in response to market forces, e.g., by corporatizing research institutes, by offering companies incentives to contract relevant activities with public laboratories or one another, and by relying more on appropriately skilled and efficient Arab consultancy, engineering and development firms.

Knowledge acquisition entails not only building on a country's own knowledge base to generate new knowledge through R&D but also harnessing and adapting knowledge available elsewhere through openness, broadly defined, including, e.g., promoting the free flow of information and ideas, establishing constructive engagement in world markets, and attracting foreign investment. A commitment to openness is particularly important in view of the current weakness of technological development in Arab countries. This means that importing and adapting technology and internalizing it by learning-by-doing may be the most practical approach in this area, pending the establishment of the necessary conditions for dynamic local technological development, namely, a large, diverse and vibrant production system and a market large enough to justify the costs of technological development. This should not prevent undertaking work on areas of technology of special importance for the region (e.g., ICT, solar energy, and water

While the costs of improving education systems may be substantial, the costs of perpetuating ignorance are incalculably greater.

desalination), which could be supported in the wider context of enhanced Arab cooperation.

Beyond the Arab world, knowledge acquisition could be enhanced through links with advanced international research centres and other R&D institutions, provided that such links help to further scientific and technological development at home rather than deepening dependency on external sources. Learning from other developing countries with experience in capacity-building in science and technology may also pay dividends and form the basis for future South-South networking.

Arab countries could also capitalize on the expertise of the one million highly qualified Arabs working in industrialized countries. Linkages could be reinforced by, e.g., building systematic databases of external Arab experts, setting up efficient channels of communication with them, providing facilities for visits to Arab countries and arrangements for consultations or temporary work assignments, using ICT to facilitate knowledge transfer, and supporting associations of highly qualified Arabs abroad. Meanwhile, efforts might be made to stem the current brain drain of highly qualified Arabs by seeking to offer them viable alternative opportunities at home, where their work contributes to building domestic human capabilities.

Knowledge communication. The convergence of telecommunications and computing has vastly expanded the ability to disseminate information and reduce costs. Broadening access for all, including poor people, to ICT can greatly facilitate the acquisition and absorption of knowledge in Arab countries and offer unprecedented opportunities for education, policy formulation and implementation, and services to businesses and the poor. Strategies for knowledge communication need to be multisectoral, sensitive to the interrelationships between the sectors of communication, media and information, and open to ICT applications in fields such as education, culture and general health. Lowering the cost of Internet access is a high priority, achievable through regulatory arrangements that promote competition and prevent monopoly—factors that are also of special importance in the telecommunications sector, whether public or privatized. With respect to human re-

sources, computer-training specialists are a priority, as is training generally, especially for women, along with professional upgrading. Finally, coordination among Arab countries is important, both to ensure compatibility and connectivity among various systems and to exploit the economies of scale of regional rather than national solutions.

AN OPEN CULTURE OF EXCELLENCE

Culture and values are the soul of development. They provide its impetus, facilitate the means needed to further it, and substantially define people's vision of its purposes and ends. Culture and values are instrumental in the sense that they help to shape people's daily hopes, fears, ambitions, attitudes and actions, but they are also formative because they mould people's ideals and inspire their dreams for a fulfilling life for themselves and future generations. There is some debate in Arab countries about whether culture and values promote or retard development. Ultimately, however, values are not the servants of development; they are its wellspring.

Values play an especially critical role in social achievements that are not driven by narrowly economic forces, from the simple (prevention of littering) to the complex (community support for the disadvantaged and the impetus to eliminate socio-economic exclusion). Governments—Arab or otherwise—cannot decree their people's values; indeed, governments and their actions are partly formed by national cultures and values. Governments can, however, influence culture and values through leadership and example, and by shaping education and pedagogy, incentive structures in society, and use of the media. Moreover, by influencing values, they can affect the path of development.

Traditional culture and values, including traditional Arab culture and values, can be at odds with those of the globalizing world. Given rising global interdependence, the most viable response will be one of openness and constructive engagement, whereby Arab countries both contribute to and benefit from globalization. The values of democracy also have a part to play in this process of resolving differences between cultural traditionalism

Arab countries should capitlize on the expertise of the million highly qualified Arabs living abroad.

Values are not the servants of development; they are its wellspring.

and global modernity. Different people will have different preferences, some welcoming global influences, others resenting their pervasive impact. In a democratic framework, citizens can decide how to appraise and influence cultural changes, taking account of a diversity of views and striking a balance between individual liberty and popular preferences in the difficult choices involved.

Several other values deserve special emphasis from a human development perspective, e.g., tolerance and respect for different cultures; respect for the rights and needs of women, young people and children; protection of the environment; support for social safety nets to protect the vulnerable; refusal to tolerate excessive unemployment; reverence for knowledge and education; and other concepts conducive to human dignity and well-being. Of these, respect for other cultures is particularly important in countries with minorities, as is the case in most Arab countries. Such respect needs to go beyond mere tolerance and incorporate a positive attitude to other people. States can neither legislate nor enforce such attitudes. They can, however, enshrine cultural freedom as a human right.

Values relating to gender equality and interdependence are important for human development. Respect for the rights and duties of children and young people are another value of particular relevance for dynamic and sustained human development in Arab countries. No generation of young Arabs has been as large as today's. Their vast and rapidly growing numbers, coupled with their vulnerability, make it essential to protect and nurture them. This is both their basic human right and Arab societies' best investment in the future.

A FUTURE BUILT BY ALL

Human development is development of the people, for the people and by the people. If development is to be people-centred, then participatory processes need to be central to its evolution. Participation takes many forms: political, economic, social and cultural. Freedom, basic human capabilities and competitive markets are critical conditions for participation. Moreover, recognition of the multidimensional nature of the development process and the multi-stakeholder nature of societies and economies argues for strong support for pluralism and inclusion.

Political participation in Arab countries remains weak, as manifested in the lack of genuine representative democracy and restrictions on liberties. At the same time, people's aspirations for more freedom and greater participation in decision-making have grown, fueled by rising incomes, education, and information flows. The mismatch between aspirations and their fulfilment has in some cases led to alienation and its offspring —apathy and discontent. Remedying this state of affairs must be a priority for national leaderships.

Moving towards pluralism, which is more conducive to genuine sustainable participation and in tune with the requirements of today's and tomorrow's world, needs to become a priority for Arab countries.

The weakening of the position of the state relative to its citizens is supporting such a shift. Two simultaneous processes are taking place. The position of the state as patron is diminishing partly as a result of the reduced benefits it can now offer in the form of guaranteed employment, subsidies and other inducements. By contrast, the power position of citizens is increasing as states increasingly depend on them for tax revenues, private-sector investment and other necessities. Moreover, human-development accomplishments that have endowed citizens, particularly the middle classes, with a new range of resources have put them in a better position to contest policies and bargain with the state.

The shortcomings of current social and economic arrangements with respect to the status of women represent a major issue for Arab countries. Women remain severely marginalized in Arab political systems and broadly discriminated against in both law and custom. Women need to be politically empowered by far greater participation. In addition, a timetable to eliminate legal discrimination should be established and followed. Adoption of the Convention on the Elimination of All Forms of Discrimination against Women (CEDAW) would be an important step in this regard. The eight Arab countries that have neither signed nor acceded to CEDAW account for nearly one third of all the countries

No generation of young Arabs has been as large as today's.

The mismatch between aspirations and their fulfilment has in some cases led to alienation and its offspring —apathy and discontent.

that have not ratified the Convention. Greater transparency, disclosure and accountability can also help to advance women's political participation and reduce customary or legal discrimination.

Finally, the discrimination imposed by sexism has parallels in the prejudice implied by ageism. Both types of bias curtail the participation of two majorities in the Arab region: women and the young. Both also emanate from patriarchal dominance that exploits divergence with respect to gender and age. Predictably, discrimination is worst when the two biases overlap--in the case of young females. Ageism runs counter to the needs of the current era when technology and globalization reward innovation, flexibility and dynamism, and it deprives young people in the Arab world of opportunities to participate in and contribute to their societies' development.

People's participation in the economy also needs to be improved. Labour-force participation in the Arab countries as a group is lower than in other regions. Among the relatively small proportion of the population in the labour force, 20 million are unemployed. These problems are even more extreme with respect to women. Those fortunate enough to participate in the economy through their labour have seen its returns decline as real wages have fallen and its contribution to output fall with dwindling productivity.

Job creation, although rapid in some Arab countries from the mid-1980s to the early 1990s, has not matched the growth of the work force. Population growth is adding about six million labour-force entrants every year, a flow that is proportionately greater than in any other region. Since the unemployment rate is also one of the highest among all regions, the task of job creation is probably more formidable in the Arab region than in any other.

Despite the scale of the task, securing people's economic participation requires a clear political commitment to full employment as a national (and regional) priority. While there is a place for special employment-generating projects, programmes and funds, broad-based growth is the major determinant of job creation. Globally, employment generation is strongly and positively correlated with growth

in per capita income. However, this generally positive relationship is not automatic. Growth can also be jobless, as the experience of some Arab countries that have enjoyed significant income growth has shown. In these cases, growth was not able to create enough jobs to match the expansion of the labour force and unemployment rose.

Where employment creation has been most successful, it has resulted from the concerted application of a deliberate, informed strategy rather than the simple assumption that employment will increase automatically with growth. Most successful job-creation policies have deliberately targeted sectors in which growth could be labour-intensive, but typically low-skill labour-intensive sectors cannot sustainably improve productivity and incomes. Long-term strategies must therefore aim to move from employment in low-skill, low-productivity sectors to more skill-intensive, higher-productivity jobs. Such strategies should exploit the opportunities and niches that globalization offers.

Policies that discourage employment creation must be reversed. Perversely, some past economic policies, such as overvalued exchange rates and artificially low or negative real interest rates, have favoured capital-intensive industry. Government intervention in labour markets, traditionally geared towards regulation, should be designed to help people to adapt to market needs and markets to adapt to human needs. In the past, some well-intentioned regulatory interventions have also had the perverse effect of discouraging employment. Several Arab governments have started reforming labour laws in areas such as job security, separation awards and wage regulations (collective bargaining and minimum wages).

In the wake of public-sector downsizing, governments need to continue to intervene to smooth the labour-market transition for those left without jobs. This is a special problem for the region because of the large share of government employment in Arab countries (much higher than in other developing regions) and the large number of redundancies needed for an efficient outcome. In some cases, the costs of massive downsizing can be unaffordable; here, multilateral agencies should continue

Government intervention in labour markets, traditionally geared towards regulation, should be designed to help people to adapt to market needs and markets to adapt to human needs.

their support for retrenchment. In addition, so-called active labour-market policies can help on the demand side (e.g., through public works programmes), on the supply side (e.g., through training and re-training), and by matching demand and supply through labour-market intermediation (e.g., through job-search assistance).

Labour is not the only means by which people can enhance their economic participation. They can also participate using capital (often combined with labour) to set up small businesses. Credit is critical for these forms of participation. However, formal credit is often available only to those who are better off; the less well-off are often asset-deprived and hence cannot offer the collateral that lenders require. Formal credit-allocation mechanisms in the Arab region tend to be overly concentrated on larger enterprises, which are often capital- rather than labour-intensive. As a result, millions of people lack the opportunity to participate in the economy by combining their innovation, skill and hard work with capital.

Microfinance is potentially useful in addressing these missed opportunities. The bottleneck that needs to be addressed is not lack of funds for on-lending but rather the lack of local capacity to deliver microfinance services efficiently. Institutional and human capacity is needed to expand outreach beyond the less than two per cent of poor households that currently have access to financial services. Estimates of the outreach gap-people needing financial services and willing to pay for them but who nevertheless lack access-range from two million to four million households. The funding gap-funds needed for on-lending-ranges from US$750 million to US$1.4 billion, less than one per cent of total lending of the formal financial sector

The market is the central arena for economic participation. Free, open, competitive markets provide efficient mechanisms for economic exchange between buyers and sellers, producers and consumers, employers and workers, creditors and borrowers. Participation through free enterprise unleashes innovation and entrepreneurship. To maximize effective operation and participation, markets need to be free from arbitrary government actions and operate in the context of macroeconomic stability and an undistorted incentive system. Some Arab governments are moving in this direction by changing their roles from participants in markets to referees and by reducing public deficits and price distortions. To date, however, the pace has been slow. Governments should consider accelerating their disengagement from productive activities while strengthening their regulatory role to ensure openness and competitiveness. They should also take steps to modernize the delivery of essential public services.

As with political participation, women's economic participation remains unacceptably low, even though their capabilities have grown significantly (although still far less than is desirable). Their opportunities both to contribute to and to gain from such participation remain circumscribed by convention and legal restrictions. With respect to employment, mainstreaming gender in national development strategies and plans can set the stage for greater female participation. The feminization of unemployment can be reversed by removing gender bias in labour markets, including gender-based occupational segregation and unequal returns on education. Women's capabilities can be better matched with labour-market demand by effectively addressing gender gaps in the quality and relevance of education and skill-training programmes.

Evidently, much remains to be done to broaden both political and economic participation in Arab countries. Some countries are already taking positive steps to increase aspects of participation; others are moving slowly, if at all. Fundamentally, raising political and economic participation is not a technical problem. Progress will depend on attitudinal change at all levels of society, from top levels of government to local communities and individual households.

A FUTURE FOR ALL

Securing a better future for all requires putting the attack on poverty at the top of national agendas in Arab countries. The Arab region has dramatically reduced poverty and inequality in the twentieth century; it can do so again in the twenty-first. Given the political commitment, Arab countries have the resources to

Women's capabilities can be better matched with labour-market demand by effectively addressing gender gaps in the quality and relevance of education

Securing a better future for all requires putting the attack on poverty at the top of national agendas in Arab countries.

eradicate absolute poverty in less than a generation. Commitment, not resources, is the binding constraint. A solid, unequivocal political commitment--based on ethical, social, political and moral imperatives as well as the region's religious and cultural traditions--to well-articulated human development objectives, including poverty reduction, is the critical ingredient for securing a brighter future for all the people of the Arab region.

The challenge of reducing poverty and inequality has become more daunting following the slowdown in economic growth since the mid-1980s and the fiscal retrenchments associated with the shift from a state-led economic model based on import substitution to a private-sector-led, outward-looking model. If poverty is to be reduced, economic growth must be accelerated. The impact of rapid growth on poverty should be particularly effective in the Arab context, where low inequality suggests that the character of growth in the past has generally been pro-poor. Nevertheless, promoting growth needs to be complemented by concerted public action if poverty-reduction efforts are to succeed. There are two reasons for this. First, such action is needed to strengthen the synergy between growth and poverty reduction, i.e., to help to increase the efficiency of translating growth into poverty reduction. Second, while growth has generally been pro-poor, it has not been automatically or consistently so.

Public action has supported pro-poor growth in the past, when a public-investment boom and rapid expansion of the public sector, coupled with large subsidy outlays financed by strategic rents from oil and geopolitics, helped to reduce poverty by increasing real wages for unskilled labour and lowering prices. Public policy also has a major role to play with respect to critical factors such as the state of the macroeconomy and the functioning of labour markets.

Another key area for public policy is the provision of social safety nets. Spending on transfer programmes needs to grow beyond its current level, which ranges from 0.2 per cent to about 1 per cent of GDP. Arguments for additionality need to be supported by greater efficiency. Transfer programmes need to be coordinated with other social programmes to

The role of public policy in building, utilizing and liberating people's capabilities remains critical.

avoid overlaps. Better management is needed to improve administration. Combined with better targeting, this can reduce leakage of benefits to the non-poor and cut administrative costs for needy beneficiaries.

Features of market-driven regional integration, such as migration and remittances, also have an important role. These flows have disproportionately benefited poor people, either directly through transfers or indirectly through the labour market. They need to be nurtured and sustained.

Poverty reduction will require drawing on the strengths and capabilities of a broad network of actors in government, the private sector and civil society. The role of public policy in building, utilizing and liberating people's capabilities remains critical. Governments need to provide an enabling environment for broad-based political support and mobilization for pro-poor policies and markets. This environment can be enhanced by research and policy analysis that identifies problems, diagnoses their causes and presents options for policy-makers, highlighting the tradeoffs and costs of each option. An increasingly dynamic and constructive civil society in the Arab region, including public and non-governmental think tanks and research institutions, has the potential to provide intellectual and analytical ammunition for operationalizing the commitment to a future for all, based on a comprehensive, multifaceted strategy for poverty reduction. Many of these institutions contribute to studies, reports and publications and undertake advocacy that seeks to influence national debates and impact policy. The 13 national human development reports that UNDP has supported in the region since 1994 are a case in point.

Finally, effective strategies for attacking poverty must focus not only on what needs to be done in principle but also on how to ensure that action is taken in practice. This means implementing improvements in such basic areas as promoting broad-based political participation, ensuring accountability and transparency in government, promoting a free flow of information and freedom of the press, and ensuring a strong role for community groups and NGOs in policy-making and legislative decision-making.

The legitimacy and strength of states and their institutions are inextricably linked to their capacity to mobilize and be mobilized in the fight against poverty. This implies that it will be essential to mainstream human development and poverty reduction within national economic policy, which in the past has too often sidelined them, especially in the context of structural adjustment. Countries that have reduced poverty while adjusting have shown that poverty reduction can be integral to the process and central to the goals of structural adjustment. This has now been accepted as a principle of international policy on adjustment although it is not yet always practised.

The basic priority for policy in Arab countries needs to be to create a virtuous cycle whereby economic growth promotes human development and human development in turn promotes economic growth. The starting point for this process must be a focus on people. The backlog of deprivation must be tackled if growth is to be restored on a sustainable basis. Tackling deprivation is a particularly urgent task for Arab countries with low levels of human development. The Human Development Report 1996 demonstrated that every country that succeeded in sustaining both rapid human development and rapid economic growth did so by accelerating advances in human development first, or by pursuing both objectives simultaneously. By contrast, countries that relied primarily on economic growth to reach the point where growth and human development become mutually reinforcing failed in the attempt because shortcomings in human development kept undermining their growth process.

In sum, human development is essential for sustained economic growth, and poverty reduction—the promise of a better future for all—is central to both. For Arab countries, such a future is both a moral imperative and an attainable goal as they move into the twenty-first century.

The basic priority for policy in Arab countries needs to be to create a virtuous cycle whereby economic growth promotes human development and human development in turn promotes economic growth.

CHAPTER 1

 Human development: definition, concept and larger context

This chapter outlines the concept and definition of human development as pioneered and popularized by the UNDP global Human Development Reports. It explains how human development is now customarily measured through the human development index (HDI), which is based on four variables covering life expectancy, adult literacy, education enrolment ratios and gross domestic product per capita. Acknowledging that the concept itself is broader than any of its measures, the chapter next considers how, in a larger context, human development includes not only basic choices but also additional choices encompassing human freedoms, human rights and knowledge. Following a discussion of several freedoms instrumental to human well-being, a key suggestion is put forth that an alternative HDI could help to measure these other key variables that vitally influence human development (Box 1.6). The chapter concludes by indicating how subsequent parts of this Report explore, in the Arab context, the larger meaning of human development characterized here.

People are the real wealth of nations. The basic goal of development is to create an environment that enables people to enjoy a long, healthy, creative life. This fundamental truth is often forgotten in the immediate concern with the accumulation of goods and money.

Preoccupation with economic growth and the creation of wealth and material opulence has obscured the fact that development is ultimately about people. It has had the unfortunate effect of pushing people from the centre to the periphery of development debates and dialogues.

The publication of the first Human Development Report (HDR) by the United Nations Development Programme (UNDP) in 1990 was a modest attempt to reverse this trend. With the introduction of the concept of human development, the construction of a composite measure for it and a discussion of the relevant policy implications, the HDR changed the way of looking at development and dealing with the issues it presents.

DEFINING HUMAN DEVELOPMENT

Human development can be simply defined as a process of enlarging choices. Every day human beings make a series of choices – some economic, some social, some political, some cultural. If people are the proper focus of development efforts, then these efforts should be geared to enhancing the range of choices in all areas of human endeavour for every human being. Human development is both a process and an outcome. It is concerned with the process through which choices are enlarged, but it also focuses on the outcomes of enhanced choices.

Human development thus defined represents a simple notion, but one with far-reaching implications. First, human choices are en-

Human development can be simply defined as a process of enlarging choices.

BOX 1.1

The equation of human development

Enlarging human choices is critically linked to two issues: capabilities and functionings on the one hand, and opportunities on the other.

The functionings of a person refer to the valuable things the person can do or be (such as being well-nourished, living a long time and taking part in the community). The capability of a person stands for the different combinations of functionings the person can achieve; it reflects the freedom to achieve functionings. Enlarging choices for a person implies formation or enhancement of capabilities. Human capabilities can be enhanced through the development of human resources: good health and nu-

trition, education and skill training, etc.

However, capabilities cannot be used unless opportunities exist to use them--for leisure, productive purposes or participation in social, political or cultural affairs. Economic opportunities can be created through better access to productive resources, including credit, employment, etc. Political opportunities need polity and other conditions.

Human development thus represents an equation, the left-hand side of which reflects human capabilities, and the right-hand side, economic, political and social opportunities to use those capabilities.

Source: UNDP, Human Development Report 1990.

---

larged when people acquire more capabilities and enjoy more opportunities to use those capabilities (box 1.1) Human development seeks not only to increase both capabilities and opportunities but also to ensure an appropriate balance between them in order to avoid the frustration that a mismatch between the two can create.

Second, as already implied, economic growth needs to be seen as a means, albeit an important one, and not the ultimate goal, of development (box 1.2). Income makes an important contribution to human well-being, broadly conceived, if its benefits are translated into more fulfilled human lives, but the growth of income is not an end in itself.

Third, the human development concept, by concentrating on choices, implies that people must influence the processes that shape their lives. They must participate in various decision-making processes, the implementation of those decisions, and their monitoring and adjustment to improve outcomes where necessary.

In the ultimate analysis, human development is development of the people, development for the people, and development by the people. Development of the people involves building human capabilities through the development of human resources. Development for the people implies that the benefits of growth must be translated into the lives of people, and development by the people emphasizes that people must be able to participate actively in influencing the processes that shape their lives.

Income poverty is only one aspect of human impoverishment; deprivation can also occur in other areas.

HUMAN DEVELOPMENT: A HOLISTIC APPROACH

Looking at development from a human-development perspective is hardly new. The idea that social arrangements must be judged by the extent to which they promote human goods goes back at least to Aristotle, who said: "Wealth is evidently not the good we are seeking, for it is merely useful and for the sake of something else". He argued for seeing the "difference between a good political arrangement and a bad one" in terms of its successes and failures in facilitating people's ability to lead "flourishing lives". The idea of better human lives as the real end of all human activities was a recurring theme in the writings of most of the early philosophers.

The great Arab historian and sociologist , Ibn Khaldoun, devoted a whole chapter in his famous work "Almuqaddimah" (Introduction to History) to "The Facts Concerning (economic), Sustenance and, Earning (of income) and their Explanation and the Fact that Earning is (tied to) the Value of Human Labour".

In this chapter, of his *magnum opus,* Ibn Khaldoun draws distinctions relevant to the different purposes to which income earned through people's labour and pursuits is allocated. To the extent that income earnings are allocated to people's necessities and needs, they will constitute their "livelihoods". If earnings are greater than people's needs, they will be surpluses that finance luxuaries and capital accumulation.

Ibn Khaldoun also distinguished between expenditure of earnings on purposes that "benefits human needs and interests", and expenditure that does not result in such benefit. The first he calls "sustenance" and connects it with the noble saying of the prophet: "the only thing you really possess of your income and wealth is what you ate, and have thus consumed, or what you wore, and have thus worn out, or what you gave away as charity and you have thus spent". In his regard, Ibn Khaldoun also quotes the Mu'tazilah – a famous School of Islamic jurisprudence - who stipulated for the use of the term "sustenance" that it must be possessed rightfully. Illegally acquired income or property was not admitted by them as something that could be called "sustenance".

Finally, Ibn Khaldoun linked income to human labour. He insisted that human labour is necessary for earning income and forming capital. He further linked civilization itself to human labour, saying: "You should know that when the human labour is all gone or decreased by regression of civilization, God will then allow earnings to terminate. Cities with few inhabitants can be observed to offer little sustenance and profits, or none whatsoever, because little human labour is available. Likewise, in cities with a larger supply of labour, the inhabitants enjoy better welfare and have more luxuries."

The same motivating concern can be found in the writings of the early leaders of quantification in economics: William Petty, Gregory King, François Quesnay, Antoine Lavoisier and Joseph Lagrange, the grandparent of gross national product (GNP) and gross domestic product (GDP). It is also clear in the writings of the leading political economists: Adam Smith, David Ricardo, Robert Malthus, Karl Marx and John Stuart Mill.

The notion of human development, as introduced in the first Human Development Report in 1990, was an extension of that long but recently obscured tradition. It questioned the relevance of the unique preoccupation with equating GNP with development and thus shifted the development paradigm. It put people back where they belong--at the centre of the development debate and dialogue--and it created an impact far beyond the expectations of its founding parents in 1990 (box 1.3).

The human development concept is broader than other people-oriented approaches to development. Human-resource development emphasizes only human capital and treats human beings as an input in the development process, but not as its beneficiaries. The basic-needs approach focuses on minimum requirements of human beings, but not on their choices. The human-welfare approach looks at people as recipients, but not as active participants in the processes that shape their lives. Human development, by encompassing all these aspects, represents a more holistic approach to development.

MEASURING HUMAN DEVELOPMENT

A concept is always broader than any of its proposed measures. Any suggested measure for any concept cannot fully capture the richness and the breadth of the concept. This is true of the notion of human development as well.

In principle, human choices and their outcomes can be infinite and change over time. However, the three essential ones at all levels of development are for people to lead a long and healthy life, to acquire knowledge and to have access to resources needed for a decent standard of living. If these essentials are not available, many other opportunities remain inaccessible.

The HDR 1990 therefore constructed a composite index, the human development index (HDI) on the basis of these three basic dimensions of human development. The HDI contains four variables: life expectancy at birth, to represent the dimension of a long, healthy life; adult literacy rate and combined enrolment rate at the primary, secondary and tertiary levels, to represent the knowledge dimension; and real GDP per capita (purchasing power parity (PPP)US$), to serve as a proxy for

A concept is always broader than any of its proposed measures. This is true of the notion of human development as well.

BOX 1.3

Impact of the human development reports

The Human Development Reports (HDRs) over the last 12 years have covered a series of key issues as their themes. These themes range from public expenditure for human development, to participation, to economic growth and human development. Such issues as gender and human development, human poverty, human development in a globalized world, human rights and human development, and technology for human development have also been addressed in HDRs.

All these reports with their analysis, data and policy discussions have had a significant impact on development thinking and practice. First, they initiated new policy debates and dialogues at the national level and influenced policy-makers to come up with new policy strategies. Second, they encouraged the disaggregation of various human-development indicators in terms of gender, regions, ethnic groups, etc. Such data clearly indicated intra-country dispari-

ties and inequalities and helped governments to direct necessary resources to formulate required policies. Third, development activists, non-governmental organizations (NGOs) and institutions of civil society have used the Reports as advocacy documents. Fourth, significant academic research has been undertaken to expand the frontiers of human development, in terms of analytical frameworks, indices and statistical work and policy recommendations. Fifth, HDRs are being used as reference materials in universities and academic institutions.

One important by-product of the global HDRs is the more than 260 national HDRs (NHDRs) produced in over 120 countries. Some of these countries have produced these NHDRs for more than five years. These NHDRs have become important catalysts for national policies and strategies; they have also served as repositories of innovative data and as crucial advocacy tools.

Source: Jahan, 2001.

the resources needed for a decent standard of living.

A number of observations can be made about the HDI. First, the HDI is not a comprehensive measure of human development. Its focus on the three basic dimensions outlined above inevitably means that it cannot take into account a number of other important dimensions of human development. Second, the index is composed of long-term human-development outcomes. Thus it cannot reflect input efforts in terms of policies nor can it measure short-term human-development achievements. Third, it is an average measure and thus masks a series of disparities and inequalities within countries. Disaggregation of the HDI in terms of gender, region, race and ethnic group can point up urgent areas for action that the average inevitably conceals. Fourth, income enters into the HDI not in its own right but as a proxy for resources needed to have a decent standard of living.

All the quantitative information about human development and its various indicators constitute what may be termed human-development accounting. This accounting has a focus dimension and a breadth dimension. The HDI, concentrating only on the basic dimensions of human development, represents the focus aspect of the accounting. All the data and quantitative information on various human-development indicators represent the breadth dimension of the accounting.

The HDI thus has a limited scope. It cannot provide a complete picture of human development in any situation. It must be supplemented with other useful indicators in order to obtain a comprehensive view. Thus it is human-development accounting, not the HDI, that can portray the complete picture. Yet the HDI has its strength. While it is a simplistic measure, as GNP per capita is, it is not as blind as a GNP per capita measure is to broader issues of human well-being.

BROADENING THE CONTEXT: FREEDOM, KNOWLEDGE, INSTITUTIONS

Human freedom is a multidimensional concept, extending far beyond the basic dimensions measured by the HDI. Leading a long and healthy life and being knowledgeable may be universal goals, but people may make additional choices and have additional aspirations that may be society- and culture-specific. The human-development concept encompasses additional choices and goals, processes and outcomes that are highly valued by people, ranging from political, economic and social freedom to opportunities for being creative and productive, and enjoying personal self-respect and guaranteed human rights. The notion of human development emphasizes enlargement of choices in these areas as well.

In the societal and cultural context of the Arab world, such wider choices regarding freedom, human rights, knowledge acquisition and the institutional context are especially critical. No notion of human development can be relevant and effective unless it addresses these crucial issues both analytically and empirically.

HUMAN FREEDOM

As noted earlier, human development is inextricably linked with human freedom. Human development emphasizes enhancement of human capabilities, which reflects the freedom to achieve different things that people value. In this sense, human development is freedom. However, this freedom, the ability to achieve things that people value, cannot be used if opportunities to exercise this freedom do not exist. Such opportunities are ensured through the existence of various human rights that key institutions--the community, the society, and the state--must support and secure.

Human development and human rights are thus mutually reinforcing and they have a common denominator: human freedom. Human development, by enhancing human capabilities, creates the ability to exercise freedom, and human rights, by providing the necessary framework, create the opportunities to exercise it. Freedom is both the guarantor and the goal of both human development and human rights.

Poverty as well as tyranny, limited economic opportunities as well as systematic social deprivation, neglect of public facilities as well as intolerance or state repression are major sources of human deprivation and thus

Human development and human rights are mutually reinforcing and they have a common denominator: human freedom.

diminution of human freedom. Many manifestations of these problems are old, but some are new; many of them can be observed, in one form or other, in rich societies as well as in poor ones. Overcoming these problems is central to the exercise of development (box 1.4).

In the context of this broader approach to well-being and for empirical purposes, five distinct types of instrumental freedom have been identified as being of special importance for policy purposes on the grounds that they contribute directly to the general capability of a person to live more freely and that they complement one another. The five types are:

• political freedoms, which relate to the opportunities that people have to determine who should govern and on what principles, and also include the possibility to scrutinize and criticize authorities and to have freedom of political expression and an uncensored press;

• economic facilities, which can be understood as the ways in which economies function to generate income opportunities and promote the distribution of wealth;

• social opportunities, which refer to the arrangements that society makes for education and health care, both of which influence the individual's substantive freedom to live better, as well as to transparency guarantees and protective security;

• transparency guarantees, which safeguard social interactions between individuals and which are undertaken on the basis of some presumption of what they are being offered and what they expect to get;

• protective security, which deals with the provision of the relevant social safety nets for vulnerable groups in society.

All these types of instrumental freedom have specific importance in the context of the Arab world not only in their own right but also as important choices that are crucial for human development.

KNOWLEDGE ACQUISITION

Acquisition of knowledge has intrinsic value by itself, but more importantly, it is an important dimension of human development because as it is a critical means of building human capability.

It is now generally accepted that knowl-edge is a core factor of production and a principal determinant of productivity and human capital. There is thus an important synergy between knowledge acquisition and the productive power of society. This synergy is especially strong in high value-added productive activities, which are becoming increasingly based on both intensive knowledge and the rapid obsolescence of know-how and capabilities. These activities are the bulwark of international competitiveness and will become more so in the future.

By the same token, a limited knowledge stock, especially if combined with poor or non-existent knowledge acquisition, condemns a country to meagre productivity and poor development prospects. In today's world, it is the knowledge gap rather than the income gap that is likely to be the most critical determinant of the fortunes of countries across the world. At the beginning of the third millennium, knowledge constitutes the road to development and liberation, especially in a world of intensive globalization.

INSTITUTIONAL CONTEXT

It is well recognized that addressing and ensuring human rights and human freedoms depend critically on the institutional context. The same is true for dynamic knowledge acquisition. Since issues of human freedom and knowledge acquisition are of prime impor-

At the beginning of the third millennium, knowledge constitutes the road to development and liberation, especially in a world of intensive globalization.

BOX 1.4

Development as freedom

Expansion of freedom is viewed both as the primary end and as the principal means of development. Development consists of the removal of various types of unfreedoms that leave people with little choice and little opportunity for exercising their reasoned agency. The removal of substantial unfreedoms, it is argued here, is constitutive of development.

However, for a fuller understanding of the connection between development and freedom, we have to go beyond that basic recognition (crucial as it is). The intrinsic importance of human freedom, in general, as the pre-eminent objective of development is strongly supplemented by the instrumental effectiveness of freedoms of particular kinds to promote freedoms of other kinds. The linkages between different types of freedoms are empirical, rather than constitutive and compositional. For example, there is strong evidence that economic and political freedoms help to reinforce one another rather than being hostile to one another (as they are sometimes taken to be). Similarly, social opportunities of education and health care, which may require public action, complement individual opportunities for economic and political participation and also help to foster our own initiatives in overcoming our respective deprivations.

If the point of departure of the approach lies in the identification of freedoms, the main object of development, the reach of the policy analysis lies in establishing the empirical linkages that make the viewpoint of freedom coherent and cogent as the guiding perspective of the process of development.

Amartya Sen

Source: Sen, 1999, preface.

tance for human development in the Arab region, recognition of the necessary institutional context and choice of an appropriate institutional framework are also crucial.

With regard to human freedoms, individual agency is, of course, ultimately central, but individual freedom of agency is inescapably qualified (enhanced or constrained) by available social, political and economic opportunities. This is true across the world, including in the Arab region. In the Arab world, there is a deep complementarity between individual agency and social arrangements. It is thus important to recognize the centrality of both individual freedom and the role of institutional and social arrangements in the extent and reach of freedom, and to see individual freedom as a social commitment.

Moreover, the five types of instrumental freedom mentioned earlier depend, each in its own way, on the effectiveness of the various institutions that Arab society provides to enable individuals to pursue the lives that they have reason to value. Respect for human rights and effective participation of the people in social and political activities must be fundamental ingredients of the institutional context of human development in the Arab world.

With respect to knowledge acquisition, the standard usage of the term "human capital" denotes attitudes, knowledge and capabilities acquired by individuals, primarily through education, training and experience. However, the concept of capital that would be consistent with the concept of human development relevant to the Arab world is far broader than conventional human capital on the individual level and far more sophisticated on the societal level.

It is perhaps more precise in the Arab world to adopt the term social capital to integrate the concepts of social, intellectual and cultural capital into a notion of capital formed by systems that organize people in institutions. This type of capital determines the nature of societal activity and its returns, paramount among which is the level of human well-being. An amalgam of conventional human capital and social capital would then constitute the notion of human capital commensurate with human development in the Arab region.

Given the critical importance of gender equality, knowledge acquisition in the information society age and environmental choices, it is worth considering how some of these aspects might be incorporated into constructing the HDI for the Arab world. Neither per capita GNP nor the HDI takes explicit account of these important choices. Box 1.6 explores the dimensions and construction of such an index as well as insights from applying it.

BOX 1.5

Measuring freedom

Since 1972/1973, Freedom House, an American non-profit organization, has published an annual assessment of the state of freedoms in countries and regions of the world. The assessment takes the form of a numerical scale measuring the extent of availability of a broad range of political and civil rights and freedoms enjoyed in reality, not in declared documents and policies. Without fully endorsing the content of the Freedom House assessment or its methodology, the "freedom index" can be used as an overall char-

acterization of the extent to which of rights and freedoms necessary for good governance are available.

An attempt is made in box 1.6 to combine the freedom index and other key variables with the HDI. To arrive at freedom scores, the Freedom House scale is transformed so that it ranges between zero (expressing absence of freedoms) to one, (denoting complete enjoyment of freedoms). The resultant freedom index is moderately and positively associated with indicators of social development.

BOX 1.6

IN SEARCH OF AN ADEQUATE MEASURE OF HUMAN DEVELOPMENT,
AN ALTERNATIVE HUMAN DEVELOPMENT INDEX, AHDI

Nader Fergany

Introduction

It is widely recognised that the standard measure of human development (HD), the human development index (HDI) does not capture the rich content of the HD concept. In fact the popularity of the HDI has sometimes meant that HD is reduced to nothing more than human resources development (HRD), an unfortunate misunderstanding. This is indicated in the present chapter and emphasised in chapter 2 in the context of analysing significant human development deficits in the Arab region. The latter analysis confirms the region suffers from significant human development deficits that nonetheless do not register on a country's standing on the HDI.

The need to construct an adequate measure of HD is now well established. Indeed, the search for a better measure of HD is thus a pressing task for the human development movement.

This exploratory analysis aims at initiating a process of innovation that could culminate in constructing an adequate measure of human development. The territory to explore is rugged and therefore calls for ingenuity as well as perseverance.

The approach of this analysis is rather simple. It uses a flexible yet robust method to compose a number of human development indicators into a human development index deemed sufficient to approximate the rich content of HD. The method used is the Borda rule, a rank sum function that calls for the minimum technical requirements of the constituent indicators. The requirement is that the indicator can be used to arrive at an unambiguous ranking of alternatives (units of analysis, countries in our case) on the dimension of human development measured by the indicator. Given the ranking of alternatives, the Borda rule assembles the rankings of alternatives on the indicators considered into a single value, the rank sum, which produces a complete ordering of alternatives on the indicators used and hence is a valid social welfare function. (Dasgupta, 1993). We call the resulting rank-sum an alternative human development index (AHDI).

This procedure produces only ranking of countries. As the objective here is to put the need for a better measure of human development on the human development research agenda, it is sufficient to produce country rankings. However, it would be a simple matter to compute AHDI values on the basis of the set of indicators proposed here .

The indicators proposed here were, in part, motivated by the human development deficits in the Arab region given in chapter 2, defined to express human functionings, hence human capabilities, or freedoms and deemed, as such, to have universal validity. In addition, availability of data for a large number of countries was also a criterion for the inclusion of an indicator .

The indicators used in this analysis are, in order:
- Life expectancy at birth, LE, as a general measure of longevity and overall health.
- Educational attainment, EA as a means of knowledge acquisition.
- Freedom score, FS, as used in Chapter 1 and 2, defined to express enjoyment of civil and political liberties, a universally sought objective as well as to reflect the freedom deficit in the Arab region.
- GEM, as computed by UNDP, to express women's access to power in society in general, as well as reflect the women empowerment deficit in the Arab region.

- Internet hosts per-capita, IH, to reflect ICT connectivity (access to ICT), to express a universally recognised requirement for benefiting from globalisation in this age, as well as to reflect the knowledge acquisition deficit in the Arab region.
- CDE, Carbon dioxide emissions per-capita (metric tons), defined as a penalty, to reflect damage to the environment .

As such the proposed indicators are universally valued functionings. In that sense, these are also developmental outcomes. Hence, the indicators proposed here have global relevance that extends beyond the Arab countries. As a result, the set of six variables seems to provide a good starting point for constructing indices of human development. The proposition is surely worth pursuing, and refining.

It can be anticipated that the utilisation of this set of indicators will, compared to the HDI, penalise Arab countries, an anticipation that would be borne out by the construction of such an AHDI. But we think that this is not a serious shortcoming. Penalised also will be any country in the world that does not perform well on the six indicators proposed, including some of the highest ranking countries on both income and HDI, which are to be, rightly, penalised for their extensive contribution to global warming through CDE thus spoiling the world's atmosphere for all.

More important in our judgement than any country's position on the AHDI is the conviction, articulated above, that the proposed indicators are genuinely valid yardsticks for measuring human development in this age of globalisation. In other words, countries, Arab or otherwise, that want to perform on human development, need to perform on freedom for all incorporating women's empowerment, knowledge acquisition, including ICT connectivity, improving health and safeguarding the environment.

As expected, the five variables: LE, EA, FS, IH and GEM are positively correlated with HDI and themselves. CDE, defined negatively to reflect damage to the environment, however, comes out negatively correlated with all other indicators

Structurally, the AHDI consists of the two fundamental human capabilities: living a long and healthy life and knowledge acquisition through education. This it can be claimed is the irreducible core of human development.

The exclusion of income from the AHDI was meant to de-emphasise the importance of average income as a measure of human development in general as well as to reflect the deficit of human capabilities relative to income in Arab countries. Properly understood, human development philosophy proposes human capabilities, especially freedom, rather than command over goods and services though income, as the ultimate means of human empowerment. It is freedom, not income that empowers human beings to achieve valued functionings. Thus, beyond the two fundamental human capabilities of health and knowledge acquisition, a human being needs to be empowered by freedom for all. It is time that average income be dethroned as the primary means of empowerment in human societies.

*This is indeed a major departure from the HDI and, from the vantagepoint of the concept of human development, a definite improvement. Freedom for all does not admit the disempowerment of any group, be it women, the poor or a religious or ethnic minority. In other words, freedom for all incorporates women's empowerment, indeed

empowerment for all.

Nevertheless, disempowerment of women remains a major impediment to human development in many parts of the world, especially in the Arab region as noted in chapter2. As a result, we believe there is a strong case for explicitly incorporating a measure of women empowerment in the AHDI to stress this aspect of freedom for all. This indirectly adds to the weight of the freedom score in the AHDI by placing an emphasis on gender equity as well as to reflect the women empowerment deficit in the Arab region.

The inclusion of two indicators of knowledge acquisition, EA and IH , is meant to reflect the emphasis on knowledge acquisition stressed throughout the report and to express the critical importance of ICT in this age of global connectivity. The two variables together give knowledge acquisition a higher weight than LE for example, reflecting the deficit of knowledge (education) relative to health (LE) in the Arab region.

The human capability of being able to enjoy a safe environment translates, on the societal level, into a measure of environmental responsibility towards the global environment.

AHDI Values

To gain an appreciation of the implication of the proposed approach to the measurement of HD we examine in some detail the results of applying AHDI.

AHDI turns out to be strongly and positively correlated with the HDI (rank correlation coefficient = +0.904). This strong correlation between the two indices perhaps indicates that they belong to the same family of measures.

However, the position of individual countries on the range of the AHDI is reshuffled thoroughly. It is important to note that the rank of an individual country on HDI reported here, does not have to tally with the rank reported in the HDR. The ranks given here are based on the Borda ranking rule and not on the values of HDI, in addition to the fact that the rankings given here are limited to the 111 countries covered by the present analysis (compared to 174 in the HDR).

This reshuffling of positions is reflected, at the level of world regions, utilising the average rank of countries of the region, in Figure 1. A higher rank represents a worse human development position.

The same mapping is presented, on the level of the 111 countries, in Figure 2. Sweden comes on top of the AHDI, while Canada is demoted to No. 3 (out of 111, it was No. 1 of 174 on HDI, 1998). The USA, UK, France and Germany do not make the top ten on the AHDI. Scandinavian countries, on the other hand, make a strong showing in the top ten on the AHDI.

Of the 14 Arab countries included in the analysis, four place in the ten lowest AHDI values: Syria, Sudan, Mauritania, and Iraq.

Jordan, Kuwait, Lebanon and UAE, in order, top the list of Arab countries on AHDI, followed by Morocco and the Comoros, Egypt and Tunisia. This order perhaps reflects differences in human welfare better than the HDI ranking.

As expected, the position of all Arab countries deteriorates, to varying extent, on moving from HDI to AHDI but, especially Kuwait and the UAE, lose place considerably. Only Jordan and Comoros essentially retain their relative placing on both indices.

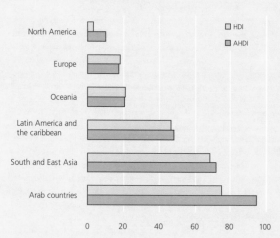

Figure 1
Average rank of countries of world regions on AHDI and HDI

□ HDI
▨ AHDI

North America
Europe
Oceania
Latin America and the caribbean
South and East Asia
Arab countries

0   20   40   60   80   100

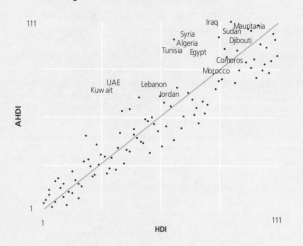

Figure 2
Ranking of 111 countries on AHDI and HD

AHDI

HDI

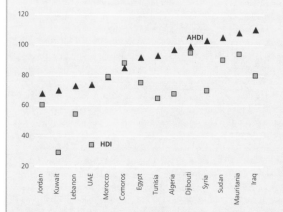

Figure 3
Ranking of Arab countries on AHDI and HDI

AHDI

HDI

Jordan, Kuwait, Lebanon, UAE, Morocco, Comoros, Egypt, Tunisia, Algeria, Djibouti, Syria, Sudan, Mauritania, Iraq

Does the AHDI Suffer Methodological Shortcomings?

The AHDI can perhaps be assaulted on 'technical' grounds: that it mixes different types of indicators: input and output, stock and flow, single and composite. All, by the way, characteristics of the HDI.

In particular, the AHDI could be assailed on the basis that it 'mixes oranges and apples,' i.e., it combines quantitative variables and a variable expressing perceptions. Strictly speaking, no technical requirement is infringed as a result. More importantly, it has to be borne in mind that this is indeed the nature of the phenomenon for which we are aiming to provide a measurable proxy. Human development is a complex syndrome that is definitely not limited to the quantifiable. Freedom is a value, enjoyment of freedom is a feeling.

At the present state of social science development, feelings are approximated by perceptions. Until social science can provide us with better tools for assessing feelings, we have to do with what is available to us. In this sense, the claimed inadequacy is in fact a confirmation of the fidelity of AHDI to the concept of human development. By comparison, the restriction of HDI to quantifiable variables of the Human Resource Development (HRD) genre opts for simplistic technical validity at the expense of conceptual fidelity.

As we have indicated repeatedly, the freedom score used here is admittedly grossly imperfect as a universally valid proxy for freedom. There is indeed room for improvement in the measurement of freedom as the ultimate yardstick for development . This is a task that begs international agencies, notably UNDP, to devote energy and resources to it. It is hoped that future issues of the AHDR devote attention to better measurement of freedom, at least in Arab countries.

The AHDI may also be criticised on the grounds that it assigns equal weights to variables that do not command equal importance in different perspectives. An HRD enthusiast could ask: 'Is not LE more important than CDE?' A global environment devotee could well counter: 'Not necessarily!' The HRD enthusiast could add: 'LE should have a higher weight than knowledge or freedom, since avoiding death is a most primordial human instinct.'

A primordial human instinct it may be, but on the scale of human values, avoidance of death might not rank very high. Is prolongation of life under suffering and oppression a blessing or punishment? Freedom fighters throughout history, have voted with their lives.

In a different point of view, since a recognised achievement in prolongation of life has been attained in Arab, as well as other developing, countries, it is natural

that attention shifts from length to quality of life. Without doubt, the ideal goal is for a long life characterised by liberty and human dignity. As a reflection of this superior human goal, the AHDI includes both indicators of life expectancy at birth and level of enjoyment of freedom.

As should be well known, assigning equal weights reflects the 'equal ignorance assumption' in statistical analysis. It is, by the way, the same principle that is used in the construction of the HDI.

However, to investigate the validity of the equal ignorance assumption, with respect to the AHDI, a principal components factor analysis on the values of the six indicators utilised, was carried out. This is one statistical technique that is normally utilised to assign an 'objective' weight to each of a set of variables in order to arrive at a composite index as a proxy for a certain multi-faceted phenomenon.

The results of the factor analysis reveal that the weights proposed by this analysis are rather close in value , a result that does not place the equal weights assumption in jeopardy.

The way forward, an agenda for innovation in the measurement of human development.

This analysis has explored the contours of a new ap-

proach that could lead to a better measurement of HD. Nevertheless, a long agenda remains. Refinements are surely possible, even recommended, in the areas of definition of indicators, measurement of indicators and construction of composite indices. A vigorous process of innovation in the measurement of human development is called for.

In particular, national and international efforts to improve data availability on human development in general, freedom and gender issues in particular, should be stepped up.

The weakness of the indicators of freedom, and of good governance indicators in general, is arguably the biggest stumbling block in the way of adequate measurement of HD. It is a block that calls for mobilising an international program for better measurement of enjoyment of freedom on a world scale.

In the same way that the purchasing power parity comparison program, an international endeavour that was led by the UN, has given income per capita a new lease on life as a measure of development or welfare, the measurement of freedom needs to be likewise improved. The UN system should play an instrumental role in this endeavour, as it did with respect to the PPP approach.

Towards Arab human development

The concept of "human development" gains special importance in the Arab context since it reflects two dimensions.

The first is a materialistic one, relating to satisfaction of human needs as reflected in the HDI's quantitative measures of income, education, and health. The second is a qualitative one in the sense of participation, democracy, freedoms, and rule of law which is consistent with the economic and social rights enshrined in the Universal Declaration on Human Rights.

The satisfaction of human needs sustains human dignity and acquires major importance in the context of once-colonized and exploited peoples. The importance of this material dimension grows with the growth of poverty in the Arab world under intensifying social polarization and the continuing waste of resources at the expense of existing and coming Arab generations. One of the requirements of human development is preserving national wealth for coming generations and preventing its exhaustion by building sustainability.

Arab countries have a vast potential to attain adequate living standards that enhance all their people's interests, especially if these countries achieve economic integration and deepen their inter-Arab trade. Economic integration will form an important mechanism for overcoming dependency and vulnerability and helping to make globalization work for Arab interests in an attempt to reach self-reliance.

Regional integration, while forming an Arab economic block in the era of massive economic clusters in the world, will also ensure the return of Arab resources to the benefit of the Arab people by helping to overcome increasing poverty.

The qualitative dimension is based on accountability and constitutes a cornerstone of human development, for there is a basic and dialectic relationship between governance and development. The Arab people face some deep ethical choices in an environment of competition, selfishness and individualistic personal ambition. These motivations divert efforts away from the common good and hinder the development process.

In some Arab countries, the absence of democracy based on participation, pluralism, separation between authorities, independence of the judiciary system, and free and honest periodic elections has formed an obstacle to the development process. This is not to deny achievements attained in the social, economic, productive, political, and cultural spheres. Nevertheless, giving democracy low priority has not helped to reinforce the necessary participation and unity needed between civic and political circles in the Arab States.

In my assessment, this democratic deficit remains a challenge to this day, in spite of some promising signs of movement towards freer societies in some cases. Giving this issue the special attention it deserves and maximizing participation in decision-making both help to create a true partnership between the official, private and civil sectors and enhance the evolution of a developmental vision that includes the interests of the poor and the marginalized.

Fostering multiparty systems, freedom of the press, constructive criticism, and periodic elections represents an important mechanism for the preservation of freedom and for invigorating people's trust in their abilities and their future. Safeguarding the rights of citizenship through the rule of law links the individual citizen, through his or her rights, to the state, guarantees two-way trust and counteracts marginalization and alienation.

Haydar Abdel-Shafy

THE ARAB HUMAN DEVELOPMENT REPORT

In chapter 2, the Report draws substantive conclusions about the state of human development in the Arab world at the end of the twentieth century by applying the yardsticks of progress represented by the HDI. It demonstrates that the institutional context of society and disabling knowledge and human-freedom deficits constitute the most critical impediments to human development in the Arab region.

Chapters 3 through 8 address what must be done to reduce constraints and increase opportunities in areas critical for human development, especially for coming generations, by focusing respectively on measures for building, using and liberating human capabilities. Chapter 3 considers the basics of life, health and habitat. Chapter 4 strongly advocates the building of human capabilities through education and proposes guidelines and action areas for reform. Chapter 5 discusses how to use knowledge acquisition to work towards the establishment of an Arab information society. Chapter 6 looks at issues of growth, employment and poverty, and how better to use human capabilities, foster growth, attack joblessness and poverty, and integrate the Arab region equitably with the global economy. Chapter 7 highlights an enabling governance and institutional framework for human development as the essential foundation for liberating people's potential in the Arab region. This institutional context, in the case of the Arab countries, extends to the perspective of Arab cooperation, which is discussed in chapter 8.

Giving democracy low priority has not helped to reinforce the necessary participation and unity needed between civic and political circles in the Arab States.

CHAPTER 2

The state of human development in the Arab region

This chapter starts with a brief discussion of the paucity of data and information on human development in the region and the challenges these gaps pose. It then summarizes the status of core human-development measures for the region compared to those for other regions of the world and over time, based primarily on the HDI. The chapter introduces three deficits that are considered to be defining features of Arab countries that impede human development. As an additional yardstick for judging the importance of some of the themes discussed in subsequent chapters, it reports on the findings of a limited survey of the opinions of young Arabs on major issues. On the basis of these various analyses, the conclusion is reached that the region is at a decisive crossroads. Some of the key challenges that the region faces are then identified.

PRELIMINARY NOTE: DATA DEFICIENCIES

The Arab region suffers from a severe shortage of detailed data and information necessary to undertake a comprehensive examination of human development, especially but not only with respect to the dimensions of institutional context and knowledge acquisition. The inadequacy of reliable, comparative and recent data from Arab sources makes it necessary at times to use international data sources. These sources can present problems. They sometimes resort to estimation to arrive at region-wide indicators where corresponding data for individual countries within those regions are not available. Another difficulty is that various international organizations classify Arab countries differently, making consistent comparisons across these classifications difficult.

The limited production and dissemination of data and information by many developing countries, including Arab countries, are unfortunate but not surprising. They reflect some of the consequences of underdevelopment, including suboptimal governmental capacity and decision-making processes, which weaken demand for data and information, in turn retarding their production and dissemination.

This Report presents as solid an assessment of the state of human development in Arab countries as can be supported by the current information base. Nevertheless, the relative fragility of the data and information base means that caution is needed in drawing conclusions from it. The Report has endeavoured to exercise due caution in this respect, and readers are invited to do likewise.

BASIC MEASURES OF HUMAN DEVELOPMENT: REGIONAL COMPARISONS

This section briefly compares Arab countries as a group with other world regions with respect to the UNDP HDI and three of its four component indicators.

As can be seen from figure 2.1, the Arab region outperformed sub-Saharan Africa and South Asia on the overall HDI and on indicators of overall health (life expectancy at birth) and educational attainment (proxied here by adult literacy). It has yet to reach the levels attained by East Asia (with or without China)

The Arab region suffers from a severe shortage of detailed data and information necessary to undertake a comprehensive examination of human development.

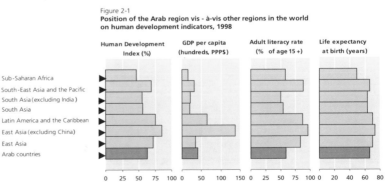

Figure 2-1
Position of the Arab region vis - à-vis other regions in the world on human development indicators, 1998

and Latin America and the Caribbean for these indicators. Evidently, it is the latter comparison, i.e., with regions that have done better, that matters in any discussion of enhancing human development in the Arab region. Comparing the region with those that have done less well could invite undesirable self-congratulation in the face of major challenges.

The relative position of the Arab region improves with respect to the per capita output indicator (PPP basis), where it outperformed the South-East Asia and the Pacific region as well as South Asia and sub-Saharan Africa. The Arab region might thus be said to be richer than it is developed with respect to basic human-development indicators.

Since a strong association exists at the global level between per capita output and the HDI, the above data could indicate that Arab countries may have invested more in building physical capital than in developing human resources. This in turn suggests the great scope for future investment by Arab countries in the formation of human capital, a major cornerstone of human development.

BASIC MEASURES OF HUMAN DEVELOPMENT: REGIONAL COMPARISONS OVER TIME

This section briefly compares the Arab countries as a group with other world regions in terms of trends in the HDI over time (figure 2.2).[1] The HDI value for the Arab region was

The Arab region might be said to be richer than it is developed with respect to basic human-development indicators.

lower than the global average throughout the period from 1980 to 1999. Over time, the region again did better than sub-Saharan Africa and South Asia. It also narrowed the gap with Latin American and Caribbean countries—but the gap remains. The East Asia and the Pacific (EAP) region showed the most rapid gains. Although the Arab region matched the EAP rate of improvement in HDI values in the 1980s, it fell slightly further behind in the 1990s.

DIFFERENCES IN THE ARAB REGION

Arab countries present a very heterogeneous picture with respect to the HDI. Of the 19 countries for which 1998 values are available (UNDP, 2000) (data were unavailable for the occupied Palestinian territory and Somalia), four large-scale oil exporters are classified as "high human-development" countries. Four other countries are included in the "low human-development" group. Somalia (for which values could not be calculated) should also be considered in this group. (These latter five countries account for about one fifth of the total Arab population.) The remaining 11 Arab countries fall into the "medium human-development" category.

To further illustrate this heterogeneity, the highest-ranking Arab country on the HDI (Kuwait) scored only slightly lower than the world leader (Canada). At the other extreme, the lowest-scoring Arab country on this yard-

Figure 2.2
Trends in the HDI, 1980-1999

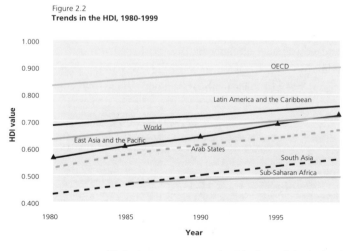

Figure 2-3
HDI values, Arab countries,

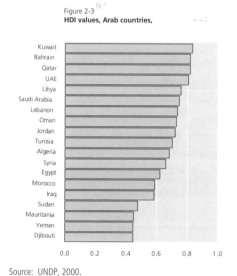

Source: UNDP, 2000.

[1] Regional averages were computed, weighted by population size, based on data derived from HDR 2001. The calculations included only those countries that have data for the entire period and only those regions where over two thirds of the regional population are represented. HDI values were available for seven Arab countries: Algeria, Egypt, Jordan, Morocco, Saudi Arabia, Syrian Arab Republic and Tunisia.

stick, Djibouti, is not much better off than the country with the world's lowest HDI value (Sierra Leone). In other words, the range of disparity among Arab countries on the HDI (figure 2.3) is almost as wide as that observed in the entire world.

THE THREE DEFICITS

As suggested in chapter 1 and as subsequent chapters will illustrate, human development in the Arab region needs to be assessed against a wider set of measures than GDP or those of the HDI. Scrutiny of Arab socio-economic systems from the perspective of Human Development in its broader sense encompassing freedom and human rights, shows that the region is hampered by three key deficits that can be considered defining features:

•   the freedom deficit;
•   the women's empowerment deficit;
•   the human capabilities/knowledge deficit relative to income.

Each of these deficits is discussed in detail below.

THE FREEDOM DEFICIT

If human development is indeed freedom, as discussed in chapter 1, the measurement of freedom should be of paramount concern in the analysis of development. However, freedom is a concept that has been notoriously intractable to measurement, and it is widely felt that the prevailing basis for assessments of such difficult-to-quantify phenomena as freedom smacks of bias and a lack of rigour. However, the inextricable links between freedom and human development make it necessary to try to quantify the presence or absence of freedom in the context of the present Report. One way to do so is to look at a set of aspects of civil and political freedoms. Of course, human freedom encompasses much more than political freedom. However, since civil and political freedoms are considered among the most important instrumental freedoms, what follows focuses on these dimensions of freedom, using the freedom index to characterize the extent of freedom in Arab countries compared to other regions in the

world, and among Arab countries themselves. At this level of aggregate analysis, this approach would seem to be acceptable if inevitably incomplete.

Out of seven world regions, the Arab countries had the lowest freedom score in the late 1990s (figure 2.4).

Figure 2-4
Average value of freedom scores, world regions, 1998-99

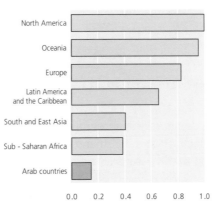

The low level of freedom in the Arab region is confirmed by a set of indicators of "voice and accountability" derived from another international database (Kaufman et al, 1999b). This set includes a number of indicators measuring various aspects of the political process, civil liberties, political rights and independence of the media. As figure 2.5 shows, the Arab region also has the lowest value of all regions of the world for voice and accountability.

Figure 2-5
Average value of "voice and accountability" indicators, world regions, 1998

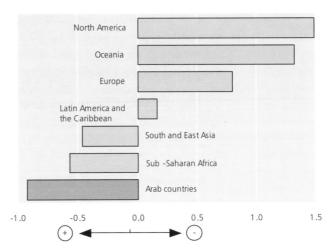

Source: A. A. Ali, background paper for the AHDR.

More telling still is figure 2.6, which shows that freedom scores for individual Arab coun-

Figure 2-6
HDI ranks and freedom scores, Arab countries, 1998

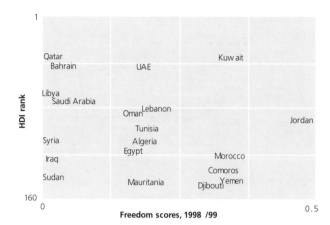

culate 1995 GEM values for only 14 Arab countries because the necessary data were not available in many Arab countries. This fact itself reflects an apparent limited concern for women's empowerment in the region.

Figure 2-7
Average GEM values, world regions, 1995

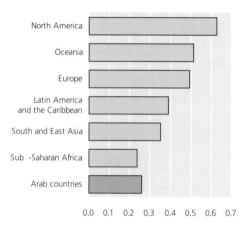

Source: data derived from HDR 1995. Regional averages are weighted by population size.

tries do not tally at all with their standing on the HDI. (If they did, country symbols in the graph would have been concentrated on the diagonal connecting the lower left and upper right corners.) Countries with essentially the same HDI value can vary tremendously in their freedom scores.

THE WOMEN'S EMPOWERMENT DEFICIT

As noted in chapter 1, gender empowerment is a critical aspect of human freedom. Applying the UNDP gender empowerment measure (GEM)[2] to Arab countries clearly reveals that the latter suffer a glaring deficit in women's empowerment. Among regions of the world, the Arab region ranks next to last as measured by GEM; only sub-Saharan Africa has a lower score.

It should be noted that Arab countries have scored important successes in girls' education although the share of girls in enrolment is still relatively low, especially in higher education, as shown elsewhere in this Report. The main reason for the low GEM values of Arab countries is the limited participation of women in political organizations, as noted in chapter 7.

As with freedom, the next stage of analysis is to see how women's empowerment in individual Arab countries as measured by the GEM relates to their country's HDI position. It is worth noting that UNDP was able to cal-

Arab countries clearly suffer a glaring deficit in women's empowerment.

For the Arab countries with GEM values (figure 2.8), no clear association is observed between the HDI and GEM. As with the freedom index, there is no correlation between the extent of gender empowerment in Arab countries and human development as measured by the HDI.

Figure 2-8
HDI rank and GEM values, Arab countries

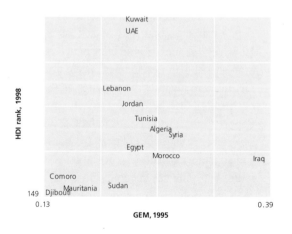

[2] The GEM measures the participation of women in economic, professional and political activities using the indicators of income per capita (PPP$), women's percentage share of professional and technical positions, and women's percentage share of parliamentary seats, respectively.

Human capabilities in the region are relatively weak and poorly utilized, as subsequent chapters will show. A subsidiary deficit in human capabilities is revealed by better results in the area of health than in educational attainment in Arab countries. This is evident from figure 2.1, which indicates that, compared to high-ranking HDI regions, the Arab region suffers smaller shortfalls for the overall health indicator used in HDI (life expectancy at birth) than for educational attainment (proxied, in figure 2.1, by adult literacy). In an age of knowledge intensity, poor knowledge acquisition, let alone its production, is a serious shortfall. A telling indicator of the poor level of educational attainment in the Arab countries is the persistence of illiteracy rates that are higher, and educational enrolment rates that are lower, than those of dynamic less developed countries in East Asia and Latin America.

This shortfall underlies the emphasis that this Report places on building and using human capabilities, markedly in relation to knowledge acquisition. One proxy for access to knowledge in this age of connectivity is the number of Internet hosts per 1,000 people. The Arab region has the lowest level of access to ICT of all regions of the world, even lower than sub-Saharan Africa (figure 2.9).

Moreover, all Arab countries except for Kuwait and the United Arab Emirates seem to be equal in their ICT poverty, irrespective of their HDI level (figure 2.10).

THE VOICES OF YOUTH

A more subjective but illuminating yardstick for the state of human development is represented by an effort to measure the concerns of youth, appropriate in a report dedicated to coming generations.

A standardized opinion poll of Arab youth was conducted under the sponsorship of UNDP country offices. The poll was originally meant to cover a limited number (24) of young Arabs (15 to 20 years of age) in each Member State of the Arab League.

In each country, the sample was to be divided equally between the sexes and roughly

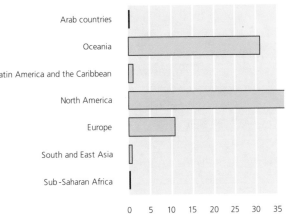

Figure 2-9
Internet hosts (per 1,000 population), world regions, 1998

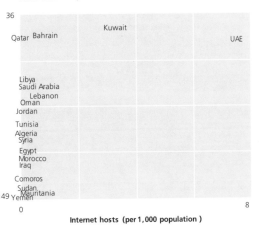

Figure 2-10
HDI rank and internet hosts per 1,000 population, Arab countries, 1998

representative of three levels of socio-economic status (above average, average, below average). Responses from only five Arab countries (Egypt, Jordan, Lebanon, Libyan Arab Jamahiriya and United Arab Emirates) were available at the time of writing. However, the views of young Saudis became available through a published source (Yamani, M., in Arabic, 2001).

The questionnaire was also distributed at the 21st Arab Children's Conference held in Amman, Jordan from 10 to 17 July 2001, an event organized by the Performing Arts Centre of the Noor al-Hussein Foundation, with backing from the United Nations Population Fund (UNFPA). Organizers of the conference allowed the lead author of the Report to speak to the participants, ages 13 to 17, and obtain their responses to the questionnaire. Thus, 112 additional questionnaires, representing youths from 14 Arab countries,

The Arab region has the lowest level of access to ICT of all regions of the world, even lower than sub-Saharan Africa

were completed. However, the new sample increases the relative representation of young Jordanians since the conference was held in Amman. It also includes individuals who are younger than the sample for which the questionnaire was originally intended.

In the following analysis (figure 2.11), the responses of younger and older groups are considered separately to see if there are differences in their views.

Figure 2-11
Key issues for young Arabs

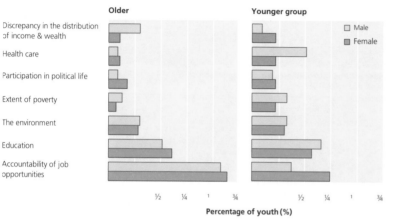

RESULTS OF THE OPINION POLL

An analysis of what the older group considered to be the most important issues among the topics considered in the Report indicates the following priorities: first, job opportunities (45 per cent of the respondents), followed by education (23 per cent), the environment (12 per cent), distribution of income and wealth (8 per cent), political participation (5 per cent), health care (4 per cent) and poverty (4 per cent). Young women expressed relatively more concern than did young men about education, work, political participation and health care.

Among the younger group, education (at 25 per cent) tops the list of concerns, followed by jobs (23 per cent), health care (15 per cent), the environment (13 per cent), poverty (11 per cent), political participation (8 per cent) and distribution of income and wealth (6 per cent).

It is noteworthy that the younger group expressed keener interest in health care, poverty and political participation, which indicates social sensitivity and early maturity among this group. Younger females expressed relatively higher concern than younger males

Overall, the poll clearly suggests that job availability is the most common concern of youth, followed by education.

about work availability and the distribution of income and wealth.

Overall, the poll clearly suggests that job availability is the most common concern of youth, followed by education. The youth of individual countries expressed concern over other problems, including drugs and inadequate health care, reliance on foreign labour and job squeezes in labour markets where expatriate and national workers compete.

Remarkably, 51 per cent of older youths expressed a desire to emigrate to other countries, clearly indicating their dissatisfaction with current conditions and future prospects in their home countries.

Among those contemplating emigration, European countries were the favourite destination (46 per cent of respondents, 21 per cent of whom chose the United Kingdom alone), followed by the United States and Canada (36 per cent), and other Arab countries (13 per cent). The implicit judgement of how liveable these young people consider Arab societies to be is evident.

The younger group expressed slightly less of a desire to emigrate, with 45 per cent indicating their wish to do so. Young women showed less desire to leave their countries than young men did. With respect to the emigration destination, the younger group differed from the older one, with North America and other Arab countries being chosen more often (45 per cent and 21 per cent, respectively) and Europe less frequently although it was still the choice of a substantial percentage (32 per cent).

In general, the younger youths, particularly girls, seem to be somewhat more attached to their countries and aware of broad social issues such as participation and poverty. The expressed priorities of young people for education, together with the influence that education can have on the thinking of young people provide a strong reason to focus, as this Report does, on education systems in Arab countries.

Clearly, the responses obtained and analysed here do not constitute a probability sample of Arab youth large enough to permit valid generalizations about the entire universe of young Arabs. The aim of the poll was, within the limitations imposed by time and finances, to obtain qualitative responses from purposive samples of Arab youth. Despite the small number of young people polled (240, including 128 in the five Arab countries and 112 at the Arab Children's Conference), of whom 53 per cent are girls, respondents had definite views on a wide spectrum of issues and expressed deep-seated concerns about, and a strong desire for, a better future. Their voices speak to many of the central issues examined elsewhere in this Report.

THE ARAB REGION AT A CROSSROADS

The conclusion from the preceding sections is that a broader approach to the concept of human development suggests that it is perhaps premature to celebrate the achievements of Arab countries as measured by the standard HDI. As this chapter has suggested, there are significant deficits in Arab countries with respect to key elements of human well-being: civil and political freedoms, the status of women in society and access to knowledge.

Indeed, as the world moves into the twenty-first century, the Arab world is at a crossroads. There are huge inter-country disparities in the region. While some countries have done well in terms of income and material wealth, human development remains low in many instances. Poverty and deprivation in their many forms remain real in many Arab societies. In some instances, as in the case of the occupied Palestinian territory, the level and degree of human deprivation under occupation reaches extreme levels. Hanan Ashrawi in her individual contribution to this Report (box 2.1) speaks to this issue :
Continued occupation of Arab territories, the political instability that ensues and poor governance in the region place major obstacles in the way of human development, particularly with respect to the non-material aspects of human well-being.

Beyond the question of occupation, millions have lost lives and livelihoods because of conflict driven by regional and extra-regional factors. Furthermore, in a vicious circle of cause and effect, conflict has both led to, and

resulted from, enormous resources being directed to the acquisition and development of arms and armies.

Political upheavals, military conflicts, sanctions and embargoes have affected many economies of the region, causing declines in productivity, disrupting markets and retarding human development. This latter impact is starkly manifested in the condition of children in Iraq, who more than any other group bear the brunt of human development under siege (box 2.2). Some countries struggling to recover from the ravages of war have emerged with substantial debts, limiting options for public expenditure. All affected countries have emerged with compounded socio-political problems that have retarded progressive moves towards liberalization and democratization.

The region's development prospects cannot significantly improve unless a dynamic process of vigorous human development is initiated and maintained. The severe consequences of a continuation of present trends means that all Arabs need to make inescapable strategic choices. These choices need to be faced directly and urgently.

The fundamental choice is whether the region's trajectory in history will remain characterized by inertia, including the persistence of institutional structures and types of actions that have produced the substantial development challenges it currently faces, or whether prospects will emerge for an Arab renaissance that will build a prosperous future for all Arabs, especially coming generations. The Arab responses to a number of derived challenges will jointly determine which of those two historical trajectories the Arab region will follow:
• First, the choice between continuation of dependency on societies that are leaders in the production of knowledge--and building a capacity to belong, from a position of strength, to the global knowledge society by establishing an effective, dynamic knowledge-acquisition system. This is one of the main keys to progress in the Arab world. There is an increasing need to strive to overcome backwardness in the area of knowledge acquisition and

It is perhaps premature to celebrate the achievements of Arab countries as measured by the standard HDI.

BOX 2.1

Human development: the Palestinian perspective
A special contribution

Cast outside the course of history, deprived of the most basic rights and requirements for a life of dignity and freedom — let alone for sustainable human development — the people of Palestine are made to endure all forms of exclusion, oppression, and exploitation.

The dual injustices of dispossession, dispersion and exile on the one hand and of occupation and enslavement on the other have rendered the Palestinians entirely vulnerable to all manner of denial and victimization.

Deprived of the right to life, land, and even historical affirmation by Israel's relentless attempts to negate Palestinian sovereignty, national identity and continuity, the Palestinian people have been engaged in the dual process of nation-building and peace-making as an act of will and as a force of human redemption.

Simultaneously engaged in the struggle for survival and liberation, we are committed to those values and endeavours that render life meaningful and imbue it with value. Traditional indicators and gauges, however, fall far short of encompassing or even adequately assessing the full scope and complexity of the challenges that confront us.

Ensuring a human-based and inclusive system of governance, generating equitable systems for economic growth and social justice, combating poverty and preventing regression in education and health standards, empowering women and children and other vulnerable sectors of society, while legislating for a constitutional democracy that would guarantee justice and the rule of law have all become integral components of our survival strategies.

The tenacious pursuit and proclamation of our human-development agenda are rapidly being overpowered by the deafening din of the occupation's military onslaughts. Imprisoned on our own lands by a multiple, and suffocating, state of siege, our homes and institutions are being shelled and bombed on a daily basis, our activists and leaders assassinated, while innocent children and adults are murdered in cold blood. Prevented from laying claim to our resources and rights, we witness our lands being confiscated and our crops and trees destroyed. Israeli military checkpoints fragment our human and territorial continuity and have become the most brutal expression of a discriminatory and pervasive system of wilful humiliation and subjugation. All rights--including the right to shelter; to educational and health services; to work; to a clean and untainted environment; to a life free from war, fear and coercion; to governance as an expression of the collective will for internal justice and to gain access to the tools of information and knowledge--have been obliterated.

No instruments have been devised to measure such wholesale destruction. A quantitative approach may be possible for the assessment of the number of hectares confiscated, trees uprooted, victims murdered or injured, jobs lost and income severed. However, the human mind has not succeeded in measuring the full import of the loss of hope and the usurpation of the future of a whole nation. Nor can the collective and individual traumas of children in the grip of horror and fear be quantified — despite the frequency of nightmares, bedwetting incidents, and uncontrollable behaviour.

The poverty level that defies any measure is the poverty of spirit and its concomitant moral bankruptcy that are the essence of the occupation. The impunity it enjoys before a global rule of law and its immunity to intervention and accountability exact a heavy toll on the measure of humanity as a whole. Such devaluation — at once of Palestinian human rights and lives and of Israeli culpability and moral responsibility — is also immeasurable. The courage to intervene, rectify and redress such a comprehensive exercise of cruelty and violation remains beyond value.

Hanan Ashrawi

to put knowledge to work effectively in Arab societies. At the beginning of the third millennium, knowledge acquisition through education/learning and research and development and its effective use are of crucial importance to the Arab world, whether with respect to their impact on good governance, on ensuring good health or on providing other prerequisites for material and moral well-being.

A related strategic choice is between preserving the present institutional context that has proved unfavourable to development and moving to build an institutional structure that supports a social contract enabling human development.

• Second, the choice between continuing to face the challenges of the region, the world and the new century individually and remain weak and marginal—and constructing institutional arrangements that can transform the huge potential of Arab integration into a reality. All human societies, including the most advanced, strive to belong to larger entities able to compete in a globalized world characterized by intense competition. This leads directly to the third challenge.

• Third, a choice between remaining on the margins of the modern world--and developing a new societal capacity, on both the national and pan-Arab levels, sufficient to ensure not

BOX 2.2:

Children in Iraq: human development under siege

"The increase in mortality reported in public hospitals for children under five years of age (an excess of some 40,000 deaths yearly compared with 1989) is mainly due to diarrhoea, pneumonia and malnutrition. In those over five years of age, the increase (an excess of some 50,000 deaths yearly compared with 1989) is associated with heart disease, hypertension, diabetes, cancer, liver or kidney diseases."

"Malnutrition was not a public health problem in Iraq prior to the embargo. Its extent became apparent during 1991 and the prevalence has increased greatly since then: 18% in 1991 to 31% in 1996 of [children] under five with chronic malnutrition (stunting); 9% to 26% with underweight malnutrition; 3% to 11% with wasting (acute malnutrition), an increase or over 200%. By 1997, it was estimated about one million children under five were [chronically] malnourished."

"The situation throughout Iraq remains one in which the child's right to survival and health care as decreed by the Convention on Rights for the Child remains subject to overwhelming risks to life and health generated by the economic hardship."

"[Before the 1990 sanctions] primary medical care reached about 97% of the urban population, and 78% of rural residents...[Now] the health system is affected by lack of even basic hospital and health centre equipment and supplies for medical, surgical and diagnostic services...In 1989, the [Iraqi] Ministry of Health spent more than US$500 million for drugs and supplies; the budget is [now] reduced by 90-95%.

only openness to the new world being shaped by globalization, a world in which distance shrinks but geography and culture remain strongly present in all spheres of human activity, but also a capacity for active participation in shaping this new world from a position of capability and security.

Wise, forward-looking and courageous responses by Arab countries to these challenges are needed to liberate the full potential of the region, capture the imaginations and minds of its young people, and transform the state of human development as portrayed by the foregoing data and in the next chapters of this Report.

Wise, forward-looking and courageous responses by Arab countries to these challenges are needed to liberate the full potential of the region.

Source: UNICEF, Situation Analysis of Children and Women in Iraq, 30 April 1998.

CHAPTER 3

Building human capabilities: the basics—life, health, habitat

Chapters 1 and 2 set the scene for the chapters that follow, which successively discuss key aspects of building (chapters 3 and 4), using (chapters 5 and 6) and liberating human capabilities (chapter 7). This chapter discusses the basic conditions for human development in Arab countries: population size and characteristics, together with issues relating to the population's health, and the physical environment in which people live. These factors are interrelated, and their status and evolution directly affect human welfare. Taken together, they have an important impact on issues discussed in later chapters, for example, developing a knowledge society, enhancing economic performance and reducing poverty. Key demographic features of the region include historically high but gradually declining fertility and population growth rates and an expected decline in the dependency ratio over the coming 20 years, reflecting a small rise in the percentage of the population over 65 but a very large reduction in the proportion of children (from around two fifths of the total to about one quarter). With respect to health, conditions vary widely from country to country, but a number of important areas for improvement stand out: reduction in infant, child and maternal mortality; better management of health care, including more attention to primary care, preventive care and behavioural factors that damage health; and ensuring access to care for the poor. With respect to habitat, while Arab countries vary very widely in topography and climatic conditions, a number of region-wide issues and concerns have emerged in recent years, most importantly, severe water and arable land scarcity coupled with environmental degradation, urbanization and air pollution, and coastal area pollution. The section on environment closes with a series of principles for meeting the environmental challenges the region faces and strategic guidelines for protecting the region's habitat endorsed by the Council of Arab Ministers Responsible for the Environment.

LIFE: DEMOGRAPHIC PROFILE[1]

POPULATION SIZE AND MAIN CHARACTERISTICS

The combined population of the region covered by this Report was about 280 million in 2000, approximately equal to that of the United States but only around one fourth of India's population and one fifth that of China. Population size varies very substantially by country, with just six countries with populations of over 20 million accounting for 200 million of the total. Egypt has the largest population (68 million), followed by Sudan (31 million) and Algeria (30 million). At the other end of the scale, Qatar has a population of 565,000, and Bahrain, Comoros, and Djibouti have a population of less than one million each. In global terms, the Arab countries account for about 5 per cent of world population; this share has approximately doubled over the past 50 years. Over this period, population increases have also varied sharply by country: at one extreme, the population of the United Arab Emirates has multiplied 36 times; at the

In global terms, the Arab countries account for about 5 per cent of world population; this share has approximately doubled over the past 50 years.

---

[1] Source of data and limitations: The data used in this section are derived mainly from "The World Population Prospects: The 2000 Revision Highlights" (United Nations, Department of Economic and Social Affairs, Population Division, 2001). United Nations data were used to ensure uniformity. However, data for the occupied Palestinian territory were not available in the United Nations sources. Therefore, data for the occupied Palestinian territory were derived from "Arab World Population, Selected Demographic and Reproductive Health Indicators" (Population Reference Bureau, Arab World Region, International Planned Parenthood Federation (IPPF), 1996). These data represent only the Arab population of the West Bank and Gaza. It is worth mentioning that United Nations data still include estimates of the population of the West Bank and Gaza with those of Jordan, which implies a slight inflation of the population of the Arab region presented here.

other, Lebanon's has grown only 2.4 times.

Some Arab countries, especially in the Gulf, have also become home to substantial expatriate populations, reflecting a combination of the oil boom and domestic labour shortages. The number of foreign workers in the six Gulf countries increased fivefold from 1.1 million in 1970 to 5.2 million in 1990. By 1990, foreign nationals constituted over two thirds of the population in the Gulf States. In Saudi Arabia, non-Saudis accounted for approximately 25 per cent of the 1999 population. Some observers have expressed concern about substantial reliance on non-Arab labour, particularly in the areas of domestic service and child-rearing.

SEX AND AGE STRUCTURE

The sex ratio (the number of males per 100 females) is around 104 in the Arab world, close to the global ratio of 102. Again, however, there are marked differences among countries, with the ratio ranging from 89 in Djibouti to 195 in the United Arab Emirates. The sex ratio is higher in the Gulf Cooperation Council (GCC) States (figure 3.1), reflecting the presence of large numbers of male foreign workers.

The age structure of the population is significantly younger than the global average (figure 3.2), reflecting the large proportion (38 per cent) of children ages 0 to14 and the relatively small proportion of those age 60 and older (six per cent). The population's young age structure means that the dependency ratio (the ratio of the economically inactive to the working age population, defined as those 15 to 64 years of age) is around 0.8, above the world average.

As with the sex ratio, country age structures vary widely, with the proportion of those under 15 ranging from 26 per cent in the United Arab Emirates to 50 per cent in Yemen. With respect to the elderly, the percentage of national populations age 60 and over varies from around eight per cent in Lebanon and Tunisia to three per cent in Qatar. Differences in age structure reflect international migration and differing fertility rates and in turn yield different dependency ratios, which are lower in the GCC countries than elsewhere in the Arab world, owing to the presence of large numbers of foreign workers.

FERTILITY

Fertility rates have declined significantly in many Arab countries but are still high by international standards. The countries covered by the World Bank's Middle East and North Africa (MENA) classification had an average fertility rate of 6.2 in 1980, which had fallen to 3.5 by 1998—still well above the world average of 2.7. Arab countries can be classified into three groups with respect to fertility rates: one at an advanced stage of demographic transition with low rates, a second in the middle of the transition process, and a third group still at early stages of transition with very high fertility rates.

The first group consists of only four countries with a total fertility rate (TFR) of less than three births per woman: Bahrain, Kuwait, Lebanon, and Tunisia. Lebanon and Tunisia share the lowest rate, 2.2 births per woman (HDR 2001). Of these four countries, three—Bahrain, Lebanon and Tunisia—have fertility rates below the global average.

The second group of countries includes nine with a TFR of between three and five births per woman: Algeria, Egypt, Jordan, Libyan Arab Jamahiriya, Morocco, Qatar, Sudan, Syrian Arab Republic and United Arab Emirates. Of these countries, the United Arab Emirates is closest to moving to the advanced stage of transition.

The remaining nine Arab countries are in

Fertility rates have declined significantly in many Arab countries but are still high by international standards.

Figure 3-1
Sex ratio **(males/females), GCC states and the Arab world**

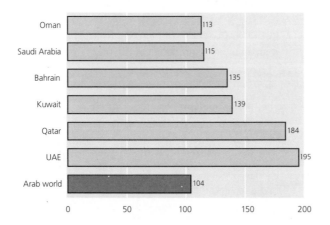

the early stage of transition, with total fertility rates of more than five births per woman. Yemen has the highest rate, 7.6 births in an average woman's reproductive life. Somalia is the only other Arab country with a TFR of over seven births per woman (7.25).

POPULATION GROWTH

High fertility rates are associated with rapid population growth. Among the Arab countries, population growth rates ranged from a low of 1.1 per cent in Tunisia to a high of 4.1 per cent in Yemen; of the 22 Arab countries, only Tunisia had a growth rate below the global average of 1.4 per cent.

POPULATION PROJECTIONS

Population projections for the period 2000-2020 were prepared under two scenarios.
• Scenario one: assuming that the total fertility rate and life expectancy at birth are constant at the estimated level for 2000;
• Scenario two: using the total fertility rate and life expectancy at birth as estimated by the United Nations for single years during the period 2000-2020.

In both scenarios, the impact of migration is assumed to be limited to the impact of past migration on the age structure of the population.

POPULATION PROJECTIONS: NUMBERS

The two scenarios yield slightly different numbers for future population size. By 2020, the Arab population is expected to be 459 million under scenario one (stable fertility at the current level), and 410 million under scenario two (figure 3.3).

Differences under the two scenarios would be the smallest for the countries identified earlier as being at an advanced stage of demographic transition, more significant for the middle group, and greatest for the group whose members still have very high fertility rates. Under the first scenario, only the population of Egypt is expected to exceed 100 million by 2020, and no other country would have

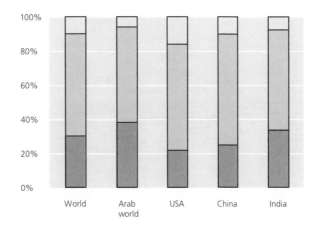

Figure 3-2
Age structure of Arab population and other selected countries

a population of 50 million. Under the second scenario, Egypt's population would not reach the 100 million mark.

POPULATION PROJECTIONS: AGE STRUCTURE

Declining fertility combined with rising life expectancy at birth will affect the age structure of the population in Arab countries. Under the second scenario, for example, while the number of children in all Arab countries is expected to grow by around 4.5 million in the period 2000-2020 (with increases in some countries such as Saudi Arabia, Somalia and Yemen and decreases in others such as Algeria and Egypt), the percentage of children in the population will fall by 10-20 percentage points in the majority of Arab countries. Taking all the Arab countries together, the proportion of children in the population is projected to fall from around two fifths to slightly over one quarter. This would represent a dramatic shift, with important socio-economic implications. For example, even taking account of a rise in the proportion of elderly (see below), the net

By 2020, the Arab population is expected to be 459 million under scenario one , and 410 million under scenario two

TABLE 3.1		
Population growth in Arab countries		
Population growth (less than 2%)	Population growth (2%–3%)	Population growth (3% or more)
Algeria	Bahrain	Mauritania
Egypt	Comoros	Occupied
Lebanon	Djibouti	Palestinian
Morocco	Iraq	territory
Qatar	Jordan	Oman
Tunisia	Kuwait	Saudi Arabia
	Libyan Arab	Somalia
	Jamahiriya	Yemen
	Sudan	
	Syrian Arab Republic	
	United Arab Emirates	

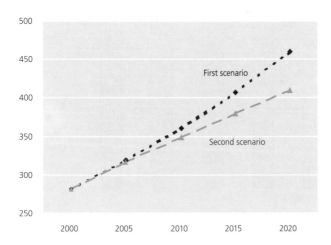

HEALTH

Building a useful picture of health in the Arab region is governed by the availability of good comparative data. Unfortunately, the data suffer from two systemic limitations: they relate mainly to the purely physical aspects of health (leaving out broader aspects of well-being), and within the physical dimension, they focus mainly on mortality indicators. The discussion that follows will attempt to look at some aspects of health where only limited data exist in order to (a) draw attention to neglected health concerns and (b) highlight the need for a more holistic social- health approach to health assessment that includes consideration of a larger set of health conditions than that covered by a pathology-oriented medical model for a few conditions. Nevertheless, it is right to begin with the aspects of health for which fairly good data exist.

MEASURES OF HEALTH STATUS

Survival

Life expectancy at birth varies very widely among Arab countries, from a low of around 45 years (Djibouti and Somalia) to a level approaching 75 years (United Arab Emirates), close to that of the high-income countries (78 years in 1998). The World Bank's World Development Indicators give an average for countries in its Middle East and North Africa classification of 68 years in 1998, one year higher than the world average.

In all Arab countries, life expectancy for women either equals or exceeds that for males, but the difference between the two sexes is 2.5 years or less in around two thirds of the countries; for the remainder, the difference is between 3 and 3.5 years. The global average difference is around 4 years, and in countries with high human development, it can be as much as 11 years. This suggests that there is room for improvement in women's chances for survival in Arab countries. One area for action is reduction of high maternal mortality rates, as discussed later in this section.

effect would be to lower the dependency ratio in all Arab countries—a potential gift to these countries because more people of working age would be able to support the non-working population with better services for all.

With respect to the elderly, the second scenario suggests an increase in the proportion of the population age 65 or older from 3 per cent in 2000 to 5 per cent in 2020. The percentage of elderly is expected to be highest in the United Arab Emirates (9 per cent) and lowest in Yemen (3 per cent).

The demographic profile described above presents both challenges and opportunities for Arab countries. Population size, growth and age distribution can be either a demographic gift or a demographic curse, depending on whether countries can use the human potential represented by their populations well enough to satisfy people's aspirations for a fulfilling life. For example, a large, rapidly growing population can be an engine of material development and human welfare when other factors conducive to economic growth—such as high levels of investment and appropriate types of technological know-how—are present. Absent such factors, however, it can be a force for immiseration as more and more people pursue limited resources and jobs. In addition, any population is only as capable of achieving its human development goals as it is blessed with good health—the topic of the next section.

Population size, growth and age distribution can be either a demographic gift or a demographic curse.

Disability-adjusted expectation of life at birth

The World Health Organization (WHO) estimates the disability-adjusted expectation of life at birth (DALE).[2] Given the nature of information in the Arab region, the range of uncertainty in these estimates is likely to be quite broad. Nevertheless, the use of the DALE is helpful in highlighting the toll on healthy lives that disease and disability take. It also suggests the importance of improving the existing information base on different types of disability.

The estimates show that the burden of disease and disability reduces life expectancy by between 5 and 11 years. Close to a third of Arab countries lose more than nine years of life expectancy to disability. It should be noted that the expectation of disability at birth tends to be higher for females than males. The excess is more than two years in about half of the countries considered. Thus females lose most of their initial survival advantage by spending more life-years in disability—again pointing up women's health as a priority for policy.

Countries with the highest survival rates are not necessarily those with lower disability. Kuwait, Oman and Qatar, for example, lose more than nine years in disability (figure 3.4). Internationally, most countries with low mortality rates tend to lose only between six and seven years in disability.

Burden of ill health

The high burden of ill health in countries with the highest survival rates is further confirmed by the recently conducted Gulf Family Health Surveys. Close to one in five adults (age 15+) in each of these countries experiences a long-standing illness or disability[3], and females tend to have a much higher burden than males. The proportion of females reporting long-standing illness exceeds that of males by more than 6 per cent and can be up to 8.5 per cent higher.

Available estimates of disability are in the neighbourhood of eight to 24 per thousand. However, it is believed that these are generally underestimates. [4]

Infant and child mortality

Both infant and under-five mortality vary greatly among Arab countries. The infant mortality rate (IMR) ranges from a low of 10.2 per thousand in Qatar to a high of 75.3 for Yemen. The under-five rate varies from less than 20 to over 100 per thousand. Bahrain, Kuwait, Qatar and the United Arab Emirates have very low child mortality (below 20 per thousand), while Djibouti, Iraq, Mauritania, Somalia, Sudan and Yemen experience extremely high levels (despite the fact that Iraq had achieved a rate in the neighbourhood of 20 before the Gulf War).

Current levels of infant and child mortality in Arab countries need to be assessed against very high past levels and the generally rapid pace of improvement. One commentator has noted that "mortality rates for children under five were reduced by nearly two thirds. The Arab region was the first region in the developing world where most countries reduced mortality rates of under-five children to the target of 70 per thousand by 1990, well ahead of the global goal" (Doraid, 2000:4). "In general, oil-rich countries made rapid progress. Nevertheless, rapid progress was not limited to the oil-rich Arab countries; Tunisia and Yemen were among the 10 countries that experienced the fastest improvements in the world in, respectively, raising life expectancy and reducing under-five mortality" (ibid.:5).

Differences also exist within countries. With the exception of the Syrian Arab Republic, the disparities between rural and urban areas are very evident. The ratio of rural to urban under-five mortality is from 1.21-fold to as high as twofold. Even countries that have been quite successful in reducing overall under-five mortality are suffering from this difference, which poses a serious challenge in terms of equity.

Close to a third of Arab countries lose more than nine years of life expectancy to disability.

---

[2] The DALE index requires information on prevalence of different types of disease and disability at each age as well as assumptions about the relative weights of the different types of disability.

[3] A person is considered to have a long-standing illness or disability if he/she is reported to have had any of the following doctor-diagnosed conditions: high blood pressure, heart disease, diabetes, stroke, asthma, joint disease, peptic disease, renal disease, liver disease, nervous disease, cancer or any long-standing condition that prevents or limits his/her participation in activities normal for a person of his/her age.

[4] They are based on general questions that are open to misinterpretation (definition problems) and that are not supported by the necessary probing to avoid the under-reporting that is characteristic of disability measures. For example, the percentage of disabled children (less than five years of age) was estimated at about 9.65 per thousand using the general-questions approach (Abdel Azeem et al., 1993), while more detailed probing produced a prevalence estimate as high as 30 per thousand (El Tawila, 1997).

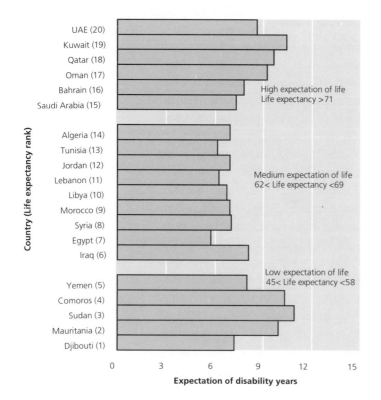

Figure 3-4
Expectation of disability years by life expectancy, Arab countries

Country (Life expectancy rank)

UAE (20)
Kuwait (19)
Qatar (18)
Oman (17)
Bahrain (16)
Saudi Arabia (15)

High expectation of life
Life expectancy >71

Algeria (14)
Tunisia (13)
Jordan (12)
Lebanon (11)
Libya (10)
Morocco (9)
Syria (8)
Egypt (7)
Iraq (6)

Medium expectation of life
62< Life expectancy <69

Low expectation of life
45< Life expectancy <58

Yemen (5)
Comoros (4)
Sudan (3)
Mauritania (2)
Djibouti (1)

0   3   6   9   12   15

Expectation of disability years

Stunting

Anthropometry measures point to a serious health challenge in Arab countries. Not surprisingly, poor and war-torn countries are reflecting high levels of moderate and severe stunting (Yemen, as high as 52 per cent; Mauritania, 44 per cent; and Comoros, Iraq and Sudan, above 30 per cent). However, many other Arab countries are also showing serious nutritional problems that are incompatible with their economic capabilities—an example of the condition of being "richer than developed" in human terms identified in chapter 2. Arab countries such as Egypt, Kuwait, Libyan Arab Jamahiriya, Morocco, Oman, Saudi Arabia, Syrian Arab Republic and United Arab Emirates, with levels of stunting of between 15 per cent and 25 per cent, need to identify and address the underlying problems of nutritional status (whether caused by dietary patterns, environmental conditions or disparities in food distribution).

Maternal mortality

High maternal mortality is a key health challenge facing most Arab countries. More than half of the Arab countries considered in this

Only two Arab countries have managed to reduce maternal mortality to a level that is low by international standards.

Report have a maternal mortality ratio (MMR) exceeding 75 per 100,000 live births, and as many as a third have an MMR exceeding 200 per 100,000 live births. Only two Arab countries (Kuwait and the United Arab Emirates) have managed to reduce maternal mortality to a level that is low by international standards (not more than five per 100,000 live births). The other Gulf countries of Oman, Qatar and Saudi Arabia have moderately low levels (between 10 and 20 per 100,000 live births), but these levels remain higher than those for countries with comparable command over economic resources.

Old age

Few data exist on the health of the older population in Arab countries. The findings of a four-country study covering Bahrain, Egypt, Jordan, and Tunisia indicate a substantial degree of ill health. Around a third of the elderly perceive themselves as unhealthy and at least 50 per cent are suffering from sight problems and having difficulty walking. Only a very small proportion (between 5 per cent and 43 per cent) scored favourably on scales of high morale or low depression.

CONTEXTUAL FORCES

Health achievements are strongly affected by a country's level of income but not shaped solely by it. The priority assigned to health investment compared to other investments plays an important role, as do the effectiveness and fairness of delivery systems. Disparities in public services and command over resources translate into unequal health attainments among and within countries. Social, cultural and other forces also play a role. Gender gaps and dynamics, for example, are key determinants of the reproductive health of women. Low educational levels, discussed in chapter 4, translate into poor management of health and lack of awareness of behavioural risks to health. Wars, displacement and political sanctions have also adversely affected health conditions in Iraq, Mauritania, the occupied Palestinian territory, Somalia, Sudan and, to some extent, the Libyan Arab Jamahiriya.

Level of health expenditure relative to GDP

With the exception of Lebanon and Qatar (with a higher percentage of expenditure) and Somalia (with the lowest), health spending ranges from 2.5 per cent to 5.6 per cent of GDP. The majority of Arab countries spend between 3 per cent and 4.5 per cent of their GDP on health. This compares with a middle-income-country average of 5.7 per cent. In Arab countries, the level of GDP helps to explain differences in per capita health expenditure (which is perhaps more closely associated with health status) and the contribution of public expenditure to total health spending.

Per capita health expenditure in (PPP) dollars ranges from as low as $11 to as high as $1,105. Gulf countries with similar life-expectancy levels spend between $334 and $1,105. The public share of total health expenditure ranges from as low as 21 per cent to as high as 87 per cent. The countries with the lowest public share include Egypt, Lebanon and Sudan. The countries with the highest public share are Kuwait and Saudi Arabia. Countries with a high proportion of public expenditure are not confined to those that are better off. The governments of some low-income countries—Comoros, Djibouti and Somalia—account for close to 70 per cent of total health expenditure (but their total health expenditure is quite small).

Figure 3.5 provides a partial illustration of the effectiveness of expenditures on health by comparing two measures of health performance with per capita health expenditure. For the countries with very low per capita health expenditure, there is no link between the level of spending and the level of mortality. Also, for high-expenditure countries, there is no simple direct relationship between survival and expenditure. Only at the middle level of expenditure (between $100 and $334) do mortality measures appear to be responsive to the level of spending. Clearly, there is a threshold that is needed to effect changes in the level of mortality. Also, above a certain level of expenditure, other factors than levels of spending help to shape performance.

Responsiveness and fairness of health systems

The World Health Report 2000 (WHO, 2000a) has evaluated national health systems in terms that emphasize two elements in system performance: goodness and fairness. The report explains that "The objective of good health itself is really twofold: the best attainable average level--goodness--and the smallest feasible differences among individuals and groups — fairness. Goodness means a health system responding well to what people expect of it; fairness means it responds equally well to everyone, without discrimination" (WHO, xi).

The report provides constructed indices measuring the responsiveness of the health system to the expectations of the population and fairness of financial contributions. Available data show that Kuwait, Qatar and the United Arab Emirates fare best in terms of responsiveness, ranking between 26 and 30 among the 191 countries investigated. The countries that fare worst on fairness in financial contributions are Mauritania, Sudan and the Syrian Arab Republic. From the point of view of fairness, Djibouti, Libyan Arab Jamahiriya and the United Arab Emirates scored the best among Arab countries, ranking between 3 and 22 in the world. The only Arab country in the sample that scored well on both responsiveness and fairness is the United Arab Emirates.

Any discussion of the responsiveness and fairness of health systems needs to be fully sensitive to the complexity of measuring these concepts and the pitfalls of comparative analysis across countries. There is a real need, however, to introduce and refine these concepts. This need arises from the recognition that the challenge to health systems in many Arab countries includes not only raising overall standards but also ensuring greater fairness and fewer disparities.

Gender and rural residence are areas on which countries need to focus in order to improve both responsiveness and fairness. Poverty is another major determinant of exclusion. Meanwhile, health-sector reform programmes are being introduced in many Arab countries. It will be critical to develop better comparative data in order to monitor closely the impact of these reforms on vulnerable and inadequately served segments of society.

Per capita health expenditure in (PPP) dollars ranges from as low as $11 to as high as $1,105.

The only Arab country in the sample that scored well on both responsiveness and fairness (of health systems) is the United Arab Emirates.

POLICY AND MANAGEMENT OF HEALTH
CARE

Health-sector reform programmes

Health-sector reform programmes share a common objective in Arab countries as elsewhere: to contain costs and increase efficiency. The occupied Palestinian territory and several countries, including Egypt, Jordan, Lebanon, Morocco and Yemen, are currently at various stages of progress in their programmes. Whereas there is little disagreement

Figure 3-5
Health measures and expenditure on health per capita, Arab countries

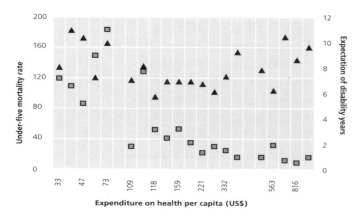

Expenditure on health per capita (US$)

▲ disability years
☐ under-5 mortality rate

with health-sector reform's goal of increasing efficiency, especially in light of increasingly limited available resources, several issues remain to be resolved in terms of implementation. In particular, the makers of health policy need to scrutinize plans for health-sector reform carefully and choose those policies and strategies best suited to their own country-specific context and needs. In the quest for total well-being, of which good health forms a critical element, the financial dimension should not be the only guiding principle; ensuring equity and accessibility for the most vulnerable groups must continue to be regarded as priority issues by policy-makers. It is only by satisfying these criteria that Arab countries can begin to realize their potential for achieving positive health for all, especially the poor. This having been said, there are certain common elements of a good health-care system that could usefully be considered by policy-makers in all Arab countries. Some of these are briefly discussed below.

A significant proportion of the health problems facing Arab populations is responsive to forms of prevention involving raising awareness and changing behaviours.

Preventive vs. curative care

Most Arab health-care systems tend to play down preventive health care and investment in preventive and primary-care programmes and actions, instead focusing mainly on curative services, generally at the secondary and tertiary levels. This is usually reflected in public-sector budget allocations and in patterns of health-sector expenditures. Focusing on curative care and hospitalization tends to increase rather than contain costs, especially when it is heavily reliant on expensive high technology.

A significant proportion of the health problems facing Arab populations is responsive to forms of prevention involving raising awareness and changing behaviours. This is a fruitful alternative to the current imbalance in typical health-care systems, under which curative and hospital care take up increasing proportions of budgetary allocations for national health, and large segments of the population are left with poorer health and overall well-being than they might otherwise achieve. If conditions amenable to education and behaviour modification are left behind or ignored, improving health status becomes harder to achieve. In the coming few years, makers of Arab health policy must by necessity begin to focus more on introducing and investing in preventive programmes and activities of all kinds while improving the efficiency of curative services and facilities.

Behavioural change for better health

As noted above, awareness and prevention programmes designed to change behaviours inimical to health can address a range of existing and potential health problems in Arab countries. These include promoting exercise and good dietary habits and cessation of smoking. The region has high rates of tobacco use, and smoking is increasing among women and younger age groups. WHO has estimated that 182,000 people in the region died from tobacco-related conditions in 1998. Other societies have shown that active anti-smoking campaigns can have a real impact on the percentage of the population that smokes. Alcohol and drug use is thought to be on the rise, especially among the young. The Arab countries have thus far been substantially spared from the scourge of HIV/AIDS, but experience elsewhere suggests that inattention can allow the virus to spread until it reaches epidemic proportions and that active prevention campaigns can have a positive impact. Meanwhile, road accidents, another behaviourally based source of death and disability, are a significant cause of death in the region; road safety campaigns can help to reduce them.

Other, more cultural behaviours common in the Arab world can also have an adverse health impact. These include intermarriage between close relatives, promotion of early marriage, and female circumcision.

Better awareness of the health consequences of risky behaviours and practices can play an important part in containing and reducing them. However, awareness campaigns and the behavioural change they are designed to promote will work best in an enabling overall environment that needs to include reasonable levels of general education, acceptable economic conditions, and positive social pressure. The growth and spread of information technology and media penetration can also be helpful in spreading the message about healthy (and unhealthy) behaviours.

AVAILABILITY AND DELIVERY OF HEALTH CARE

This is a very large topic and several aspects of it have already been touched on (for example, levels of health spending, questions of fairness, programmes for health-sector reform, and the need for more emphasis on primary care). Only a few other aspects will be touched on here.

Health manpower.

A health-care system ultimately depends on the people who deliver it: doctors, nurses and paramedical personnel. On the whole, Arab countries do not appear to suffer from a shortage of physicians, but they do appear to face severe shortages of nurses and paramedical personnel, particularly at the level of primary care. Yet while there may be no overall shortages of physicians, there appear to be serious disparities in the distribution of doctors between urban and rural and rich and poor areas. Policy-makers will need to grapple with issues of health manpower as part of the drive towards both efficiency and equity in health systems.

Poverty and access to health care.

Poverty both contributes to ill health and can be a barrier to access to care. Unless the special problems facing the poor are explicitly included in system design, they can be left out and effectively denied access. Since the poor are typically politically weak and without a voice, their needs may be ignored in favour of those of the better-off. A major challenge for Arab countries in the coming years will be balancing the requirements of different social groups while maintaining a commitment to efficiency and equity.

Community involvement for health-care delivery.

A trend currently gaining support worldwide is the drive towards having communities actively involved in all aspects of their own health care—from needs identification through resource identification, planning, resource allocation, implementation and monitoring. Ownership of health programmes has proven to be an important determining factor in their success, allowing people control over a sector vital to their own well-being. This drive towards community ownership is usually

Policy-makers will need to grapple with issues of health manpower as part of the drive towards both efficiency and equity in health systems.

BOX 3.1

The silent threat: HIV/AIDS

By most conservative estimates, more than 400,000 people are thought to be living with HIV in the Eastern Mediterranean Region. This is almost double the estimates of previous years, and is due to revised calculations for Djibouti and Sudan in light of new evidence of increased spread in these countries.

All countries of the Region reported new HIV and AIDS cases during the year 2000. The cumulative number of AIDS cases in the Region since 1987 has reached 10,479, of which 1,263 were notified in 2000.

Information on HIV/AIDS in the Region remains insufficient. In many countries, the epidemiological surveillance system is still weak and the reporting is often delayed and incomplete. Drug transmission accounts for only 4 per cent of cases although there is growing concern with this route of transmission. The high geographical mobility among populations within the Region exposes migrants to the disease and calls for better-targeted prevention and care efforts.

In general, the HIV epidemic in the Region appears to be advancing slowly; however, applying global figures to the Region masks the wide diversity in the level and patterns of the HIV epidemic in different countries. Countries suffering from complex emergencies are the hardest hit.

In all countries, success in fighting AIDS rests on the political will to deal with it as a real threat that requires addressing vulnerability wherever it exists and creating open environments that enhance the well-being of the people and communities living with the disease.

Source: Excerpted from the WHO Progress Report on AIDS in the Eastern Mediterranean Region, 48th Session of the WHO Regional Committee for the Eastern Mediterranean, July 2001.

linked with a strong commitment to the importance of primary health care and is based on the assumptions that communities are best placed to know and identify their own needs and that they are the best monitors and evaluators of programmes intended to serve them. To be effective, however, community involvement requires the presence of established grass-roots and community structures capable of undertaking the relevant tasks.

This section has been able to touch on only a few of the issues with respect to health status and policy in the Arab countries. Much has been done to improve conditions, but much remains to be done. In this regard, it is critical to remember that health-care systems do not exist in a vacuum; their efficiency and effectiveness are determined by a range of external factors. One of the most important is habitat—the physical environment in which people live. This is the topic of the next section.

HABITAT

KEY CHARACTERISTICS AND ISSUES

The Arab region covers a vast territory, from the Gulf in the east to the Atlantic Ocean in the west, from the mountain ranges of Lebanon and the Syrian Arab Republic in the north to the equatorial plateau and the plains of Somalia in the south. This massive expanse encompasses a diverse range of ecological systems. At the risk of over-simplification, some distinction can be made between the northern regions of the Arabian Peninsula (Iraq, Jordan, Lebanon, occupied Palestinian territory and Syrian Arab Republic) and the Gulf countries (Gulf Cooperation Council members plus Yemen), and also between the Nile basin countries and the North African States that have no major rivers. The Arab world has coastal areas abutting three semi-closed bodies of water (the Mediterranean, the Red Sea, and the Gulf) that suffer from varying degrees of pollution.

Despite this diversity, countries of the Arab region face a number of common problems, in varying degrees of severity, with respect to habitat. These problems fall into two categories: resource scarcity and habitat pollu-

tion. Taken as a whole, the Arab world is extremely water-scarce; it suffers from a shortage of arable land and land scarcity is being exacerbated by degradation and desertification; rapid urbanization is creating major problems of air pollution; and major cities are located on coastal areas and are creating coastal-area pollution. All these problems contribute in their own ways to reductions in the quality of life (especially for the poor), to hampering aspects of human capability, and to heavy economic costs that countries can ill afford. Each is briefly discussed below.

Water scarcity

The Arab world suffers from an increasing scarcity of usable water resources and is considered one of the most water-stressed regions in the world. The World Bank has identified 22 countries that are below the water poverty line, defined as those that have less than 1,000m³ per person per year. Of the 22, 15 are Arab countries. The Bank has estimated that, for the countries in its Middle East and North Africa classification, their average renewable water resources will fall from just above the 1,000m3/year-level in 1997 to 740m3/year by 2015. Several countries are already mining non-renewable sources. Physical shortages are compounded by problems in water quality caused by the dumping of pollutants into rivers and streams and by run-offs of agricultural chemicals.

A number of factors exacerbate the water difficulties of the region, including the following:

• About 85 per cent of countries in the region share their total available water with at least one other country either as riparians or by sharing a common aquifer. More powerful upstream and downstream countries have been able to determine the water shares of the other riparian or aquifer-sharing countries. Equitable water-sharing is often compromised by politics.

• The rapid increase in population in the region is putting increasing pressure on water availability per capita. Meanwhile, the persistently high share of water used in agriculture (including ambitious, intensive irrigation programmes) is starving other users, industrial and domestic—in the case of the latter, also

The Arab world suffers from an increasing scarcity of usable water resources and is considered one of the most water-stressed regions in the world.

helping to worsen health problems. Current shortages can only worsen, even without factoring in any impact of climate change.

• Conservation and reuse programmes are weak, and no country in the region has effective water-demand management systems and economic instruments to rationalize the use of water.

Land scarcity and degradation

Land suitable for agriculture, grazing and forestation is also scarce. Cultivated land per capita in Arab countries averaged only 0.24 ha. in 1998, compared to 0.4 ha. per capita in 1970. Unsustainable agricultural practices, natural factors (such as wind and floods) and pillaging of firewood have led to the loss of productive land and desertification.

Urbanization and air pollution

Although there are marked differences in degree of urbanization between countries (table 3.2), the pace of urbanization was rapid during the second half of the twentieth century. In 1950, only about a quarter of the Arab population was living in urban areas; the figure had risen to 50 per cent by the end of the century. During the period 1990-1995, all countries had urban growth rates at or above the global average of 2.5 per cent.

Fueled by heavy rural-urban migration as well as natural increase, late twentieth-century urbanization created major air-pollution problems in Arab cities. The transport, industrial and energy sectors have had substantial adverse effects on human health through the use of leaded gasoline, in a fleet of aging vehicles, inefficient use of fossil fuels in power generation, and industrial emissions of particulates and sulphur oxides.

Coastal area pollution

As noted earlier, some large cities in Arab countries are located in coastal areas. Land based-pollution, including discharge of wastewater into the sea, is creating coastal-zone degradation, which in turn is costing countries $1billion to $2 billion a year in lost tourism revenues.

MEETING THE ENVIRONMENTAL CHALLENGE

Countries are attempting to grapple with these and other aspects of natural-resource scarcity and habitat degradation, but the problems that many of them face remain acute. Awareness has grown that it is as critical to focus on conserving resources as on attacking pollution and that sustainable development needs to observe three environmental principles:

1. Non-renewable natural resources should be used efficiently, not wastefully, since they cannot be replaced;[5] investment is necessary in securing alternative resources.

2. Renewable resources should be used at a pace that permits them to reconstitute themselves in order to avert the risk that they will become scarce or unavailable.

3. Pollutants and waste matter need to be disposed of at rates that the environment can safely accommodate.

The ways in which these principles are observed will vary according to country circumstances and ecosystems, but in all cases, they will require effectively managed environmental programmes. Environmental management is a relatively new concept for all countries, and all are grappling with some of the special problems that it poses. These include:

• the expanding scope of the environmental systems to be managed. Over the years, this scope has grown to encompass the province, the city, the State, communities of neighbouring States and the entire planet. Each of these domains has overlapping problems as well as solutions;

• the changing quality standards that any environmental management system seeks to maintain. As knowledge deepens about the causes of undesirable environmental phenomena, previously acceptable standards may seem inadequate; [6]

• the fact that formal tools for the achievement of societal goals, such as legislation, can be ineffectual in the environmental sphere,

No country in the region has effective water-demand management systems and economic instruments to rationalize the use of water.

---

[5] Man has, throughout the ages, tried to increase his share of non-renewable resources. As his scientific and technological knowledge grew, he turned the material existing in nature to resources (iron ore was not used until the late dynasties in ancient Egypt; oil was not used as a fuel until the second half of the nineteenth century; aluminum was used only at the beginning of the last century, and this applies to uranium and silicone as well).

[6] A recent example is the ongoing debate in the United States over the permissible level of arsenic in potable water and the cost involved in maintaining this ratio in various areas.

Figure 3-6
**Available water resources (billion cubic meter),
Arab region, 1996**

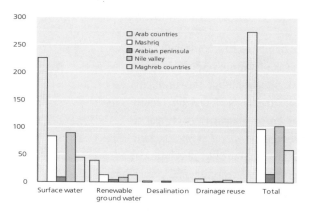

Figure 3-7
**Projected total water demand (billion cubic meter),
Arab countries of west Asia**

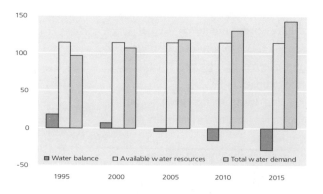

Figure 3-8
**Cultivated area per capita (ha), primary energy consumption
(quadrillion BTU) and carbon dioxide emissions (million metric
tonnes of carbon equivalent), Arab region, 1980-1999**

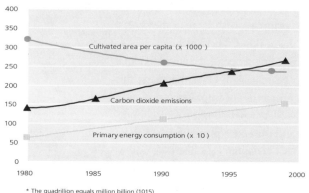

* The quadrillion equals million billion (1015)

TABLE 3.2
Urbanization, by Arab country

Urban population (less than 50%)	Urban population (50–80%)	Urban population (more than 80%)
Comoros	Algeria	Bahrain
Egypt	Djibouti	Kuwait
Morocco	Iraq	Lebanon
Somalia	Jordan	Libyan Arab Jamahiriya
Sudan	Mauritania	Oman
Yemen	Syrian Arab Republic	Qatar
	Tunisia	Saudi Arabia
		United Arab Emirates

[7] A quadrillion equals a million billion (10[15]).

[8] This section is based mainly on the report entitled "Future of Environmental Work in the Arab World", prepared by Osama El-Kholy in collaboration with Mostafa Kamal Tolba and Kamal Thabit (El-Kholy, O., 2001). The Council of Arab Ministers Responsible for the Environment, at their extraordinary meeting in Abu Dhabi in February 2001, approved this report, considering it a reference for future programmes of Arab environmental protection.

particularly in developing societies. Laws can be difficult, and sometimes impossible, to enforce. Environmental goals may more helpfully be met by other means, such as public-awareness campaigns, societal pressure, economic incentives and technical assistance.

• other constraints on environmental management and action, such as prevailing social values, the power of vested interests, the problem of externality, or limited expertise in environmental matters in many countries.

• the emergence of new global environmental issues. Arab countries are both affected by, and have a role in, influencing emerging problems such as ozone-layer depletion and changing global weather patterns. At the same time, global changes affect different areas differently. Changing rain patterns affect countries on the Nile River differently from countries in North Africa. Rising sea levels affect Egypt differently from Bahrain or countries on the eastern coast of the Mediterranean. Arab countries will need to keep abreast of research in these areas in order to minimize future risks.

Meanwhile, a revival of Arab interest in the environment has taken place at the government and public levels as well as in academic and research institutes. The strategy for environmental protection outlined in the next section reflects recent thinking on how the Arab countries might move forward in this area of special importance for human development.

*A STRATEGY FOR ENVIRONMENTAL
PROTECTION*[8]

The strategy proposed here embodies a number of broad guidelines that can be drawn on to design programmes of action. These guidelines are in turn based on two pillars: (a) areas of strength and weakness in current Arab environmental conditions; and (b) a broad understanding of recent developments in various fields of environmental work. The ecological diversity of the Arab world calls for different methods and treatment of environmental problems in different countries, but the guidelines are broad enough for general application.

Features of the strategy

In light of the analysis offered above and the ongoing changes in the world, the proposed strategy for Arab environmental action would have the following six dimensions:

1. *Working within two timeframes.* Tackling all the many and varied environmental problems facing Arab countries at once is impossible. Therefore, plans of action aiming to protect and mend the environment must take place on two levels:

• first, the formulation of short-term plans, covering up to, say, five years;

• second, the formulation of longer-term plans, taking into account short-term plans but tackling problems requiring sustained effort over a longer timeframe.

2. *Prioritizing work on a rigorous scientific basis.[9]*

3. *Halting the causes of environmental degradation.* Much effort is often spent on treating the effects of environmental degradation before giving proper consideration to halting its causes. Such effort is self-defeating. Of course, there are cases, especially when the effects are severe, where efforts should be divided between treatment of the effects and elimination of the underlying causes of the problem. In such cases, substantial effort will be needed. Displacing environmental problems from one area to another or postponing dealing with them will always be costly. The best approach is to address problems at an early stage.

4. *Bolstering Arab ability to use the tools of modern environmental economics.* Mastering modern tools of analysis can provide the policy-maker with an accurate estimate of the damage incurred by inaction and delay and could help to ensure that environmental problems are treated speedily and effectively. Such tools include the calculation of externalities and the amendment of GNP statistics to show resources lost, environmental damage and the discounted value of investment over time.

These tools are available and are becoming better and easier to apply. They can be of considerable help to the Arab decision-maker, helping her/him in making rational and confident decisions on environmental matters.

5. *Adopting a strategy for cleaner production.* A strategy for cleaner production covers a wide range of topics, including radically and tangibly reducing the consumption of natural resources, avoiding the use of highly toxic or environmentally harmful substances, and improving product design and manufacturing so as to reduce emissions, refuse and waste and encourage recycling. It also considers the system of social values and the conditions under which social demand for products or services has been generated. It then tries to adjust this system to reduce unnecessary luxury consumption that wastes resources and harms the environment.[10] Industrial countries are seeking to achieve, in the short run, what is known as coefficient 4, and in the long run, coefficient 10. The former involves producing twice the output with half the input of natural resources and energy. The latter refers to producing the same output with one tenth of the relevant input. The cleaner-production strategy involves a dynamic understanding of the concept "cleaner", the point being that the target is constantly changing: with improvements in technical know-how and the understanding of environmental problems, better modes of production and consumption become possible.

6. *Increasing popular participation in environmental-protection action plans.* The basic question in dealing with environmental issues has been, and still is, how to achieve an appropriate balance between the requirements of development and its pressure on the environment on the one hand and the need to protect the environment on the other. To achieve this balance, substantial changes may need to be made in development plans. These changes may in turn conflict with the interests of one social group or another. Therefore, every ef-

Displacing environmental problems from one area to another or postponing dealing with them will always be costly.

---

[9] The Abu Dhabi Declaration, issued by Arab environment ministers in February 2001, stated that the following environmental problems are of high priority: the acute shortage of water resources and the deterioration of their quality; the shortage of land and the deterioration of its quality; inefficient use of natural resources; the increase in urban areas and the attendant problems; and the deterioration of marine, littoral and wet zones.

[10] When the United Nations Environment Programme came up with the concept of "cleaner production", the latter was defined as "the constant application of a preventive environmental strategy on operations and products with the aim of minimizing risks for humans and the environment". In production operations, cleaner production involves conserving raw material and energy, non-use of toxic raw materials, and reducing the quantity and toxicity of all emissions and refuse during the production operations. As for the products, the strategy focuses on reducing their environmental effects throughout their lifecycle, from the extraction of raw materials to their final disposal. The primary goal of cleaner production is the non-generation of waste. Cleaner production can be achieved by the application of knowledge and technological development and/or a change in social conditions and values.

fort should be made to gain public backing for these changes. Such backing will need to be based on public awareness of the dimensions of environmental problems, and of why a given approach is needed to deal with them. Public opinion on suggested options should be probed and taken seriously because it is the public that is affected by both problems and their solutions. Without public support, efforts at environmental protection cannot succeed in the long run.

Three factors are critical in mobilizing public opinion with respect to environmental issues. One is to integrate environmental awareness into education and training at all levels and in all fields, starting with the earliest stages of education and continuing through graduate studies (engineering, management, economics and law) and research institutes. The second is to mobilize the mass media--written, audio and visual—together with artists and writers to draw the public's attention to environmental issues and to enlist their backing. The third is to promote public participation in legislation and in compliance with it once it is passed.

This is no easy task in societies where public participation is limited in both law and practice with respect to making and implementing decisions, but it is of critical importance if environmental legislation and action plans are to bear fruit.

Suggested programmes for protecting the environment in the Arab world

The proposals below take into account the above strategic guidelines and are consistent with the priorities for Arab environmental work that received unanimous approval by Arab environment ministers and that were summarized in the Abu Dhabi Declaration issued in February 2001.
Scarcity and degradation of the quality of water resources.

The proposed programme in this area would aim to boost the socio-economic return on a unit of usable water. This would involve the establishment of a central institutional entity charged with managing the use of water in various sectors of society, thus eliminating the existing fragmentation of water-affairs management. Currently, management is divided among numerous executive agencies that may lack an overall water policy or the ability to implement it.

The proposed programme would have three main elements:
• rationalizing the use of available water resources;
• preserving the quality of these resources;
• providing additional resources from unconventional sources.

Strong, sustained programmes should also be designed to raise public awareness of the importance of water, the gravity of the current situation and the need to implement the measures needed to deal with it. With respect to specific measures, emphasis should be placed on the feasibility and ease of implementation.
Scarcity and degradation of the quality of land.
Since most of the land mass of Arab countries is desert, with arable land not exceeding one seventh of the total land area, the focus of discussions of land availability and quality is often exclusively on agricultural or grazing land. Agriculture and animal husbandry are of considerable importance in providing food domestically, and the majority of land use is dedicated to these two functions. However, the critical need is to develop a comprehensive, logical planning system for all forms of land use, including the use of different types of land (including land whose quality has deteriorated) for different purposes. At the same time, the reasons for such quality deterioration should be carefully studied, and plans for adopting coordinated programmes to arrest degradation in both the short and long term in Arab countries should be drawn up. A comprehensive national plan for various types of land use should take into account the type of land, priorities for land use, the relevant socio-economic returns, and the expected increase in the need for different uses in the future. Special emphasis should be given to the participation of concerned parties in preparing and implementing land-use plans.
Urbanization.
As noted earlier, urbanization presents many environmental problems. In addition to air pollution and attendant health problems, urban development has encroached on some of the best and scarcest agricultural and grazing land in the Arab world. Programmes

Public opinion on suggested options should be probed and taken seriously because it is the public that is affected by both problems and their solutions.

aimed to confront the negative impact of urbanization, which has been accelerated by the high rates of population growth, will need to be implemented differently in accordance with individual conditions, but there should also be a place for the exchange of available expertise in this area.

Coastal areas.

Arab countries have coasts on seven bodies of water, three of which are semi-closed. Coastal areas are inhabited by over half the Arab population and are thus of considerable importance as habitat. They are also important as sources of tourism revenue, which helps to create employment that is generally labour-intensive. However, unregulated tourism and the consequences of other forms of human activity (pollution from land sources, the destructive landfill of marine habitats, oil and industrial activities) also contribute substantially to the degradation of coastal areas. To resolve these problems, much higher levels of marine conservation efforts are needed. They will need to involve collaborative action by national and local governments and the private sector.

INSTITUTIONAL FRAMEWORK FOR ENVIRONMENTAL PROTECTION

Most Arab countries have followed a command-and-control approach to environmental affairs. This approach, which had been unsuccessfully tried in industrial countries, has also failed in Arab countries. An alternative, more effective approach is needed.

Experience in many developing and industrial countries suggests that it is wise to begin with indirect tools (for example, self-surveillance) and postpone the use of direct intervention until it becomes clear that indirect tools have proved ineffective and other measures are needed.

Direct action should be taken to help those who are called upon to comply and to change their behaviour. Such help (for example, technical assistance and expertise) should be provided before enforcement action is taken. Other features of an effective institutional framework include:

• maximizing the willingness of the community to comply and the resources required for compliance;

• persuading people of the value of their extra effort and helping them to make that effort;

• using market mechanisms (for example, eco-labelling) to raise community awareness of the environmental effects of products and services;

• involving groups affected by pollution or the waste of resources in implementing and checking compliance (self-surveillance) with environmental specifications;

• maintaining government responsibility for enforcing compliance (even with self-surveillance in place);

• addressing and vigorously punishing deceit and fraud;

• establishing a rigorous, comprehensive and credible surveillance system.

ARAB COOPERATION IN ENVIRONMENTAL AFFAIRS

The interdependence of environmental systems and their two main aspects (resources and pollutants) makes it necessary for nations to cooperate in taking care of these systems. Some Arab countries have experience going back decades in conducting such cooperation (e.g., through agreement, or disagreement, on the way to use joint water resources). Despite mixed experience in this area, countries could consider three levels of regional collaboration on wider environmental matters.

Inter-governmental efforts

Enhancing the performance of the Council of Arab Ministers Responsible for the Environment is a matter of urgency. The Council needs to be able to examine relevant environmental matters in a rigorous, efficient way and to provide decision-makers with optimum but realistic options for addressing regional and international environmental issues. It needs to function efficiently, tend to joint environmental resources, settle potential disputes among Arab countries over the shared use of these resources, enhance Arab cooperation and defend Arab interests at international forums. One question it needs to address is any possible disparity or conflict of Arab interests (over energy policies and climate change,

Most Arab countries have followed a command-and-control approach to environmental affairs. This approach, which had been unsuccessfully tried in industrial countries, has also failed in Arab countries.

for example). The Council needs to define these differences, assess their scope, narrow them and, if necessary, keep them from surfacing at international forums.

Scientific efforts

Environmental research and study are still scattered among a number of Arab States. This has weakened research in important areas linked to protecting the environment in Arab countries, such as use of solar energy, particularly in water desalination.

Establishing new agencies is not necessarily the best way to boost joint Arab scientific efforts, but it is advisable to divide tasks and exchange expertise and information. Centralized Arab entities could be of help in those instances where the cost of installations exceeds the ability or needs of any single Arab country.

Stimulating Arab scientific work is the responsibility of Arab governments. What Arab business can do, with a reasonable amount of spending and effort, is to develop and market viable environmental technology. This could boost the efficiency of the use of environmental resources and curb or reverse pollution. Arab governments should provide the necessary incentives to enable business to carry out this task.

Non-governmental efforts

In some rare and laudable cases, NGOs have exhibited expertise and knowledge of environmental issues, adopted environmental issues of interest to the public, and defended them with conviction and determination.

However, without a larger number of civil associations working to protect the environment in Arab countries, the effectiveness of the federation of these associations set up in the late twentieth century will remain limited unless efforts are made to strengthen such associations as a popular force in support of governments and professional organizations in their efforts to overcome environmental problems.

As with the preceding sections on people and health, this brief discussion of some of the issues associated with habitat, the physical environment in which people live, has identified problems with which Arab countries must contend in the coming years. However, countries are far better equipped to tackle these problems than they were ten or even five years ago. Above all, knowledge about both problems and possible solutions has greatly improved. It is worth re-emphasizing, however, that success in preserving precious resources and dealing with unacceptable pollution will depend on an aware, committed and, above all, educated population—the topic of the next chapter.

Establishing new agencies is not necessarily the best way to boost joint Arab scientific efforts.

CHAPTER 4

 Building human capabilities: education

Chapter 1 emphasized the importance of knowledge acquisition as a cornerstone of human development. This chapter focuses on building human capabilities for knowledge acquisition in Arab countries through education. The assessment of the state of education using such indicators as enrolment and illiteracy rates and per capita expenditure reveals tangible achievements but also significant areas for further progress in the Arab countries as a whole. In addition, a mismatch between educational output on the one hand and labour-market and development needs on the other could lead to Arab countries' isolation from global knowledge, information and technology at a time when accelerated acquisition of knowledge and formation of advanced human skills are becoming prerequisites for progress. To address these and other quality issues, a radical vision of education reform is put forward, including strategic directions and policies and specific areas for educational expansion and improvement.

THE STATUS OF EDUCATION

Arab countries have made great strides in education, particularly since the middle of the twentieth century. Nevertheless, educational achievement in the Arab countries as a whole, judged even by traditional criteria, is still modest when compared to elsewhere in the world, even in developing countries.

LITERACY

While education has made headway among the younger generations, illiteracy has proved difficult to eradicate. Therefore, the overall educational achievement among adults in Arab countries remains low on average. Arab countries have nevertheless made tangible progress in improving literacy: the estimated rate of illiteracy among adults dropped from approximately 60 per cent in 1980 to around 43 per cent in the mid-1990s.[1] However, illiteracy rates in the Arab world are still higher than the international average and are even higher than the average in developing countries. Moreover, the number of illiterate people is still increasing, to the extent that Arab countries embark upon the twenty-first century burdened by over 60 million illiterate adults, the majority of whom are women (figures 4.1 and 4.2).

Most importantly, the illiteracy rates for the more vulnerable social categories, such as women and the poor, are relatively higher, particularly in the rural areas. Girls and the poor, especially in the countryside, suffer from more intense deprivation of education, especially at the higher levels. In other words, differences in literacy follow the same patterns as differences in enrolment in basic education by gender, social status and locale. Therefore, differences in enrolment in basic education aggravate disparities in educational attainment by gender, social status and rural/urban residence. It should be noted that illiteracy among males in Arab coun-

Educational achievement in the Arab countries as a whole, judged even by traditional criteria, is still modest when compared to elsewhere in the world, even in developing countries.

BOX 4.1

Gibran: on teaching

No man can reveal to you aught but that which already lies half asleep in the dawning of your knowledge.

The teacher who walks in the shadow of the temple, among his followers, gives not of his wisdom but rather of his faith and his lovingness.

If he is indeed wise, he does not bid you enter the house of his wisdom, but rather leads you to the threshold of your own mind.

The astronomer may speak to you of his understanding of space, but he cannot give you his understanding.

The musician may sing to you of the rhythm which is in all space, but he cannot give you the ear which arrests the rhythm, nor the voice that echoes it.

Source: Kahlil Gibran, The Prophet.

---

[1] The data in this section are derived from the statistical yearbooks of UNESCO (1996 and 1998). It has been noted elsewhere in the Report that education statistics in the Arab countries are often incomplete.

tries is not expected to disappear before the end of the first quarter of the twenty-first century, and for women, not until 2040.

PRE-SCHOOL EDUCATION

The steady affirmation by recent scientific research of the importance of the early years of childhood in configuring the human brain and shaping its faculties underscores the need to concentrate on pre-school education. However, this is another area in which the Arab countries fall behind developing countries.

Despite a doubling of the number of children who enrolled in pre-school education in the Arab countries between 1980 and 1995, the figure for 1995 did not exceed 2.5 million,

corresponding to an enrolment rate that was below the average for developing countries. Moreover, the percentage of children enrolling in pre-school education actually fell over this period (from 4.8 per cent in 1980 to 4 per cent in 1995). Furthermore, despite the steady increase in the percentage of girls in pre-schooling, the percentage was also less than the average for developing countries (42 per cent versus 47 per cent in 1995).

ENROLMENT IN FORMAL EDUCATION

The data on enrolment in the three levels of education[2] in Arab countries show a steady quantitative increase. The number of students enrolled in all three levels combined jumped from 31 million in 1980 to approximately 56 million in 1995. However, the rate of increase in enrolment for the three levels slowed during the 1990s compared with the 1980s (figure 4.3).

Available data on school enrolment for the first level of formal education indicates that to date, the Arab world has been unable to absorb new generations of Arab citizens. There is also an apparent bias against females whether the comparison is made with developing countries or the world as a whole.

The mid-1990s witnessed higher total enrolment rates for the secondary and tertiary levels in the Arab countries (54 per cent and 13 per cent, respectively) compared to developing countries (49 per cent and 9 per cent, respectively). However, these percentages are lower by far than those prevailing in the industrialized countries for that period (106 per cent[3] and 60 per cent, respectively). Arab countries are not expected to catch up with the industrialized countries' mid-1990s enrolment levels for the three levels of education before 2030.

Despite the substantial quantitative expansion of education in Arab countries, including education for girls, female enrolment rates are lower than those for males, particularly at the tertiary level (higher education). The Arab countries also lag substantially behind other regions of the world in female tertiary enrolments (figure 4.5).

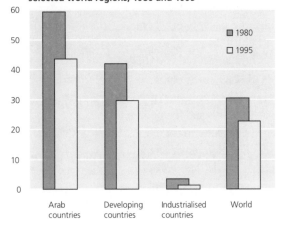

Figure 4-1
Illiteracy rate (%), Arab countries and selected world regions, 1980 and 1995

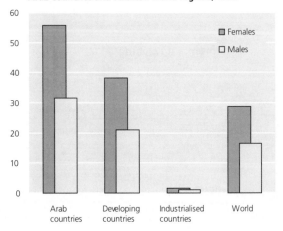

Figure 4-2
Illiteracy rate (%) by gender, Arab countries and selected world regions, 1995

[2] According to the standard international definition, an educational level consists of six educational grades.

[3] The gross enrolment rate could exceed 100 per cent.

EDUCATION SPENDING

There are indications that rising expenditure on education in the Arab world began to taper off after 1985. Education spending increased, in current prices, from US$18 billion in 1980 to US$28 billion in 1995. However, the rate of increase since 1985 has been much slower than that during the period 1980-1985, unlike the situation in both developed and developing countries (figure 4.6). On the basis of the rather defective indicator often used in international comparisons--education expenditure as a percentage of GNP--Arab countries do better than developing and developed countries alike and the percentage was on the rise between 1980 and 1985. However, the percentage was lower in 1995 than in 1985.

A better indicator for the purpose of this analysis is per capita expenditure on education. At current prices, this indicator rose over the years from 1980 to 1985. However, this rise was followed by a deterioration during the latter half of the 1980s. Figure 4.7 shows the contrast between this situation and that of both developing and industrialized countries, especially the latter (which had been spending substantially on education to start with). While Arab countries continued to spend more on education per capita than developing countries as a group, their relative edge has been eroding since the mid-1980s. In addition, per capita expenditure on education in Arab countries dropped from 20 per cent of that in industrialized countries in 1980 to 10 per cent in the mid-1990s. The slowing rate of growth of education spending took place in the context of the macroeconomic difficulties in which many Arab countries found themselves after the mid-1970s, together with the ensuing structural adjustment programmes, which put substantial pressure on spending, including rates of growth of education expenditure.

EQUITY AND AFFORDABILITY

There is a danger that the education systems in the Arab countries will be split into two unrelated parts: very expensive private education, enjoyed by the better-off minority, and poor-quality government education for the major-

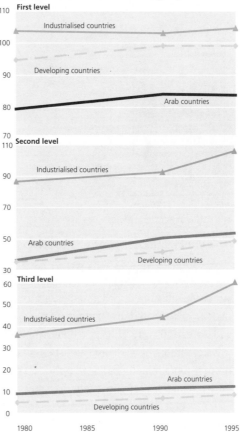

Figure 4-3
Gross enrolment ratio (%) by level of education, Arab countries and selected world regions, 1980-1995

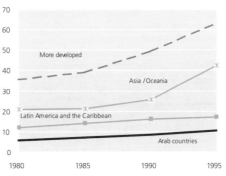

Figure 4-4
Higher education students, per 100 thousand inhabitant, Arab countries and selected world regions, 1980-1995

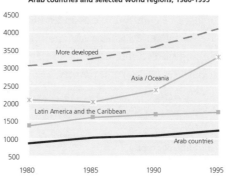

Figure 4-5
Females' gross enrolment ratio in higher education, Arab countries and selected world regions, 1980-1995

While Arab countries continued to spend more on education than developing countries as a group, their relative edge has been eroding since the mid-1980s.

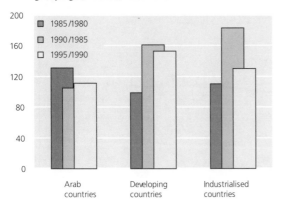

Figure 4-6
Relative total expenditure on education (at current prices) of Arab countries and selected world groupings (Indexed) 1980-1995

■ 1985/1980
□ 1990/1985
□ 1995/1990

Arab countries
Developing countries
Industrialised countries

Problems of quality and relevance have led to a significant mismatch between the labour market and development needs on the one hand and the output of education systems on the other.

ity—and even the latter can be costly for the less well-off in view of cost-recovery policies adopted by Arab countries in the context of structural adjustment programmes, a problem that is exacerbated by the phenomenon of widespread private tuition. Unfortunately, private tuition has become indispensable in order to obtain high grades on public qualifying examinations for enrolment in higher education, especially with respect to the disciplines considered most likely to lead to better professional and career prospects. The result is that these disciplines are becoming almost exclusively the preserve of financially privileged groups. Thus, education has begun to lose its significant role as a means of achieving social advancement in Arab countries, turning instead into a means of perpetuating social stratification and poverty.

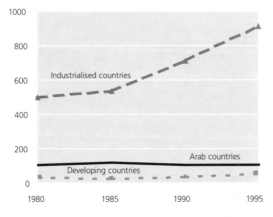

Figure 4-7
Public expenditure on education per capita (in current US$), Arab countries and selected world regions, 1980-1995

Industrialised countries

Arab countries

Developing countries

1980   1985   1990   1995

Source: UNESCO, 1996 and 1998a.

QUALITY

There are many signs of decreasing internal efficiency of education in the Arab world, including high failure and repetition rates, leading to longer periods spent at different stages of education. However, the real problem lies in the quality of education. Despite the scarcity of available studies, complaints concerning the poor quality of education abound. The few available studies identify the key negative features of the real output of education in Arab countries as low level of knowledge attainment and poor and deteriorating analytical and innovative capacity.

Problems of quality and relevance have led to a significant mismatch between the labour market and development needs on the one hand and the output of education systems on the other. This situation leads to poor productivity, a distorted wage structure and a meagre economic and social return on education. The prevalence of unemployment among the educated and the deterioration in real wages for the majority of them exemplify this problem. Poor quality has become the Achilles heel of education in the Arab world, a flaw that undermines its quantitative achievements.

The most worrying aspect of the crisis in education is education's inability to provide the requirements for the development of Arab societies. This could mean not only that education loses its power to provide a conduit for social advancement for the poor within Arab countries but also that Arab countries become isolated from global knowledge, information and technology. If the current situation is allowed to continue, the crisis can only worsen--this at a time when accelerated acquisition of knowledge and formation of advanced human skills are becoming prerequisites for progress. If the steady deterioration in the quality of education in the Arab countries and the inability of education to meet the requirements of development are not reversed, the consequences for human and economic development will be grave. Comprehensive action to reform education systems is therefore urgent. A strategic vision for such reform is presented below.

EDUCATION REFORM [4]

Education is a key factor in today's knowledge-intensive world. As education stimulates a critical outlook and creative skills, it simultaneously accelerates the pace of change, development and progress. Education and progress should therefore be mutually reinforcing. To help to achieve this goal, this section proposes a radical revision of education systems in Arab countries as they move into the twenty-first century.

TEN PRINCIPLES

The following 10 normative statements define the philosophy underlying a new education structure that puts humanity at the centre of the cultural process.

• The individual should be central to the learning process. Without implying indifference to the community or absence of cooperative behaviour, the dignity of the individual should be respected.

• Modern knowledge is power. The critical faculties of Arab youth should be encouraged as both a guide and an approach to better societal structures.

• Without denigrating higher values and established creeds, intellectual and cultural heritage should not be immune to criticism and change in the face of scientific evidence. Dialogue should be valued as an indispensable process, one that is as likely to end in agreement as in creative disagreement.

• Creative human effort lies at the heart of progress. Arab education systems should be restructured to give precedence to creativity and the dignity of productive work.

• The spirit of challenge should be stimulated in the Arab people, who should shape their future through creative responses to their natural and human surroundings.

• Equal educational opportunities should be made available to all children. Disadvantaged groups should be able to participate in the various levels of the education process in a manner commensurate with their abilities rather than the financial and social means of their

parents. At the earliest stages of this process, a degree of affirmative action would be required through fellowships, tuition loans, health care and proper nutrition.

• Education should aim at promoting, in a cohesive and harmonious manner, students' physical, emotional and societal well-being as well as their acquisition of knowledge.

• Education should help children and youth to understand themselves and their own culture, past and present, creatively and in the context of a world where cultures can flourish only through openness and dialogue.

• The objectives of the education process should be derived from the global vision of twenty-first-century education. Education should integrate the Arab people into the age in which they live, an age governed by the exactness of science--its causality, rigour and method.

• Education should help the young to cope with a future of uncertainty, acquire flexibility in the face of uncertainty and contribute to shaping the future.

THREE STRATEGIC DIRECTIONS

Strengthening the education systems in Arab countries requires action in three broad areas: enhancing human capabilities, creating strong synergy between education and the socio-economic system; and formulating a programme for education reform at the pan-Arab level.

BOX 4.2

Education in Lebanon

The educational system in Lebanon is considered one of the most advanced in the Arab region in so far as quality and gender equality are concerned. The gender gap in enrolment has been bridged, that is, female enrolment has become a bit higher than that of males at the preparatory and secondary stages of education. Illiteracy rates in Lebanon are the lowest in the Arab region.

The rise in enrolment rates and the curbing of illiteracy are achievements realized during the past 25 years, in the course of which Lebanon was mostly in a state of war. That was the outcome of an undeclared partnership between the public and private sectors of education and determination on the part of Lebanese families to get their children educated.

The educational context in Lebanon, however, still faces the problem of low compatibility with the requirements of the labour market. Reforming curricula, particularly the introduction of new subjects dealing with civil education, and social and technical topics in the early stages of education, might be appropriate steps towards tackling this problem.

Source: National report prepared for the AHDR, 2002.

Education should integrate the Arab people into the age in which they live, an age governed by the exactness of science--its causality, rigour and method.

---

[4] This section is based largely on "A vision for the future of education in the Arab world", a document prepared for the Arab League Educational, Cultural and Scientific Organization (ALECSO).

Enhancing human capabilities

Strong human capabilities are critical to the achievement of progress in the Arab world. To create such capabilities, it will be necessary to achieve three main objectives:

- full (100 per cent) enrolment in basic education and an extension of mandatory schooling to at least 10 years, with simultaneous efforts to expand post-basic education;
- creation of an institutional system for adult education that continues for life and that is flexible enough to allow for constant improvement. Its purposes would be to eliminate illiteracy and institutionalize the principle of lifetime education for graduates of the education system;
- quality enhancement of all phases of education to pave the way for renewal, excellence and creativity and incorporate modern knowledge and technology into Arab societies.

The creation of quality education should be given the priority it deserves if the Arab world is to achieve its full potential. This will mean both allocating increased resources to education and using resources more efficiently.

It might be necessary to seek higher financial contributions to education, particularly higher education, from those able to pay. This could be accomplished through either tuition fees for well-off students or the use of tax incentives to motivate businesses and the rich to make donations and endowments to education institutions, with objectives much broader than providing assistance to outstanding poor students. The private sector in particular has an interest in supporting education since it needs to secure the supply of human skills and aptitudes necessary to improve its productivity and maximize profits. This interest should be translated into more attention to, and increased finance for, all types of education.

Good education, particularly at the higher levels, is expensive. Arab countries, particularly the poorer ones, cannot afford to match the level of education spending prevalent in industrialized countries. While spending alone cannot solve the education crisis, appropriate policies, combined with a favourable public context and sufficient funding, can. It may be argued that the main challenge facing Arab countries is that of devising an alternative education system that can provide good education at the right cost. This is an area calling for more innovation.

Addressing the improvement of education at the pan-Arab level, discussed later in this chapter, could help to alleviate financial constraints that could be overwhelming at the national level.

Creating strong synergy between education and the socio-economic system

Many of the factors affecting the quality of education relate to the education-learning process in its broader sense. Education is a societal effort involving the interaction of various forces active in society. There is little benefit from maintaining a single-sector outlook, which narrows the scope of interest in education and curbs efforts to improve it. Education should become a concern for society as a whole, for government agencies generally (rather than one or two ministries) and for business and civil society, particularly in local communities. This synergy is particularly important with respect to institutions of higher education.

This societal synergy would harmonize education systems--their structure, input and output--with the needs of production, development and progress. It would also help in resolving the financial problems of education. Moreover, this societal partnership, if effectively created, could alleviate the structural tension that might develop between the education system and the needs of business and production. Improved planning and cooperative efforts among all sectors of society (the state, the private sector and civil society) would be necessary to harmonize the systems of education and employment.

There is little hope for education reform unless a strong synergy emerges between schools and local communities. Embedding schools in society requires multiple channels for interaction between the school and the community as a whole, not simply the parents. The demand side of education, represented by families and business, also needs to be understood, particularly as the role of market forces increases in Arab countries. Plans and re-

The main challenge facing Arab countries is that of devising an alternative education system that can provide good education at the right cost.

forms that ignore the demand side are bound to fail. At the same time, the role of education as a vehicle for social progress should be maintained.

The diversification of education means, among other things, a change in the pace of school life so that it remains in tandem with the realities of life outside the classroom. There should be room for part-time education and for the possibility of alternating between school duties and student participation in the socio-economic activities of the local community.

Unconventional schools, such as one-room or one-teacher schools, deserve to be part of the educational diversification process. They could meet the need to expand education in distant areas and help to eliminate the remaining pockets of education deprivation in small communities.

The question of encouraging the private sector to venture into the field of education is often broached in the context of structural adjustment. Certainly, building human capabilities can benefit from an education system that is national, vibrant, non-governmental and non-profit. However, such a system should be capable of competing with state-run education. In particular, it should operate under strong guarantees of quality, enforced through a rigorous system of quality control through accreditation.

In the current institutional context, it is difficult for the profit motive to provide for the educational needs of the weaker social groups, a majority in the Arab world. The deprivation of these groups is likely to increase if the state fails to guarantee their education. However, in cases where for-profit enterprises provide education services, partnerships between the state and society should regulate this activity to ensure that it serves the public good and ensures quality.

Formulating a programme for education reform at the pan-Arab level

Effective Arab cooperation is one of the keys for dynamic development in the Arab world. This is true for human development in general and for building human capabilities through education in particular. The considerable disparity in human and other resources among Arab countries means that some of them would find it difficult, if acting alone, to make tangible progress in the expansion and improvement of education. While there has been considerable Arab cooperation in education for decades, the outcome of this cooperation has been modest to date. The regional challenges facing Arab countries call for strong synergy in efforts to build the human and technological abilities of Arab countries. Furthermore, Arab cooperation in education can promote social integration in a manner conducive to higher forms of Arab cooperation in the future.

The creation of high-quality human resources is an abiding need in all Arab countries. National efforts have achieved a high degree of quantitative expansion in basic education, particularly in richer and less populated Arab countries. The need to boost quantity remains high in poorer Arab countries, particularly with regard to higher education. It should be noted that eliminating the last pockets of education deprivation is harder than initial achievements in expanding education. Nomadic and desert communities pose special difficulties in this respect. Previous educational expansion has also created problems of quality in both rich and poor Arab countries. Improving quality represents a greater challenge than the mere expansion of numbers.

A pressing need exists for a purposeful programme of action to improve education across the Arab world, based on national programmes but designed within the framework of effective Arab cooperation. This programme should also go beyond government action to strong partnerships between states, the private sector, and civil society.

Arab education reform and the avoidance of disastrous isolation from active involvement in the world of the twenty-first century require the establishment of a supranational education authority. The closer Arab countries come to building this authority, the more they will be able to resolve their current development crisis and acquire the capacity to participate in shaping the new globalizing world.

Arab education reform should be a main and permanent item on the agenda of Arab summit meetings. There is still much room to

Building human capabilities can benefit from an education system that is national, vibrant, non-governmental and non-profit. However, such a system should be capable of competing with state-run education.

create pan-Arab education institutions and enhance the efficiency of existing ones, both governmental and non-governmental. Existing development institutions also need to pay serious attention to education reform. The horizons are limitless, the challenge immense, and current efforts are meagre at best.

Higher education, perhaps one of the most important areas of Arab cooperation in education, deserves special attention. The need for such cooperation is as great as its expected returns. Graduate studies, research and publication are among the areas that should be given priority in such cooperation efforts. Virtual networking among education institutions using ICT and the creation of knowledge networks among researchers would be effective means of building collaboration. Stimulating Arab cooperation requires that pan-Arab dimensions take precedence over national rivalry in higher education.

The list of areas for possible Arab cooperation is extensive. In addition to higher education, it includes curriculum development, textbook production and teacher training, areas in which a common language represents a major advantage. Cooperation in some of these areas can lead to opportunities for private-sector activity--as in the case of textbooks, for example, where the size of the market depends critically on the extent of Arab cooperation in curriculum development.

The Arab League Educational, Cultural and Scientific Organization, suitably strengthened, is the obvious choice to play a leading role in the institutional structure of a pan-Arab education-reform programme. Other Arab institutions should also be mobilized for this task, particularly the Arab development funds. Arab NGOs could also be created to revitalize education and learning.

POLICIES FOR EXPANDING AND IMPROVING EDUCATION

A comprehensive, cohesive renovation of the structure, content and tools of education would release creative potential and revitalize Arab society. The following policies could bring about this renovation:

• *Self-education, or learning to learn.* Self-education means many things, but for the most part, it means greater focus on the tools of education. In the case of basic education, these tools are reading, writing, verbal expression, arithmetic, problem-solving, elementary science and social sciences. The tools also include manual and technical skills, values and a proper attitude towards work and production as well as the capacity for the autonomous search for knowledge. Self-education should aim to provide learners with knowledge, abilities and attitudes that will equip them for life-long learning and continual development.

• *Diversification of education and renewal of its framework.* This policy calls for making education opportunities available to all age groups. Workers should have the chance to learn through part-time study and through teaching and training centres in the workplace. In cases where students must work, part-time teaching should be made available. For this to happen, guidance in education should be taken seriously. The present education system grades and selects but does not guide.

• *Benefiting from modern education technology and ICT.* These technologies have an important role to play in formal education and an even more significant role in informal and casual education. They can provide learners with strong tools enabling them to engage in self-teaching, encouraging learning and stimulating their potential and talents. Arab satellite television stations, if well used, could make a considerable contribution to remote learning.

• *Constant evaluation of education.* The success of educational efforts in meeting the needs of learners and society as well as the requirements of comprehensive development needs to be measured. This measurement is the launching pad for innovation, which in turn calls for evaluation since the latter paves the way for further renewal and improvement. Special focus should be placed on modern methods and concepts used in the evaluation of educational attainment, such as portfolio evaluation, summative evaluation, and self-evaluation.

• *Teacher-centred renewal.* The teacher should play a multifaceted role, e.g., as guide, source of learning and knowledge, coordinator of the learning processes, evaluator of the

A comprehensive, cohesive renovation of the structure, content and tools of education would release creative potential and revitalize Arab society.

outcomes of learning, and judge of the individual learner's aptitudes and preferences.

Teachers should be prepared for profound changes in the structure, methods and goals of education. They should become familiar with self-learning, be willing to perform in tandem with other teachers and cooperate with parents and the local community. Teachers should be adept at using the new methods of evaluating students and providing education guidance. They should also be mindful of the link between basic education and the needs of society and the workplace. This calls for a new type of teacher. Therefore, a radical change is needed in the methods of preparing and training teachers.

The professional structure of education needs to be improved though the creation and strengthening of professional associations that formulate the codes of ethics for the profession, endeavour to enhance teacher performance, protect teachers' interests and participate effectively in the improvement of education in general and teacher training in particular.

A grade-based professional career structure for teachers should be introduced, with each grade having a clearly defined level of responsibility, independence and set of incentives. This will encourage excellence in teaching. A system for awarding professional teaching licences could be of considerable help, but only if it is combined with a set of verifiable criteria. The government, teachers colleges and the teachers association should jointly decide upon these criteria. A system of periodic re-licensing could also be put into effect, with teachers undergoing refresher training as needed.

- *Development administration, not management administration.* An innovative education administration, capable of leading the process of renewal, is indispensable. This calls for decentralized administration, the empowerment of local management, greater educational freedom for management and continual updating of management's knowledge of new trends in education. Administrators should apply education methods that enhance the spirit of solidarity and teamwork, consolidate the concepts of democracy and citizenship, strengthen the link between education and the workplace,

encourage constant and continuous education and serve local communities.

Democracy and the decentralization of education administration should be encouraged. Only then would schools become active participants in the improvement of education. Only then would the role of the local community in shaping and running the schools become substantive.

- *Effective participation of various societal groups in learning,* particularly basic education. Families, NGOs, the business sector and local communities should be able to take part in policy-making, finance and supervision. As noted earlier, private education (particularly non-governmental and non-profit) must be encouraged but kept under close supervision to ensure quality.

AREAS FOR EDUCATIONAL EXPANSION AND IMPROVEMENT

This section describes, in some detail, suggested policies in selected areas crucial to the expansion and improvement of education: adult education; pre-school education; children with special needs, particularly the gifted; technical and vocational education; higher education; and cultivation of talents in early childhood.

Adult education

Adult education is concerned with the continued improvement of the abilities and skills of the graduates of various phases of education. One of its main functions is to ensure the continued development of the abilities and skills of graduates of literacy programmes so as to avoid a relapse. Adult education is one of the requirements of contemporary society, but it has hitherto not been given the attention it deserves.

Defining various consecutive phases of adult education will help Arab countries to tackle the crucial issue of continuing education and self-learning. The successive phases of adult learning need to evolve in tandem with the explosive growth of knowledge that is the dominant characteristic of today's world.

Broader societal resources should be allocated to eliminate illiteracy and educate adults. These resources should not be limited

Teachers should be prepared for profound changes in the structure, methods and goals of education.

to finance but encompass other societal resources, such as students in higher education.

There will always be a need for large numbers of teachers, supervisors and guidance experts who are qualified in adult education and this need is likely to grow with time. Therefore, deep reform of the professional structure of adult education is required so that it is appropriately linked and coordinated with the Arab system of teacher training and the professional organization of the teaching profession.

Pre-school education

The development of the abilities of the child is a multifaceted, comprehensive, continuous process that takes place through interaction with natural and social phenomena. The ability of children to learn depends greatly on the age at which they are enrolled in pre-school education, the number of years they spend at this level and the quality of teaching. However, pre-school education has not received the due attention of Arab governments and is rarely a priority.

Pre-schooling should not be a miniature replica of elementary schooling, with graded classes and set syllabuses. A pre-school should be a transitional institution that provides children with space in which to play and learn, stimulates their physical growth and the development of the senses, helps them to adjust to their peers and stimulates their mental, emotional and social abilities.

International and national experience shows that parental awareness and integration of the parents into the formulation of education programmes encourage them to improve their communication with their children. This enhances their awareness of the multiple needs of the child, provides them with new abilities and exposes them to new modes of education, which leads to more successful interaction in the family, the pre-school and, later on, the school.

Children with special needs

Arab education systems need to pay attention to all their citizens, providing them with the opportunity to grow and take an active part in social life according to their individual abilities and encouraging them to fulfil their maximum

The ability of children to learn depends greatly on the age at which they are enrolled in pre-school education, the number of years they spend at this level and the quality of teaching.

potential. To achieve this goal, substantial improvements are needed in the teaching of children with special needs, including those who must grapple with physical impairment. It is also essential to focus on the education of gifted students since they are likely to play an important role in innovation, a prerequisite for progress in the age of knowledge and technology. This valuable potential deserves the wholehearted support of the education system; at the same time, however, attention paid to gifted students should not mean neglect of others.

Technical and vocational education

Of all the categories of education, technical and vocational education is the closest to the workplace and every effort should be made to keep it so. This has too often not been the case in Arab countries, where this category of education has become distant from the hands-on experience of the workplace, alien from the everyday needs of production.

Most technical professions now require a high level of education and a longer period of general education. Demand for traditional manual skills has declined and interest in the worker's social, communication and mental skills has risen. Technical and vocational education needs to take account of changing patterns of demand. It is desirable for graduates of technical and vocational education programmes to have several broad-based skills that can be applied in multiple professional disciplines. They should be able to use their skills in new fields and take initiative in unconventional situations rather than remain confined to localized vocations and a narrow range of professions.

Standards of technical training should be adaptable to the needs of production. Technical and vocational education should be linked to the labour market and the needs of development. This calls for continuous revision of the content of technical and vocational education. Standards used to determine the required skills and knowledge should be continually monitored and revised. Business, specialized education centres and professional societies should take part in this process of continuous adaptation.

Higher education

Four main policies are urgently needed for a serious reform of higher education.

- The responsibility of the state should continue, but higher education should be liberated from the domination of both government and the unregulated profit motive. The government's responsibility for higher education does not mean that institutions of higher education should be government-owned. Such institutions should be governed by independent boards with quadripartite representation (the state, the private sector, civil society and academia). The profit motive should be regulated to ensure the public interest, and the creation of non-governmental, non-profit organizations should be encouraged.

As part of its responsibility for higher education, the state should: (a) increase government and societal funding of higher education; (b) increase the efficiency of the use of resources in institutions of higher education; and (c) maximize the knowledge and societal return on these institutions. To accomplish these tasks, institutions of higher education should be financially accountable, and strict accreditation systems should be put in place and rigorously monitored to ensure quality.

- Higher education should be expanded. As noted earlier, there is a wide gap between Arab countries and the developed world with respect to enrolment in higher education. Building human capabilities in the Arab world requires expansion of this level of education. However, expansion needs to be carefully designed, especially in the case of existing institutions, where expansion in the past has led to a deterioration in quality. Institutions of higher education, both old and new, should be of high quality, diverse and flexible, with a focus on the fields and institutional forms required for scientific and technological progress. No new institutions, public or private, should be created unless they offer higher standards of quality than the existing ones.

- In a related area, a powerful shake-up to improve quality is needed in the existing institutions of higher education. As part of an integrated plan to improve quality, salaries of higher-education faculty and staff members should be increased, teaching and research capacities should be enhanced, and facilities should be improved to accommodate the size of the enrolment. Effective programmes should be implemented to improve the capabilities of faculty and staff through training, research and study programmes at home and abroad, especially in preparation for assuming faculty positions. Competition must be established as an essential, ongoing condition in the filling of faculty posts; tenure should be confined to professors with exceptional performance; academic ranks higher than professor should be created; and the creation of scientific professional organizations for academics and researchers should be encouraged.

The quality of higher education can be improved only by freeing the system from repetition, increasing its flexibility and making it more adaptable to the needs of development. This task calls for coordination with state institutions, the private sector and civil society.

There is also a need for reform of the rules governing enrolment in institutions of higher education. Rather than relying solely on the scores of public examinations, institutions of higher education should introduce a system of admission tests, tailored to the needs of each institution. This may also alleviate the problem of private tutoring by reducing the pressure on students to scramble for higher scores in general public examinations, in turn reducing the cost of education.

As an important component of the accreditation system, a target standard of quality should be set for new institutions of higher education and it should be strictly enforced. As noted earlier, new institutions should be created only if they can raise the general level of quality by competing with existing institutions.

A powerful shake-up to improve quality is needed in the existing institutions of higher education.

BOX 4.3

Assuring the quality of higher education

Today's global information marketplace requires a different kind of education, one that imparts the competencies, attitudes and intellectual agility conducive to systemic and critical thinking within a knowledge-driven economy. The calibre of their higher-education systems vitally influences how countries and people perform in this environment.

The UNDP Regional Bureau for Arab States is supporting an initiative to help to raise the local and global competitiveness of Arab higher education. Using international standards and benchmarks, this pilot project aims to introduce Arab universities to the methodology and practice of independent quality assessment of selected academic courses. It will also develop systems of statistical data management to strengthen university strategic planning. Some 40 Arab universities across the region have joined in and will benefit from the first phase of this initiative.

• A versatile, flexible system of higher education that is compatible with the needs of development should be established. To achieve versatility, basic programmes should not be replicas of old ones. At the policy level, greater attention should be paid to institutions of higher education that are not part of universities. For example, an open university could be created that would offer a range of programmes from single courses to higher scientific degrees, an approach totally different from that of existing universities in Arab countries.

In view of the accelerated obsolescence of technological skills in the modern world, higher education should encompass the concept of lifelong education through various modes of continuing learning. This should be achieved through collaboration with the state, private sector and civil society. Versatility also means an emphasis on the productive function of institutions of higher education, a function that can boost both their financial and research resources. Autonomous, multidisciplinary R&D centres should be created in active partnership with the state, private sector and civil society.

Flexibility on the individual level means the freedom to leave and to return to various institutions of higher education. Flexibility on the institutional level means that the structure of institutions and the content of their programmes are continually revised by governance boards to guarantee a quick response to local and international developments. Quadripartite representation in the governance of institutions of higher education would be of great value in supporting this type

Higher education should encompass the concept of lifelong education through various modes of continuing learning.

of flexibility.

Cultivation of talents in early childhood

Talent can be considered as a predisposition for excellence and innovation in various spheres of human activity, one of which is academic achievement. In developing countries, especially in poor communities, children are often deprived of the family and societal environment needed to enrich their physical and emotional experience in ways that encourage the emergence of talent.

Overcoming these barriers so as to cultivate talent consciously in Arab countries could be achieved through a two-pronged approach: a sustained, widespread programme designed to instruct and educate parents and caregivers in child-rearing methods conducive to the emergence of talent; and a guarantee by the state, assisted by other social agents, that no child is denied the opportunity to develop his or her talents because of modest means.

This may mean rethinking the concept of security that underlies, for example, social assistance or social safety nets, which traditionally have been geared to guaranteeing basic food commodities to those in need. In a knowledge-intensive age, and one where knowledge rapidly becomes obsolete, the concept of security--for individuals and society equally--may need to be enlarged to include optimizing opportunities for the emergence of talent in childhood.

More specifically, education reform should include discovering, fostering and monitoring talent by, for example, introducing into schools special programmes for children who display a talent. This would broaden the

---

BOX 4.4

Gibran: on children

Your children are not your children.
They are the sons and daughters of Life's longing for itself.
They come through you but not from you,
And though they are with you, yet they belong not to you.
You may give them your love but not your thoughts, for they have their own thoughts.
You may house their bodies but not their souls, for their souls dwell in the house of tomorrow, which you cannot visit, not even in your dreams.
You may strive to be like them, but seek not to make

them like you
for life goes not backward nor tarries with yesterday.
You are the bows from which your children as living arrows are sent forth.
The Archer sees the mark upon the path of the infinite, and He bends you with His might that His arrows may go swift and far.
Let your bending in the Archer's hand be for gladness;
For even as He loves the arrow that flies, so He loves also the bow that is stable.

Source: Kahlil Gibran, The Prophet.

base for talent stimulation and enhancement and allow all children to develop the talent they potentially possess. Under this model, talented children could also advance through the various grades and curricula at an accelerated pace. Activities outside the schools should also be undertaken, including, in particular, the development of web sites (especially in Arabic), through the Internet and local networks in order to sharpen and enhance talent. Such web sites have a tendency to develop into virtual self-learning sites and would be a creative alternative, in a knowledge society, to segregating talented children in special brick and mortar schools.

This chapter has presented a number of strategic directions and policies for building human capabilities in Arab countries through revitalized education systems. These systems are the foundation on which societies must rely for the full use of human capabilities. The next chapter looks at a key area for the use of capabilities built by education systems that are responsive to the knowledge society of the twenty-first century: scientific research and technological development (R&D). It explores the relationships between research (as both a generator and user of knowledge), development (as a consumer of knowledge), and ICT (as a channel for the dissemination of knowledge).

Using human capabilities: towards a knowledge society

Chapters 3 and 4 dealt with building human capabilities in Arab countries. This chapter and the next take the analysis a stage further to consider key areas for using human capabilities in the service of human development and welfare. This chapter focuses on utilizing capabilities in two areas that have assumed increasingly critical importance in today's knowledge-intensive world: scientific research and technological development (R&D) and information and communication technology (ICT). It considers Arab countries' progress to date in both of these areas to be relatively weak. With respect to R&D, it discusses the limited nature of R&D output and its use in Arab countries, noting some of the problems these countries face (the cost of technological development, combined with the absence of strong social demand, a large market or important societal actors interested in promoting such development, coupled with weak links between the productive sector and the education systems). It then puts forward a series of proposals for building effective R&D systems, based on a more conducive environment for their development, and an agenda for priority action. Turning to ICT, similar weaknesses are observed. For example, compared with other developing regions, the Arab region comes last with respect to web sites and Internet users, the two indices relevant to the level of information development and representative of society's involvement in ICT. It notes a range of other problems and proposes elements of an ICT strategy for overcoming them and substantially enhancing both quality and access.

STATUS OF SCIENTIFIC RESEARCH AND TECHNOLOGICAL DEVELOPMENT (R&D)

Effective systems for scientific research and technological development (R&D) are both products and drivers of education systems, especially higher education. The latter is the main source of the knowledge workers who are employed by the former, while strong R&D can, in turn, promote education/learning, especially with respect to advanced knowledge in the higher-education sector. As chapter 4 has shown, Arab higher education is urgently in need of upgrading, and its current shortcomings are reflected in weaknesses in Arab R&D. The status of R&D in the Arab world has been characterized in a variety of ways (Zahlan, A., in Arabic, 1999). Among its most important features are the following:

- In the Arab world, there is a strong correlation between the crisis in the process of development on the one hand and inappropriate technology policies on the other. A very large investment in gross fixed-capital formation of some $3,000 billion over the past 20 years has had poor returns in per capita income despite massive increases in the numbers of school and university graduates.

- Arab countries have some of the lowest levels of research funding in the world, according to the 1998 World Science Report of the United Nations Educational, Scientific and Cultural Organization (UNESCO). R&D expenditure as a percentage of GDP was a mere 0.4 for the Arab world in 1996, compared to 1.26 in 1995 for Cuba, 2.35 in 1994 for Israel and 2.9 for Japan.

- The establishment of national science and technology (S&T) systems in Arab countries is crucial for development and security. However, countries have typically acquired

Arab countries have some of the lowest levels of research funding in the world.

technology via turnkey contracting and continued reliance on foreign consulting and contracting firms, thus perpetuating technological and economic dependency, limiting employment opportunities and raising the cost of technology acquisition.

OUTPUT INDICATORS

Science and technology output is quantifiable and measurable in terms of number of scientific papers per unit of population. The average output of the Arab world per million inhabitants is roughly 2 per cent of that of an industrialized country. While Arab scientific output more than doubled from 11 papers per million in 1985 to 26 papers per million in 1995, China's output increased elevenfold from one paper per million inhabitants in 1981 to 11 papers per million in 1995. The Republic of Korea increased its output from 6 to 144 papers per million inhabitants over the same period. India's output, by contrast, barely changed over the period 1981-1995: its output increased from 17 publications per million inhabitants in 1981 to 19 per million in 1995.

In 1981, China was producing half the output of the Arab world; by 1987, its output had equalled that of Arab countries; it now produces double their output. In 1981, the Republic of Korea was producing 10 per cent of the output of the Arab world; in 1995, it almost equalled its output. On a per capita basis, the output of the Arab world is within the range of the top R&D-producing group in the developing world: Brazil, China, and India.

Many of the significant technology-rich industries in the Arab world have been parachuted in as "black boxes".

The quality of scientific capabilities is measured by the number of citations received, based on the idea that the more often a scientific paper is referred to, the higher its quality and importance. Table 5.1 shows the number of papers cited per million inhabitants for selected countries. The Arab countries not mentioned in the table had no frequently cited publications. The right-hand column of the table suggests that the Arab countries included are within the range of other developing world countries but evidently lag far behind industrialized countries.

MAKING USE OF OUTPUT: CONNECTIVITY, EXTERNAL LINKAGES, TECHNOLOGICAL DEVELOPMENT

Connectivity, outsourcing, subcontracting

Benefiting from research and technological output depends critically on a robust system of national and international linkages among practitioners. Brazil, China and the Republic of Korea have established system linkages and policies in order to benefit from their national knowledge base. They have adopted technology policies that have enabled them to sustain a high rate of growth combined with a high rate of technology acquisition. By contrast, the connectivity of Arab scientists within the Arab world is poor at the national and regional levels. The connectivity of individual Arab scientists with international science is better simply because international relations in science provide the means for cooperation.

As noted earlier, many of the significant technology-rich industries in the Arab world have been parachuted in as "black boxes" via international consulting and engineering development organizations (CEDOs). However, these installations are not linked to local or regional CEDOs and R&D organizations. Until such connectivity is established, such installations cannot contribute to the scientific and technological development of the Arab world.

During the past 30 years, there has been a massive transformation of industrial firms in OECD countries; outsourcing and subcontracting have contributed to breaking down the vertically integrated firm. Integration has instead taken the form of joining a global web

BOX 5.1
Science as a Western phenomenon and the history of Arab science
(abridged from the Arabic version)

That classical science is in essence European whose origin can be traced to Greek philosophy and science was promoted by the Orientalist movement of the eighteenth century, starting from a eurocentric conception of the world and, contrary to the tradition in the history of philosophy and science, maintained intact during the last two centuries.

Although reasons have been advanced to justify the exclusion of "Eastern science" from the chronology of the scien-

tific mind and these have been subject to criticism in this century, particularly in the last 20 years, the eurocentric conceptualization is the strongest element of this ideology.

Is time not ripe yet to abandon all anthropocentric characterizations of classical science as well as "miracles", be they Greek or Arab, so that an objective history of science can be written without resort to false axioms that barely hide anthropocentric motives?

Source: R. Rached, The History of Arab Mathematics: between Algebra and Arithmetic (in Arabic), Centre for Arab Unity Studies, Beirut, April, 1989.

of technological expertise; meanwhile, outsourcing has promoted the transfer of technology to Asian and Latin American subcontractors along with the transfer of employment from high-cost to low-cost countries. A number of Asian countries in particular have successfully secured a considerable share of subcontracting from major transnational corporations. This contributed to the formation of the celebrated Asian Tigers and others, such as Indonesia, Malaysia and Thailand. Few Arab countries have benefited from the globalization of outsourcing.

Challenges for Arab countries

This unfortunate state of affairs reflects the absence of well-developed national science and technology systems in Arab countries. Without such systems, including the necessary institutional and system infrastructure, domestic performance and external economic relations stand to suffer considerably. One reason why inter-Arab trade is so low (by some estimates as little as six per cent of Arab countries' total trade) may be the lack of capabilities of the science and technology system. However, opportunities exist for remedying this situation. Because of the widespread availability of knowledge, latecomer countries (including Arab countries) have the opportunity to leapfrog over earlier stages of research and technological development; they do not need to re-invent the wheel and repeat the mistakes of early researchers. Catching up can involve learning to adapt old technologies to the current state of science, based on creative R&D, imagination and ingenuity. Doing so would help to redress the problem noted earlier of poor returns on past investments in human resources, R&D and gross fixed-capital formation—which is a function of poorly developed connectivity and currently weak science and technology systems.

Connectivity remains critical. Effective R&D/S&T systems are complex, knowledge-intensive webs of organizations and institutions. In fulfilling one of their key functions—to produce, diffuse and convert knowledge into useful and desired outputs—the quality and efficiency of the connections that link the various components of the system are as critical as the components themselves.

TABLE 5.1			
Active research scientists, frequently cited articles and frequently cited papers per million inhabitants, 1987			
Country	Research Scientists	Articles with 40+ citations	Number of frequently cited papers per million people
United States	466,211	10,481	42.99
Switzerland	17,028	523	79.90
Australia	24,963	280	17.23
Israel	11,617	169	38.63
Republic of Korea	2,255	5	0.12
India	29,509	31	0.04
China	15,558	31	0.03
Egypt	3,782	1	0.02
Saudi Arabia	1,915	1	0.07
Algeria	362	1	0.01
Kuwait	884	1	0.53

The successful pursuit of activities in these fields involves individual scientists, teams of experts, national and regional institutions and international organizations. The nature of the connections between the various components varies from one field to another, but each successful community displays a variety of linkages, which are mutually reinforcing and have complementary roles.

International and regional connectivities

Science and technology are global activities. An enormous amount of international cooperation is required to sustain them. Globalization reached science and technology long before it reached the political and economic spheres. Scientific cooperation is dictated by the universal nature of science. International cooperation between scientists and technologists takes many forms. In the case of Arab countries, there are strong practical incentives for R&D/S&T cooperation. For example, as discussed in chapter 3, most of the Arab world lies in an arid zone where water is scarce; this gives countries a common interest in issues relating to water use (including both conservation and tapping unconventional resources), water management, and water-efficient agriculture. Likewise, several Arab countries are oil and gas producers, which provides common technological challenges and opportunities for sharing experiences. Arab countries also share a number of problems, e.g., in health and the application of codes and standards. Hitherto, however, Arab countries have been unable to benefit

Arab countries have the opportunity to leapfrog over earlier stages of research and technological development.

Level of technological achievement in Arab countries

Technological development is rather weak in the Arab countries. This is evidenced by the relative position of Arab countries on the UNDP technology achievement index (TAI) (HDR, 2001), which referred to the late 1990s.

The TAI could be calculated for only five Arab countries: Algeria, Egypt, Sudan, Syrian Arab Republic and Tunisia, another indication of the poverty of data on knowledge acquisition in Arab countries.

None of these were classified as "leaders", a category that included countries such as Israel and the Republic of Korea. Sudan was classified as "marginal-ized", while the other four Arab countries were classified as "dynamic adopters", in the same category as Brazil.

In spite of significant internal variability and compared to leaders in the world, Arab countries in general clearly lag behind in technology creation (measured by patents granted to residents) and diffusion of recent innovations (measured by the share of high- and medium-technology exports in total goods exports). On the other hand, Arab countries fared relatively better on diffusion of old innovations (measured by telephone lines relative to population).

from their commonalities because they lack institutional R&D/S&T connectivity, in ironic contrast to the significant level of collaboration between Arab scientists and their colleagues in non-Arab countries.

The dilemma of poor technological development

In spite of important achievements in specific areas (e.g., aspects of extracting and processing oil in Kuwait; water desalination in Saudi Arabia; the design of sugar production lines in Egypt; and some successes in military manufacturing in Egypt, Iraq and the Syrian Arab Republic), technological development is remarkably weak in the Arab countries (box 5.2). A critical factor explaining this weakness is that technological development is a costly process, requiring a sufficiently extensive, dynamic productive base to create a strong social demand for technological development as well as a market large enough to justify its cost. Lacking these prerequisites, Arab countries have a dearth of important societal actors, whether in government or the private sector, who have a sufficiently strong interest in promoting technological development. It is instructive to note that the exception to this rule is in the military sector, where there was sufficient demand from the state, especially in Egypt and Iraq, and willingness to bear the cost. Unfortunately, however, these efforts have not spread to civilian applications.

Stimulating R&D requires a focused effort to create an enabling social, academic, commercial and regulatory environment .

TOWARD A EFFECTIVE R&D SYSTEMS

Building effective national R&D systems requires broad-based attitudinal change, involving a clear policy commitment from national authorities, wide public respect for science and knowledge and a keen desire on the part of society to keep up with scientific progress. Organizationally, the development of successful long-term R&D policies requires cooperation between R&D institutions, universities, and industry. Components of the R&D continuum need to be fostered concurrently. These components include educational systems; institutions dealing with basic, applied and interdisciplinary research; information services; funding institutions; professional societies; consulting firms; technical support systems; procurement services; and the public at large. Such cooperation fosters critical synergies and promotes the harmonization of complementary approaches, theories, analyses and applications. The evolving role of universities is especially important in R&D strategies. Theoretical research will certainly continue to be their primary responsibility, but without strong participation in applied research activities, they cannot truly contribute to the progress of analytical methods or to the enrichment of theories.

AN ENABLING ENVIRONMENT FOR R&D

Stimulating R&D requires a focused effort to create an enabling social, academic, commercial and regulatory environment to support research and technological development. The key drivers of change in these four spheres are discussed below.

Social environment

The attitude of society and individuals towards creativity, innovation and change deeply influences scientific progress. This attitude can be changed through policies that modify the rules of the social game and provide incentives for embracing change and reform. Among the most effective incentives for changing attitudes is the provision of real opportunities for social recognition, reward and advancement for those who work in the areas of knowledge and innovation. In many societies around the world, local and national competitions, peer reviews, government medals or other forms of recognition of merit, well-publicized research grants and other similar schemes help to elevate the successful scientist's stature, thereby providing incentives for further research and holding up appropriate models for younger generations of scientists. The entrepreneurial spirit must also be kindled in order to sustain R&D within society. However, it should be recognized that many R&D activities are long-term in nature and offer limited immediate rewards although the returns on long-term endeavours should be substantial.

The success of R&D policies also requires a dramatic change in the attitude of scientists and researchers towards their own productivity. Universities, specialized research centres, consulting firms and professional associations need to focus more on performance, efficiency and results. Higher efficiency can be achieved through a better distribution of roles, choosing research objectives that better match the real-life challenges Arab countries are facing, and stronger institutional and professional collaboration that optimizes the use of resources.

An R&D culture grows out of a social infrastructure of experimentation and entrepreneurship with solid recognition of achievement and appropriate rewards. Support for experimentation requires the allotment of facilities, time and resources for such activity in the research community and at all levels of the education system. Experimentation also depends on tolerance of failure within a society. This tolerance is a critical element of the R&D process. Hence, an Arab R&D culture must evolve that does not frown on failure but rather encourages perseverance and dedication.

Academic environment

Experimentation. Arab scientists pioneered the structured experimentation process (commonly known in Western culture as the scientific method and represented by the concept of algorithms, derived from the Arabic Al-Khwarizmi). Although this is a rudimentary, well-understood process, modern Arab curricula have devoted too little time and attention

to this central pillar of research and development. Additional academic attention needs to be given to approaches to structured reasoning (deductive, inductive and statistical) that provide the tools for formulating experiments and analysing their results.

Access to information. Arab students have long had to work with outdated materials and scientific journals, reflecting inadequate university and library funding for critical periodicals. Academic institutions will need to do much more to provide access to up-to-date materials either through hardcopy library access or through the vast, instantaneous knowledge base afforded by the Internet. In this respect, digital communication has greatly alleviated the physical and monetary constraints of most academic institutions in the region.

Global collaboration and external validation. Research is an activity conducted by a global community without boundaries and the scientific research process depends vitally upon collaboration. Indeed, the Internet itself was initially developed by geographically distributed research institutions to enhance their collaboration on joint research projects. In addition, external validation of local research is critical for providing an objective measure of accomplishment. Exchange programmes, external review boards, advisory councils and joint research councils provide means for measuring and validating achievements. One particularly successful example of this process is the Indian Ph.D. qualification process, which stipulates the review of original doctoral work by external academics who are in the forefront of their respective academic fields.

In essence, the role of academic institutions in furthering R&D efforts across the countries of the Arab region should focus on: (a) identifying core regional and global research needs; (b) collecting and disseminating global knowledge; (c) marshalling commercial and government resources; and (d) developing human resources for the next generation of R&D leaders.

Commercial environment

Both long- and short-term incentives for individual researchers are commercial drivers of effective R&D. Researchers need to be supported by a solid, guaranteed career path in

An R&D culture grows out of a social infrastructure of experimentation and entrepreneurship.

addition to substantial rewards for spectacular breakthroughs.

The Arab world lags significantly in private investment in R&D, reflecting the legacy of a closed, controlled economic environment. The pressures of increased global competitiveness brought about by WTO and enhanced global communication necessitate increased private-sector investment in R&D as a key global differentiator and source of competitiveness. However, many Arab firms have limited resources and will need to pool them to develop effective R&D programmes. Arab government and academic institutions can usefully work with private companies to identify focus areas for investment by both the private and public sectors, based on core needs, competencies and existing experience.

Most R&D endeavours require long-term efforts and resources. These are difficult to sustain in a commercial world ruled by profit and loss. Private-sector effort needs to be bolstered by regulatory support for R&D, through favourable tax treatment and substantial economic rewards for pioneering achievements—which should be protected by intellectual property laws and supported by capital markets. This process will need to be spurred further by the development of risk capital through venture funds and other early-stage financing for unproven products and services. The availability of such investment resources is primarily dependent on effective regulatory/tax incentives and increased sophistication in portfolio management by individuals and financial institutions. Active capital markets are related factors.

Finally, guilds, unions and other professional institutions have a critical role to play by defining the agenda that matches human resources with existing market needs. These institutions will need to be increasingly engaged in defining the future of their respective professions, promoting specialization and collaboration and identifying appropriate research agendas. Furthermore, these institutions can also serve as a mechanism for building cooperative networks to support long-term initiatives beyond the scope of individual commercial entities.

Private-sector effort needs to be bolstered by regulatory support for R&D, through favourable tax treatment and substantial economic rewards for pioneering achievements.

Regulatory environment, legislation and financing

Government regulations, national initiatives and financial incentives can have a significant impact on the development of R&D within the region. In particular, weak national legislation on intellectual property rights can lead private firms to refrain from investing in the production of knowledge at the national level, with spill-over effects at the regional and world levels. Regulatory frameworks that protect intellectual property help to promote both the expansion of research-based knowledge and the economic growth that will help to fuel further R&D expenditures. This suggests the need for a serious review of existing legislation on intellectual property rights.

Significant attention has been devoted to the concept of intellectual property and property rights. Although protection of these rights may have a short-term detrimental impact on certain regional economies, they are critical to the development of the individual and commercial incentive structure that drives innovation in R&D. While a limited number of scientists and academics are motivated purely by the intellectual rewards of investigations and theories, many more are motivated by potential economic and social recognition for their achievements. Protection of intellectual property constitutes a significant driving force of R&D by providing a legal framework for individual recognition and for obtaining substantial returns from inventions that impact a large product set or have significant applicability across a range of platforms.

Adequate financing is essential for successful R&D policies. Arab countries cannot hope to catch up with the developed world, or even to compete with many countries in the developing world, without a substantial increase in R&D spending. Arab governments should seek to increase gradually the share of R&D in GDP from the current meagre 0.5 per cent to 1 per cent, 1.5 per cent and eventually 2 per cent within the next decade. Otherwise, they will be in danger of falling technologically further and further behind the developed countries.

While governments can encourage greater private R&D spending by significantly reducing duties, tariffs and taxes on activities directly or indirectly relating to R&D, public funding will likely be the main source of support for R&D for a long period to come. Nevertheless, the private sector needs to become aware that its contribution to R&D spending is in its own best interest as a key source of improvement of its output to meet the standards set by global markets and of adaptation to constantly evolving technologies. In addition, technology-based expansion of private firms into competitive global markets would strengthen Arab private sectors by encouraging the employment of highly qualified professionals, increasing efficiency and promoting further technological change.

Government agencies and regulatory frameworks can also play a major role in marshalling the region's resources towards the development of local, national and regional research agendas. Specialization through competency centres will need to be promoted on a regional level to ensure optimal capital use (for example, an Egyptian focus on information technologies and agricultural genetics, and a Saudi Arabian focus on materials sciences and plastics). At the same time, Arab countries stand to gain much from pooling some of their financial and human resources. An Arab science foundation should be created with the objective of attracting funds and channelling them to high-level common Arab research projects. Finally, government agencies can spur technological development through direct sponsorship. For example, more than 45 per cent of all R&D efforts in the United States over the last 20 years have been funded directly by government agencies. The European Union has followed a similar model and has established several continent-wide initiatives in strategic areas of R&D. Expenditure on R&D as a percentage of GDP in the developed world has exceeded the amounts spent within the Arab region more than sevenfold.

MOBILIZING ARAB MINDS ABROAD

Arab societies lose valuable human resources through the emigration of highly qualified citizens—estimated to number about one million working in countries of the Organisation for Economic Co-operation and Development by the end of the twentieth century (Zahlan, in Arabic, 1999). Moreover, it now appears, in contrast to previous estimates, that the Arab brain drain intensified in the fourth quarter of that century. This phenomenon could be addressed by a two-pronged approach.

First, the brain drain could be turned into a brain gain if Arab governments, instead of focusing on repatriation efforts, were to actively engage highly qualified expatriate Arabs in domestic R&D programmes through knowledge transfer and liaison work with regional R&D institutions. Measures to maximize the brain gain for countries of origin might include:

• reinforcing links with highly qualified Arabs working abroad by building systematic rosters, setting up efficient channels of communication, providing facilities for visits to Arab countries, and supporting Arab culture in expatriates' countries of residence;

• accessing the knowledge of highly qualified expatriates through consultations and temporary work assignments. ICT-based networks offer innovative approaches to the rapid transfer of geographically distributed knowledge and expertise;

• direct support by Arab countries to associations of highly qualified Arabs abroad.

Second, as discussed in the previous section, Arab countries could also work to counter the brain drain by creating better incentives at home for qualified scientists. This would entail enhancing their social stature and offering them rewarding careers in professional and financial terms. Historical experience shows that both trends take root in societies undergoing a renaissance involving more effective use of human capabilities. Thus human development considerations and countering the brain drain can be mutually reinforcing.

PRIORITIZING AN R&D AGENDA FOR THE ARAB REGION

Arab countries cannot be active across the entire spectrum of R&D. Their financial and human capabilities are modest, and their research output does not exceed one per cent of the world's total. They can, however, make significant contributions if they concentrate

The brain drain could be turned into a brain gain if Arab governments, instead of focusing on repatriation efforts, were to actively engage highly qualified expatriate Arabs in domestic R&D programmes.

Knowledge determines the wealth of nations and defines the liveable state in the age of globalization.

There is a quiet revolution occurring in the midst of the welfare state. The source of its economic wealth is shifting from physical capital to human intelligence augmented with ICT. This reverses important relationships. In the past, labour was ineffective without sophisticated physical capital. In future, physical capital will be ineffective without sophisticated labour and, labour market and migration laws permitting, labour, especially educated and skilled labour, will be able to walk out on capital at any time. States and communities will have to compete for highly educated and skilled workers. This will reverse another relationship, that between the state and a large share of its citizens. Reluctant public handouts from the welfare state may no longer suffice to persuade people to settle down, pay taxes and raise families in a given country or region. The world may be shifting from the handout-based reality of the welfare state to the rights-based reality of the liveable state.

The liveable state will have to accommodate the values and interests of highly educated and skilled workers. It is likely to pursue a higher quality of life. The state will be characterized by low inflation; effective financial systems; easily accessible, competitive local markets attached to global markets; low transaction costs for businesses; and independent, efficient judiciaries that protect the rule of law, including private-property rights and sanctity of contracts. Systems for the creation and adoption of technology, for the free exchange of ideas and knowledge also fit in this mix. Highly educated and skilled workers are likely to favour human rights and freedoms protected by the rule of law and to demand open access to the public sphere, political participation and a public expenditure programme that efficiently buys the public goods that they want. Strong public opinion will bestow legitimacy only on administrations that are service-oriented, responsive, efficient, transparent and accountable. Facilities for affordable access to health care, lifelong education and ICT may become a standard. So may tolerance, peaceful coexistence, social cohesion and a clean environment.

The importance that liveable states attach to human solidarity will determine the scope and breadth of the social safety net. Therefore, while equality of opportunities is bound to increase with education and the prevalence of ICT, equality of outcomes is likely to continue to remain an open question.

J. Szeremeta

The market for R&D efforts in the Arab world... should be evaluated in the context of global competitiveness.

their efforts on a prioritized core agenda of activities that maximizes the benefits to their societies. While a specific list of such activities cannot be determined a priori, some general prioritizing principles can be defined, as follows:

• *Build a small number of specialized centres of excellence.* The model here is that of the development of highly focused centres of competence that have dramatically surpassed others comparable in both scientific and commercial excellence. These include Silicon Valley, United States, in computer hardware and applications; Murano, Italy, in shaping, colouring and forming glass; Seoul, Republic of Korea, in micro-mill development for steel and its alloys; Bangalore, India, in software engineering and development; and Switzerland, in its focus on miniature mechanical structures (including watches, sensors and sophisticated automotive components).

• *Focus on fields in which distinctive capa-*

bilities exist. Arab countries should focus on fields in which they are capable of reaching world-class scientific standards, in which they already have experience, and which are critical for their economies, such as water desalination, solar energy, petrochemical and phosphate industries, computer software, data processing and genetic biology. Arab countries have reliable accomplishments in these fields—for example, water desalination in the Gulf States, computer programming in Egypt and Jordan, the phosphate industry in Morocco and Tunisia, or the petrochemical industry in Saudi Arabia. Building on experiences, cumulative knowledge and tested practices is an essential foundation for an effective R&D system.

• *Promote global competitiveness.* Reduced tariffs brought on by WTO will significantly reduce the economic protection of many local industries. Thus, superior products and services on a global rather than a regional, national or local scale will increasingly drive effective competition. The market for R&D efforts in the Arab region should go beyond the regional context and be evaluated in the context of global competitiveness.

• *Focus on human-resource-intensive rather than capital-intensive R&D.* The region's competitive advantage lies primarily in the availability of high-quality human resources. Conversely, the region is lacking in access to cheap capital, primarily as a result of a poor property-rights regime. This situation requires an increased focus on R&D endeavours that require limited capital outlay but significant brainpower. These are the so-called "knowledge sciences". The most obvious candidate is information technology, but other fundamental research subjects such as mathematics, theoretical and device physics, and economics can also be pursued with limited capital.

• *Learn from the global R&D community.* Various other government and regional institutions are engaged in extensive R&D promotion. Significant lessons can be learned from these institutions, e.g., Europe's Esprit programme, the Defense Advanced Research Projects Agency (DARPA) in the United States, and the United Nations International Telecommunication Union (ITU). Arab institutions must engage these and other international entities and seek to contribute to and excel in them.

The second half of this chapter focuses on a topic intimately connected with R&D/S&T systems: information and communication technology (ICT).

ICT AND THE DIGITAL DIVIDE

Aspects of the digital divide: information, knowledge, technology

Information and communication technology (ICT), a product of R&D and an increasingly important factor in the knowledge economy of the twenty-first century, can be both a unifying and a divisive force. Its divisive aspect has come to be known as the "digital divide", which refers to the differences between those who have digital access to knowledge and those who lack it. The term, coined in the United States, is based on statistical surveys that relate the possession of ICT resources by individuals, schools and libraries to variables such as income level, age, ethnicity, education, gender and rural-urban residence. The inception of the term in the United States had an impact on its definition, measurement and ensuing recommendations. The concept is now widely used in comparisons involving various countries, provinces, groups and regions.

Reactions vary concerning the digital divide. In the final analysis, its existence is undeniable, but it is not an entirely technological issue. Technology has always been, and will continue to be, a social product. ICT is emphatic testimony to this fact. Inasmuch as the digital divide calls for technological solutions, it calls for societal innovation, or post-technological innovation, so to speak (box 5.5). The digital divide is thus linked to the whole cycle of knowledge acquisition.

Clearly, there is a basic difference between information and knowledge. Information, even in abundance, does not add up to knowledge. Historically, the world complained about too little information; today, the complaint is about over-information, or information overload, which presents problems of its own. The tremendous amount of information available on the Internet is overwhelming unless it is organized, sifted and filtered through the use of appropriate tools to extract concepts and knowledge that are useful in problem-solving.[1] Moreover, valuable knowledge is still surrounded by a host of technical, legal and administrative barriers.

True knowledge is what empowers people to cope with a fast-changing, complicated world. It is knowledge about life, and knowledge as a way of life. Therefore, the concept of knowledge should go beyond scientific knowledge and embrace the full triad of knowledge about science, humanities and art. Indeed, the latest cultural trend in the information industry is to promote the latter two types of knowledge. This is a matter that should be taken into account in developing Arab human resources, as must a parallel issue: knowledge for whom?

This having been said, to understand the various aspects of the digital divide, the phenomenon should be discussed along two axes (figure 5.1).

The horizontal axis represents the full cycle of knowledge acquisition, which consists of five stages: accessing information, organizing information, extracting knowledge, applying knowledge and generating new knowledge. The vertical axis represents the components of the information industry: the content, processing and distribution of information. Of these three, content is the most important.

The common definition of the digital divide, and of ways to close it, focuses on the shaded area indicated by (1) in the figure. However, the focus of attention should be shifted to the shaded area designated by (2). A change in the perception of the digital divide is essential because it affects the choice of infrastructure and the way in which required human resources are developed.

Many studies have been carried out on the reasons for the hampered flow of knowledge in Arab countries. At this point, a key factor to grasp is that knowledge in the age of information is closely related to, and dependent on,

Technology has always been, and will continue to be, a social product.

A change in the perception of the digital divide is essential because it affects the choice of infrastructure and the way in which required human resources are developed.

[1] A good example is that all the data relevant to the human genome project are published on the Internet. However, there is a huge gap between the availability of this mass of biological data and the extraction of knowledge from it in order to discover the causes of a certain disease and create new medications.

BOX 5.4

Social innovation: going against the grain

Social innovation, with regard to technological application, is a matter of finding solutions that are creative, different from those in current use, and even heading in the opposite direction from common ICT practice in advanced countries. For example:

• From the Internet to the mass media, not the reverse. The Internet is being used extensively as a form of mass media. The common practice is for the content of the mass media (press, radio, television) to be placed on the Internet, but the opposite is also possible. The Sri Lankan radio station has been successfully taking information from the Internet and broadcasting it to its listeners, for example. A specialized team in the radio station scans the Internet on behalf of the local population, looking for information that may be of interest to them. The station receives questions from the public on any topic and airs the answers after conducting an Internet search. The local radio service has thus brought the Worldwide Web home to people who cannot explore Internet sites themselves. This successful experiment has attracted much attention from development organizations and international forums.

• The cyber café as a centre for added intelligence, not for entertainment and e-mail. Cyber cafés are usually used for distance correspondence, chatting or electronic games. The Republic of Korea has succeeded in spreading the use of the Internet by establishing a great number (20,000) of Internet cafés. Most of these cafés focus on the use of the Internet for recreational purposes and as a means of escaping social traditions concerning relations between the sexes. These cafés could be used as added intelligence centres, providing information services to local individuals and institutions. The personnel of the cyber cafés could look for the information on behalf of their customers, sift through the load of information, and summarize the results. These cafés could then be linked together and with popular cultural centres, youth clubs and local government decision-making centres in order to promote communication and transparency. Such cafés could thus become a popular nucleus for electronic government.

• Arabic language-processing systems as a model for processing the English language. The systems designed to process the English language electronically dominate the methods of processing other human languages. These systems have proven ineffective when used for Arabic for a simple reason: the computation of the Arabic language, compared with English, is much more complicated on each level of the language matrix: the letter, word, phrase, and text. Arabization efforts were at first confined to incorporating Arabic into systems designed for English. This is an illogical approach because it aims to incorporate the complicated into the simple. It prompted some Arab researchers to design a computerized model using the Arabic language as a superset, supplanting English. It has been proved that this model can be easily adjusted to handle English. This is a rare opportunity to apply advanced technology and artificial intelligence in the computation of the Arabic language in a manner that can be applied to other languages.

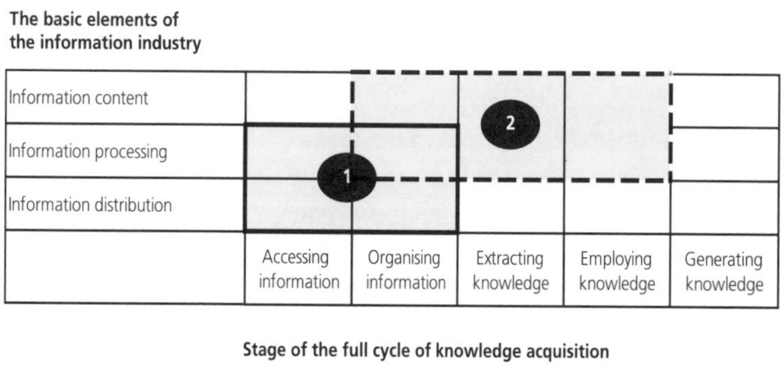

technology. In other words, the functions of generating and using information are dependent on the prevalent state of technology. Hence, technological limitations may mean that state-run Arab R&D institutions may not be able to play their full role in generating knowledge. Meanwhile, the manufacturing and services sectors in Arab countries still lack the technological maturity and the R&D departments that are capable of generating new knowledge.

Despite these impediments, several positive factors could result in the doubling of the ability of Arab countries to generate new knowledge in the information age:

• Information, by its very nature, is renewable. ICT will accelerate the rate of this renewal, thus increasing the opportunity for Arab countries to catch up in the course of the advancement of knowledge.

• The products of information are closely related to the market. This gives workers a growing role in designing, developing, selecting and marketing these products. Therefore, many local innovators will have the chance to contribute to the process of technological development.

• Modern information techniques have underlined the importance of the humanities, a discipline in search of a new methodology that transcends that of natural sciences. Arab scientists have a chance to take part in bringing about this shift in knowledge because the humanities are actually expected to inspire natural sciences in terms of future methodology (Ali, N., 2001:20).

THE DIGITAL DIVIDE BETWEEN THE ARAB REGION AND OTHER DEVELOPING REGIONS

Numerous studies have examined the digital divide between various parts of the world, measuring it through a barrage of statistical indices, including the number of stationary telephone lines, personal computers (PCs), web sites and Internet users and their ratio to the total population. As expected, the Arab world ranks low on some of these indicators. For example, Arabs represent 5 per cent of the world population but only 0.5 per cent of Internet users (Dewachi, 2000).

Figure 5.2 provides graphic comparisons

Figure 5-1
Dimensions of the digital divide

The basic elements of the information industry

	Accessing information	Organising information	Extracting knowledge	Employing knowledge	Generating knowledge
Information content			2		
Information processing		1			
Information distribution					

Stage of the full cycle of knowledge acquisition

between Arab countries and other parts of the developing world. The Arab region does not score too badly with respect to telephone lines and personal computers per thousand people, but it ranks last with respect to web sites and Internet users, the two indices that are more relevant to the level of information development and representative of society's involvement in ICT.

How the factors involved in the development of informatics interact and their weight in either expanding the digital divide or narrowing it are region-specific. This is true not only in the developing world but also in more advanced regions. For example, despite the similarities between the United States and European Union countries, many in Europe objected to the evolution of the European Union into an information society along the lines of the United States model (Bangemann, 1994). The latter is based on the establishment of a network of information superhighways, with priority given to technological and economic aspects while cultural and social ones are ignored. If Europeans have such concerns, what approach should be taken by the Arab region, where economic, social, and cultural disparities are much more pronounced? Current Arab policies for the most part have adopted a model based on copying and imitation. However, Arab countries need a different model to take them into the information society. The pressures of catching up with the information bandwagon should not eclipse the fact that Arab countries need an innovative vision that fits their special circumstances.

Some of the reasons for the wide digital divide separating Arab countries from the advanced world include the following:

- ICT, by its nature, is highly susceptible to monopoly and merger because of the means of central control it provides, together with the easy manoeuvring of symbolic assets and the easy flow of the products of informatics that it offers.

- Transition to the knowledge economy has reinforced the role of profits in the knowledge-production process, leading, in turn, to a rise in the cost of obtaining information resources.

- Building infrastructure for the information superhighways is costly.

- A growing brain drain, both actual (emigration) and virtual (through the Internet), is depriving the Arab world of its top ICT specialists, who are being aggressively sought by foreign companies. This situation, if allowed to continue, could lead to the exclusion of Arab countries from the field of R&D.

- The fast pace of change in ICT increases the important of technological planning. However, could lead to technocrats taking control of strategic development decisions. These technocrats often ignore the social and cultural aspects of ICT planning. Very few Arab experts combine ICT knowledge with awareness of its social and cultural implications.

- A situation is evolving with ICT that is reminiscent of the severe imbalance in the distribution of wavebands between advanced and developing countries with regard to telecommunications. Cyberspace is becoming a crowded place and powerful players are taking up much of the room, with their web sites dominating most regions, cities, and groups.

Despite all the impediments that have led to the widening of the digital divide between

Arab countries need a different model to take them into the information society.

Cyberspace is becoming a crowded place and powerful players are taking up much of the room.

Figure 5-2
Indicators of the digital divide among Arab countries and developing world regions

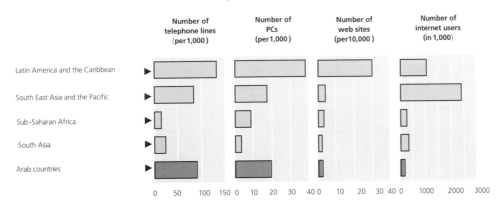

Source: Development Indicators, World Development Report, World Bank, 2001.

Arab countries and the advanced world, there is one factor that should be exploited to the utmost: the ongoing cultural and social orientation of the information industry. This is particularly true with regard to the Arabic language.

THE DIGITAL DIVIDE AMONG ARAB COUNTRIES

Figure 5.3 presents indicators of the digital divide in Arab countries according to the countries' HDI rankings. It shows extreme disparities among Arab countries regarding informatics. There is a strong correlation between the digital divide and the level of HDI if the three categories of the latter (high, medium, low) are considered. However, the correlation becomes weaker within each category because the variables affecting human development differ from those affecting informatics.

Aside from economic factors, the main reasons for the digital divide among Arab countries are:
- absence of national information policies;
- weakness of the role of Arab League agencies and other regional organizations;
- lack of interest of Arab financial institutions in information projects, where feasibility studies are normally undertaken on a purely economic basis without taking societal returns into account;
- the required considerable increase in education budgets, particularly after the expansion of ICT use in education.

Success in closing the digital divide within the region will be critical for success in narrowing the divide between Arab countries and the rest of the world. This suggests that countries might consider forming an Arab information bloc.

THE DIGITAL DIVIDE WITHIN EACH COUNTRY

There are no studies or statistics that address the various aspects of the digital divide within individual Arab countries. Given the interplay of social and technological factors, however, such a divide certainly exists. The impact of social factors on ICT will vary from country to

country, but education levels and age composition of the population are likely to be central determinants of the digital divide. Other factors significantly influencing the digital divide within countries include:
- language. Most of the information currently on the Internet is in English, a language that most of the population do not know well;
- absence of remedial education and rehabilitative adult-education programmes;
- cultural aspects, particularly with respect to gender. It is still common in many Arab countries to limit women's employment to certain areas despite the fact that ICT and the Internet, on the whole, provide opportunities for Arab women by giving them access to work from home.

The influence of language deserves special attention.

The linguistic divide

Language plays a crucial role in the information society. It is central to culture and culture is central to the information society. Language has a particularly key role in certain ICT areas, especially with regard to artificial intelligence. More generally, language is a recurring topic in the debate over globalization, especially now that the Internet has made its political, cultural and economic importance universally clear. Concern over the future of linguistic diversity in the information age is evident from the currency of such terms as "language divide", "extinction of languages", "linguistic racism", and "language wars". Some people have become pessimistic enough to list language among the victims of the information age,[2] along with other entries on the list of victims such as cultural diversity, local values and national sovereignty. Conversely, some see in the Internet a chance to revive languages, protect languages spoken by minorities, stimulate linguistic communication across cultures and promote language creativity and the arts related to it.

Linguistically, the world of ICT is at a watershed. It can maintain linguistic diversity, a choice that entails difficult communication and hinders the flow of information and knowledge, or it can turn to a standard unified language, most likely English. The Director-General of UNESCO has described this latter

Linguistically, the world of ICT is at a watershed.

[2] A book was recently published entitled The Death of Language.

possibility as a great catastrophe. Arabic, meanwhile, has its own watershed. It can become a means for Arab countries to catch up with the information train, or it can lead to a wider linguistic divide between the Arabs and the rest of the world at various levels, including linguistic studies, lexicology, language education, the professional use of language, the documentation of language and language computation.

MAIN FEATURES OF THE CURRENT ARAB INFORMATION ENVIRONMENT

Policies, legislation and organization

The absence of national information policies. All Arab countries lack information policies that delineate targets and priorities, coordinate the various sectors and formulate strategic alternatives with regard to the creation of infrastructure and the development of human and information resources. The organizational and legislative frameworks for production and services institutions in various fields of information and communication are also lacking. Nevertheless, over the past few years, political leaderships in Egypt, Jordan, the Syrian Arab Republic and the United Arab Emirates have shown interest in the information industry. This has led to the formulation of national plans to promote infrastructure, encourage foreign and local investment, provide Internet services to schools, and establish free zones for ICT technology, such as the Dubai Internet City (box 5.5), the Smart Village in Egypt and the Silicon Hills in Jordan.

The absence of a pan-Arab information policy. In view of the absence of national information policies, the absence of a pan-Arab information policy is hardly surprising. Arab attempts at integration in the field of information have been confined to the sectoral level. A series of strategies has been designed by the Arab League Educational, Cultural and Scientific Organization, an organization that has paid particular attention to informatics relating to education, culture and the media. However, these efforts have never found their way into national policies relating to information, culture, media and education. In most

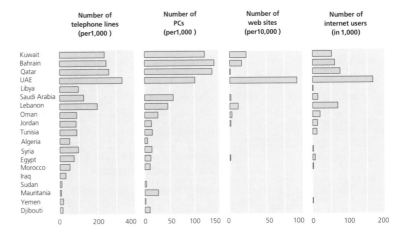

Figure 5-3
Indicators of the digital divide among Arab countries, by HDI rank

Arab countries, these sectors are mainly monopolized by governments, and the political sensitivity assigned to them hinders Arab coordination in the field of informatics.

As a result of the absence of a strong, effective policy at the national and regional level, the field of informatics in Arab countries suffers from the following impediments:

• prevalence of an isolationist sectoral outlook and the absence of coordination between sectors. This sectoral outlook conflicts with the current tendency to merge the information, media and culture sectors;

• uncoordinated procurement of communication systems, which impedes the unification and linking of Arab countries. Incompatible mobile phone systems, to give one example, mean that users may not be able to use their phone sets in the roaming mode. Recently, the need to coordinate decisions concerning the procurement of communication systems became all too evident; now such coordination seems likely once the old, incompatible systems have been phased out.

Restructuring of the telecommunications sector

Since 1995, most Arab countries have been restructuring their telecommunications sectors, substantially motivated by the introduction of mobile phones and Internet services. The restructuring is usually implemented in three phases: corporatizing state-run communications agencies; privatizing the agencies; and deregulating the sector and allowing free competition. Despite these efforts, restructuring is slow and a monopolistic, or semi-monopolistic, pattern still dominates the area of conven-

A monopolistic, or semi-monopolistic, pattern still dominates the area of conventional telecommunications.

tional telecommunications (figure 5.4).

Restructuring is taking place in the absence of both an economic model for the telecommunications corporate sector and a clear division of labour between various types of ownership (state, public, cooperative, private). Countries will need to guard against the risk that restructuring could permit the emergence of the untrammelled profit motive and the potential for monopoly to undercut the provision of affordable and equitable service.

More generally, rapid changes in ICT require prompt legislative action, something for which few Arab legislatures are equipped. This has led to the appearance of an organizational or legislative gap whose problematic nature is compounded by the fact that those who are in charge of legislation and organization lack knowledge of the technical aspects of ICT and must rely on the help of technical specialists, who tend to make recommendations on purely technological and economic grounds without taking into account the social and cultural aspects of informatics. Also, legislative efforts to date have focused on the telecommunications sector, with little attention to legislative questions relating to the convergence of telecommunications, information and content.

The element of content

Content is the most important component of the information industry, but Arab policymakers have not yet taken this fact to heart; as just noted, their focus is mainly on telecommunications infrastructure. Some studies have already pointed to the poor use of information resources in decision-making. Meanwhile, the meagre use of scientific and technological information has been linked to the low level of R&D activities in general. Even when questions of content are broached, its quality and sources are not linked to cultural trends in the information industry, nor is the distinction made between the type of content relevant to the information industry and that needed in decision-making and R&D.

The position of Arab countries is also unsatisfactory with respect to cultural heritage and creativity. In the case of heritage, Arab countries lack the means of controlling their old and new information assets, including scripts, documents, films, voice and video recordings, music and songs. Most of these resources have not been digitized. As for new creative content, Arab countries suffer a serious shortage in its production. The rate of film production has dropped from hundreds to scores. Most of the material transmitted on Arab TV channels is imported. Similarly, Arab news agencies with some recent exceptions, import most of their reports from the four major news agencies, almost becoming sub-agencies. There are no reliable figures on the production of books, but many indicators suggest a severe shortage of writing; a large share of the market consists of religious books and educational publications that are limited in their creative content.

The figures for translated books are also discouraging. The Arab world translates about 330 books annually, one fifth of the number that Greece translates. The cumulative total of translated books since the Caliph Maa'moun's time (the ninth century) is about 100,000, almost the average that Spain translates in one year (Galal, S., 1999). Meanwhile, there are some encouraging initiatives involving the publication of the content of Arab magazines and newspapers on the Internet and their distribution on CD-ROMs.

BOX 5.5

The Dubai Internet City

Dubai announced plans to set up its Internet City in October 1999. Less than a year later, the city was ready to host local, regional and international ICT companies.

The Dubai Internet City has gained a reputation, among Arab information free zones, for its advantages in terms of:

• availability of quality infrastructure. The Emirate of Dubai seeks to establish a sophisticated communication network covering all of Dubai: the schools, homes, shops, offices, hotels and restaurants;

• support given to the project at the highest political levels;

• success in attracting leading international companies to set up regional offices there;

• location in one of the regions most known for its use of ICT (figure5.3): the United Arab Emirates, Bahrain and Qatar;

• linkages with the Media City and the Wahat al-Fikr (oasis of the intellect) project in other cultural areas. This strategy is linked with the trend to merge information and media on the one hand, and ICT and culture on the other;

• assignment of the management of Dubai Internet City to a group of young people of the Emirate of Dubai who have superb qualifications as well as experience in ICT and business administration;

• presence of the annual GITEX fair in Dubai, indisputably the most important Arab event in ICT;

• provision of services that go beyond infrastructure to include R&D in the field of informatics. The City is planning to set up several units for R&D in advanced fields of informatics;

• its character as a microcosm of globalization: a mosaic of nationalities, languages, values, products and services.

However, if Arab states have been reluctantly ceding their monopoly over the telecommunications sector, they are still clinging to their monopoly over the content of information. Efforts to introduce elements of electronic government (Dubai, Jordan) are usually confined to administrative affairs and the provision of government services to the public. There are no attempts to use the Internet as a means of achieving a higher level of political transparency or enhancing democratic performance. The Internet has not yet been used as a way to transcend the official media and serve all social classes.

Using ICT in education and training

Egypt, Jordan, Saudi Arabia and the United Arab Emirates have formulated ambitious plans to introduce computers at various stages of education. There are additional plans to introduce Internet services in a communications laboratory in each school. These plans face several obstacles, however, including insufficient training of teachers; a severe shortage of educational software in Arabic; inability of curricula to cope with the diversity of education and learning methods (distance learning, learning through participation, collaborative learning); and inability of school administrations to manage modern educational technology.

On the other hand, the existence of several government and non-governmental centres for ICT that have proved their competence means that these obstacles to using ICT in educational contexts could in principle be overcome without resorting to foreign expertise for the use of ICT in education.

There are no real opportunities for using ICT to train adults in the workplace. Most Arab workplaces lack a technological environment conducive to ICT training. The language barrier is also a deterrent for the great majority since learning and training via the Internet require some knowledge of English.

Software development for ICT

It is customary to classify software on two levels: operating and productivity-enhancing software and application software. Operational and productivity-enhancing software include operating systems governing the

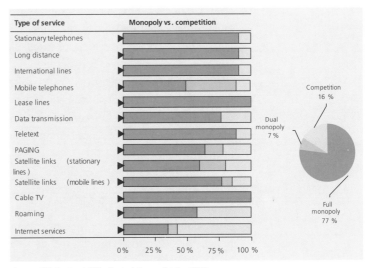

Figure 5-4
Extent of monopoly in telecommunications in Arab countries

Source: ITU, Regional Office for Arab States, October 2000.

operation of the computer, data networks, programming languages and productivity-enhancing programmes, such as word processing and databases. Successful attempts have been made to Arabize the operating and word-processing systems, but these efforts were terminated owing to fierce competition by transnational companies and the absence of standardization. It is now hard for the Arab world to compete in this field.

Numerous studies have indicated the importance of work on the computation of Arabic and the Arabization of ICT. One recent study by the Economic and Social Commission for Western Asia (ESCWA) examined the importance of Arabization, its prospects, priorities and relation to the knowledge economy. Several Arab countries have established specialized ICT centres and institutes, including the Electronics Research Centre, affiliated with the National Research Centre in Egypt, founded in 1963; the Regional Institute for Communication and Information Studies in Tunisia, founded in 1986; and the Higher Institute for Applied Sciences and Technology, affiliated with the Syrian National Research Centre.

These centres have made significant contributions to the computation of written and voiced Arabic language, electronic translation, educational software, multimedia, encryption, security systems and the design of national information networks and geographic and administrative information systems. The

The Internet has not yet been used as a way to transcend the official media and serve all social classes.

Egyptian Centre has carried out several studies in microelectronics and robotics. However, these centres have not succeeded in establishing a joint research programme, sharing resources, or coordinating research programmes to avoid duplication despite all the opportunities the Internet provides in this respect. Very few attempts have been made to use the opportunities for cooperation presented by international cooperation agreements.

Application software includes educational, administrative and financial software, information services and databases. A considerable number of companies specialize in multimedia and electronic publishing; these are mostly software development companies and a few educational and media publishing houses. One of the most popular application programmes relates to religious heritage, reflecting the importance of the cultural factor. Information services in the Arab world are rather modest, owing to the lack of resources and personnel and weak demand.

PROMOTING ACCESS TO ICT

The acquisition, (including extraction and collection), manipulation, analysis and dissemination of information will powerfully drive economic prosperity in Arab countries as elsewhere within the coming decades. The world economy is increasingly based on information-intensive services that yield higher value added than traditional manufacturing enterprises. However, it is critical that the indispensable tools of information technology--the computer terminal, associated software and the Internet--be accessible to as wide a variety of individuals within Arab society as possible. Through free-form participation, these tools can engage the minds of many budding scientists and researchers throughout the region not only in the field of information technology but in all fields of research. ICT is by far the most important enabler and equalizer of technology access available today.

Many users in the Arab world today complain of the shortage of Arab content and information resources on the Internet. Remedying this situation would have many benefits, including helping to build an in-

creased sense of community and participation on-line, through, e.g., content embodying symbolic heritage, including texts, music, films and databases, as well as new creations by writers, thinkers, artists, and composers. Some would suggest increased Internet expenditure, control and direction from institutional and government entities to ensure that culturally relevant content is produced, as a way of helping to avert a cultural onslaught from abroad. Such initiatives should be largely unnecessary: increased accessibility of, and participation in, the medium will naturally enrich the Internet with Arab information and culture. The more Arab journalists, writers, poets, engineers, scientists, doctors and philosophers are introduced to the medium, the more such people will publish their own content, making cyberspace a richer place for Arab and non-Arab users alike. However, getting the most value from this upsurge of information will require enabling commercial and regulatory frameworks. The potential value is great and the economic rewards are significant, as shown in table 5.2.

Current barriers to access

The position of the Arab region vis-à-vis ICT is characterized by several features prevailing in other parts of the developing world, including:

• a marked concentration of ICT in a few countries;

• access patterns that coincide with social divides, i.e., wealth, education, age, gender and urbanization;

• large deficits in connectivity, capability and content;

• weak linkages in infrastructure and a mismatch between ICT and the production system.

However, Arab countries face some additional problems, including:

• the increasing importance of the linguistic dimension in ICT, especially after the spread of the Internet;

• the culture surrounding the use of information in general. In some countries, the benefits of an open information culture of direct exchanges among citizens, between citizens and government, and internationally have not yet reached a critical mass;

• e-government, e-commerce and decision support systems are either non-existent or in their infancy.

MAKING ICT AVAILABLE TO ALL

Policies and organization. The Arab world needs an effective information policy. This policy should:
• have a multisectoral outlook. In particular, it should be sensitive to the increasing tendency to merge the sectors of communication, media and information;
• acknowledge the importance of the integration of Arab information in Arabic, especially with regard to the sharing of resources;
• emphasize that ICT is a tool for communicating knowledge and take into account that the computation of the Arabic language is a basic starting point for this approach;
• acknowledge the role of content in its broad sense;
• give priority to the use of ICT in education, training and public health as well as to the creation of a viable infrastructure for an Arab cultural industry.

Strategic planning agencies should be created for information development. These agencies should have units specialized in monitoring the technological development of ICT and evaluating technological programmes, products and producers. This should be coupled with the training of specialists in societal adaptation policies relevant to ICT.

Telecommunications infrastructure. Policies for the restructuring of the telecommunications sector need to guarantee deregulation and open up competition to encourage local and foreign investors to contribute to infrastructure development. At the same time, a measure of government regulation should be maintained to guarantee a minimum level of public telecommunications services for people with limited income and those residing in rural and distant areas. In addition:
• Innovative alternatives should be explored with the aim of reducing the cost of building infrastructure. For example, it is possible to establish a multi-tiered telecommunications system (with regard to speed) while maintaining connectivity and compatibility among system levels. It is also possible to create

TABLE 5.2
Information industry in the United States and the European Union, 1994 (in billions of dollars)

Information-industry sector	European Union	United States
Content of information	186 (34%)	255 (45%)
Distribution of information	165 (30%)	160 (28%)
Processing of information	193 (36%)	151 (27%)
Total	544 (100%)	566 (100%)

Source: UNESCO, Information Annual Report for 1998.

inexpensive and quick-to-build wireless communications or wireless local loops (LLPs) for local use.
• Specialists in departments of planning and organization should be trained in matters concerning the restructuring of the telecommunications sector and in examining various economic models for privatizing and liberalizing it.
• Arab countries should coordinate their telecommunications systems in order to guarantee their compatibility and connectivity.
• Telecommunications service charges should be adjusted to ensure access regardless of financial ability.

A spirit of participation. Participation in, and a sense of societal responsibility for, the process of information development and policy, planning, implementation and follow-up should be developed. This requires a clear definition of goals and full commitment by the political leadership and the government. NGOs should be encouraged and trained to use the Internet in polling opinions, rallying support and coordinating positions so that their web sites become alternative channels of expression to State-loyal official media. The purpose is to empower these organizations to become popular fact-finding bodies, able to present their views and uncover instances of social dysfunction, corruption and failure of development efforts.

Development of human resources. A full study should be made of the process of introducing computers into Arab schools in order to identify areas of success and failure. In particular, national plans should aim to develop specialized personnel for training as computer teachers. Training in the use of ICT as an educational tool should involve a blend of educational and methodological principles, the theory of knowledge and technical aspects.

ICT is a tool for communicating knowledge... the computation of the Arabic language is a basic starting point.

Efforts should be made to develop Arabic-language software for general education, adult training and upgrading of professional skills. Programmes for adult training should be linked with the actual needs of the labour market and should be coordinated with the introduction of ICT in the workplace.

The Internet should be used to the maximum extent possible in the training of women in order to attract Arab women to participate in the development process. Emphasis should be placed on the social and development sides of communication, not simply the technical.

The number of technological support centres should be increased. The Egyptian experience of creating a group of such centres in the provinces, with UNDP funding, is useful in this regard. The Technology Access Communication Centre (TACC) is providing training in electronic trade, office management, and other skills to Egyptians with limited means, adults, and small and medium-sized businesses.

The skills of social innovation should be fostered. Developers and implementers should realize the importance of innovation in the age of information and encourage their personnel to adapt technology applications to local needs. Information awareness can be spread through the media in a subtle approach that links ICT with day-to-day life.

The element of content. Content should be considered a major component in the mod-ern information industry. Laws should be passed to protect national archives, including unclassified documents produced by national and pan-Arab institutions. Heritage assets, including text, pictures, films, music and radio and TV recordings, should be digitized. Developers and users should be informed of the available Arab sources of content and the importance of these sources in providing attractive multi-media products and services. A model that might inspire this effort is the INFO2000 programme of the European Union.

R&D for ICT. Priority should be given to research that addresses the ICT trends discussed earlier in this chapter and that advances the computation of the Arabic language. A network of specialized research institutes should be created to tackle the processing of the Arabic language and the new branches of ICT. These centres could be hosted in existing Arab research institutions. Opportunities for cooperation with the European Union in ICT research should be exploited, especially with regard to automatic translation, management of information resources, and the digitalization of cultural heritage.

This chapter has discussed using human capabilities in Arab countries in order to move towards a knowledge society, a keystone of human development. Chapter 6 continues the focus on the use of human capabilities in three

Developers and implementers should realize the importance of innovation in the age of information.

BOX 5.6

Imam Ali bin abi Taleb: (556-619 A.D.) knowledge and work

● No vessel is limitless, except for the vessel of knowledge, which forever expands.

● If God were to humiliate a human being, He would deny him knowledge

● No wealth equals the mind, no poverty equals ignorance, no heritage equals culture, and no support is greater than advice.

● Wisdom is the believer's quest, to be sought everywhere, even among the deceitful.

● A person is worth what he excels at.

● No wealth can profit you more than the mind, no isolation can be more desolate than conceit, no policy can be wiser than prudence, no generosity can be better than decency, no heritage can be more bountiful than culture, no guidance can be truer than inspiration, no enterprise can be more successful than goodness, and no honour can surpass knowledge.

● Knowledge is superior to wealth. Knowledge guards you, whereas you guard wealth. Wealth decreases with expenditure, whereas knowledge multiplies with dissemination. A good material deed vanishes as the material resources behind it vanish, whereas to knowledge we are indebted forever. Thanks to knowledge, you command people's respect during your lifetime, and kind memory after your death. Knowledge rules over wealth. Those who treasure wealth perish while they are still alive, whereas scholars live forever; they only disappear in physical image, but in hearts, their memories are enshrined.

● Knowledge is the twin of action. He who is knowledgeable must act. Knowledge calls upon action; if answered, it will stay; otherwise, it will depart.

Source: Ali bin abi Taleb, Nahj Al-Balagha, Interpreted by Imam Muhammad Abdu, Vol. 1, Dar-Al-Balagha, Beirut, 2nd edition, 1985.

areas that are equally central to both the process and the goals of the human development effort: restoring economic growth, promoting full employment, and attacking poverty in Arab countries.

CHAPTER 6

Using human capabilities: recapturing economic growth and reducing human poverty

Building and using human capabilities effectively represent the engine of sustainable growth and poverty reduction. At the same time, economic growth (or lack of it) influences prospects for enhancing human development, of which persistent poverty is the antithesis. Thus, achieving sustained and equitable economic growth is intimately connected with both the process and the goals of human development. This chapter continues the discussion of the use of human capabilities in the region by reviewing the record with respect to growth, unemployment and poverty and proposing a way forward for Arab countries. It begins by examining the pattern of economic growth in the region in the last three decades, observing that sensitivity to oil markets, the low efficiency of physical capital and poor labour productivity resulted in fluctuating performance and, during the 1980s, a period of quasi-stagnation. It next considers the interrelationships between growth, average income levels, income distribution and inequality, unemployment and poverty. In doing so, it illustrates and discusses an apparent anomaly between the relatively low levels of extreme poverty in Arab countries compared to other regions and some indications of widening income disparity. After characterizing the extent, main causes and different forms of unemployment in Arab countries, it suggests that renewed growth is a necessary, although not a sufficient, condition to meet the challenge of full employment, fully use human capabilities and overcome poverty. The latter part of the chapter proposes specific policy measures towards these ends, based on mobilizing the full human and economic potential of the region.

ECONOMIC GROWTH

GENERAL TRENDS

GDP in all Arab countries combined stood at $531.2 billion in 1999—less than that of a single European country, Spain, ($595.5 billion). Over the period 1975–1998, real GDP in the Arab world[1] (in the geographically selective sense adopted here) rose from $256.7 billion in 1975 to $445.7 billion in 1998 in constant prices. The average annual rate of growth over the period as a whole was 3.3 per cent.

At first glance, this result seems respectable, slightly above the world average (2.9 per cent). The countries of East Asia and the Pacific (EAP) and South Asia (SA) have done better, with averages of 7.4 per cent and 5.2 per cent, respectively, but the region has out-performed Latin America and the Caribbean (LAC) and sub-Saharan Africa (SSA), with rates of 3 per cent and 1 per cent, respectively.

However, the period average masks wide variations by sub-period. Arab countries saw very strong growth during the second half of the 1970s: 8.6 per cent (1975-1980), followed by a very sharp drop between 1982 and 1990 (0.7 per cent)—the so-called lost decade—and then a return to more modest averages (3.3 per cent) between 1990 and 1998. Figure 6.1 illustrates the pattern over time and shows that the overall trend was downward over the period as a whole.

Moreover, several time cycles can be distinguished within sub-periods, each with an average duration of three to four years, with very

GDP in all Arab countries combined stood at $531.2 billion in 1999—less than that of a single European country, Spain, ($595.5 billion).

[1] The analysis presented, covering the entire period considered, does not include six Arab countries that account for a little less than 15 per cent of the population of Arab countries and about 20 per cent of the GDP of all Arab countries. Data are not available for these six countries as follows: for the Libyan Arab Jamahiriya, Qatar and Somalia during the period 1975–1998; for Lebanon and Yemen during the period 1975–1989; and for Iraq since 1990. Scattered data could be found for these countries at different points in time and from different sources. Three sub-periods were chosen for the analysis over time: 1975-1980, 1980-1990 and 1990-1998. The Arab countries were classified into three subgroups according to the level of income per capita: high-, middle-, and low-income. For comparisons with other regions of the world, the following four regions of developing countries were adopted: East Asia and the Pacific (EAP), Latin American and the Caribbean (LAC), South Asia (SA), and sub-Saharan Africa (SSA).

sharp variations in the late 1970s and 1980s but less dramatic fluctuations in the 1990s. This irregular, saw-tooth pattern of growth has consequences for material welfare, especially that of vulnerable populations, and for human development in general.

The fluctuating economic growth pattern

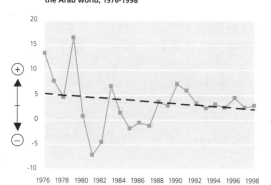

Figure 6-1
Annual growth rate in GDP (1995 US$), the Arab world, 1976-1998

in the Arab world reflects mainly movements in the oil market on which it strongly depends. Throughout the period as a whole, long-run trends present a parallel picture of decline (figure 6.2), and fluctuations around the trend show distinct similarities up to the early 1990s, after which both the oil price and GDP growth fluctuated less and the connection between the two weakened.

The second factor that explains the irregular and highly fluctuating nature of economic growth is the pattern of agricultural production—although sharp variations in agricultural output have had less effect on the GDP growth rate since 1993. Thus, growth in the 1990s, while still sensitive to oil and agriculture, became less irregular.

FACTOR PRODUCTIVITY

Physical capital formation and efficiency

Between 1975 and 1998, the rate of gross investment (gross fixed-capital formation relative to GDP) was, on average, 24.6 per cent despite negligible foreign direct investment (FDI) over the period (box 6.1). The long-term trend for investment is similar to the long-term decline in GDP growth (figure 6.3). Averages by sub-period show a steady reduction: 27.3 per cent for 1975–1980, 25.1 per cent for 1980–1990 and 21.9 per cent for 1990–1998.

The contribution of investment to growth depends not only on the rate of investment but also on the efficiency with which it is used. The correlation between the rate of economic growth and investment efficiency is quite strong and significant on a world scale, as can be seen in figure 6.4, where the Arab world as a whole (the AW symbol in the chart), lies in the lower-left quarter of the graph, indicating relatively low levels of both investment efficiency[2] and growth.

Thus, despite a quite strong capital-accumulation effort, the Arab world shows weak investment efficiency (in terms of the productivity of physical capital) associated with a rather weak level of growth.[3] It should be

The fluctuating economic growth pattern in the Arab world reflects mainly movements in the oil market on which it strongly depends.

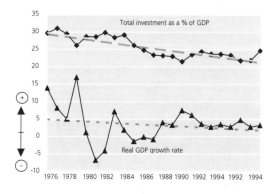

Figure 6-2
Annual growth rate in GDP and oil price (1995 prices), the Arab world, 1976-1998

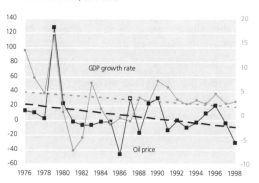

Figure 6-3
Real GDP growth rate and total investment (as a %of GDP): Arab countries, 1976-1998

[2] Knowing that the rate of growth is, by definition, equal to the product of the rate of investment and marginal productivity (average) of capital, the latter, which encompasses the efficiency of physical capital, becomes equal to the rate of growth divided by the investment rate.

[3] East Asia and the Pacific, Egypt, Jordan, the Syrian Arab Republic, Tunisia and the United Arab Emirates exhibit a rather balanced relationship between the two factors as opposed to Latin America and the Caribbean, sub-Saharan Africa, Djibouti, Morocco and Saudi Arabia, where relatively weak growth is associated with a relatively weak rate of investment efficiency.

noted, however, that a significant component of investment by Arab countries during the last quarter century was in infrastructure, generally urgently needed, occasionally superfluous, but normally not yielding quick direct returns. More generally, however, a restoration of strong growth cannot be expected to materialize without significant improvement in the efficiency of gross investment in fixed capital.[4]

Labour productivity

In addition to the low efficiency of investment, growth in Arab countries has been seriously hampered by low and declining labour productivity. Low productivity is a major challenge for the region. According to World Bank data (1998/1999 World Development Report), GNP per worker[5] in all Arab countries combined was less than half that of two comparator developing countries: Argentina and the Republic of Korea.[6] Dividing Arab countries into three groups (each of which accounts for about one third of the Arab work force) according to the share of oil in GNP sharpens this picture. In the first group of nine Arab countries that are richest in oil resources, productivity barely exceeds half the level in the two comparator countries; for the middle group with respect to oil's share in GDP (Egypt, the Syrian Arab Republic and Tunisia), productivity is less than one sixth of the comparators'; in the oil-poor Arab countries (Djibouti, Jordan, Lebanon, Mauritania, Morocco, Somalia, Sudan and Yemen) it is less than one tenth. This result suggests that excluding the effect of oil revenues might reduce productivity estimates for Arab economies to a greater extent than the simple overall comparison given above.

More important than measures of the level of productivity, however, are measures of changes in it over time. World Bank estimates of total factor productivity in the Middle East and North Africa (MENA) region showed a steady decline (-0.2 per cent a year) from 1960

to 1990, compared to rapid acceleration in other parts of the world (World Bank, 1995: 4).

Data from the 1998/1999 World Development Report permit comparisons of GDP per worker[7] in nine Arab countries with that in faster-growing developing countries during the periods 1980-1990 and 1990-1997. On this basis, annual productivity is estimated to have risen by 15 per cent in China, 8 per cent in the Republic of Korea, and 6 per cent in India but only 4 percent in the Arab countries.

Low levels of growth and productivity can be partly explained by the fact that Arab countries lag behind faster-growing developing countries in a key human-capabilities variable discussed in chapter 4: years of education. A comparison with the three Asian Tigers is revealing. In 1960, per capita output in Arab

Growth in Arab countries has been seriously hampered by low and declining labour productivity.

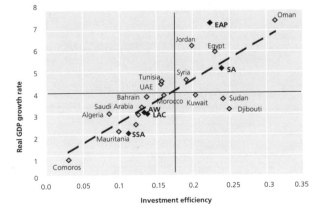

Figure 6-4
Real GDP growth rate and investment efficiency, Arab countries and selected world regions

---

[4] Efficiency varies between Arab countries. It is relatively high and associated with higher-than-average growth in Egypt, Jordan, Oman and the Syrian Arab Republic. The opposite situation prevails in Algeria, Djibouti, Mauritania and Saudi Arabia.

[5] As a preliminary indicator of productivity, dictated by the availability of newer data from one main source. Since the estimate of the labour force in developing countries is incomplete owing to the exclusion of women and children, especially in non-formal economic activity, it is expected that assessing productivity by this method would result in an overestimate.

[6] The GNP of the Republic of Korea outstrips that of all Arab countries combined (although the population of that country is less than one fifth of the total Arab population).

[7] A better reflection of productivity than GNP.

countries was higher than that of the three Tigers. The latter were, however, more advanced in terms of years of education, with a difference in educational attainment of around three years.[8] Over the period 1960-1992, the difference in educational attainment actually doubled, to 6 years. Not surprisingly, GNP per worker in Arab countries dropped to less than half of that in the Republic of Korea.

At the sectoral level, the United Nations Industrial Development Organization (UNIDO) provides comparative data for the industrial sector. Industrial labour productivity in the region (proxied by the organization's North Africa and West Asia region) was estimated in the early 1990s to be roughly the same as in 1970 (when it had been close to European and Japanese levels). In the face of rising productivity elsewhere, this has meant a significant relative decline. According to UNIDO (Industry and Development: Global Report, 1992/1993), Arab industrial labour productivity per worker fell as a percentage of the North American level in constant 1985 dollars from 32 per cent in 1970 to 25 per cent in 1980 and 19 per cent in 1990. It is noteworthy that the decline took place after the oil boom, which started in 1974, after an investment of $2,000 billion in gross fixed-capital formation by 1992 and after a massive expansion in educational systems at all levels (Zahlan, 1994:107-108).

TRENDS IN PER CAPITA INCOME (REAL GDP PER CAPITA)

As noted earlier, the Arab world did achieve an average growth of real GDP of 3.3 per cent

over the period 1975-1998. However, the impact of growth on the welfare of the population is related to the rate of growth of the latter, as noted in chapter 3—and population growth was very high (2.8 per cent) on average during the past quarter century although it gradually fell off over time (3.1 per cent for 1975–1980, 3 per cent for 1980-1990 and 2.6 per cent for 1990–1998).

While the relationship between real GDP growth and population growth is complex, for the geographically selective set of Arab countries discussed here, it has meant that real per capita income for the period 1975–1998 as a whole grew very slowly, by around 0.5 per cent a year—in effect, a situation of quasi-stagnation. Meanwhile, the global average increase was more than 1.3 per cent a year, implying a relative deterioration in the average standard of living in the Arab region compared to the rest of the world. In regional terms, only sub-Saharan Africa did worse than the Arab countries; over the past quarter century, having seen an actual fall in real GDP per capita. Latin American and Caribbean countries saw a modest average improvement of 1 per cent while South Asia averaged a 3-per cent rate; the best performer, East Asia and the Pacific, achieved 5.9 per cent growth.

With respect to sub-periods, Arab GDP per capita grew strongly between 1975 and 1980, from $1,845 to $2,300, an average annual rate of increase of 5.6 per cent. Between 1980 and 1990, growth collapsed, with a negative rate of 2.3 per cent a year, exemplifying the sharp deterioration of economic and social conditions in the Arab world during that decade. By 1990, GDP per capita stood at $1,500; it improved slightly during the decade, reaching $1,653 in 1997, an annual rate of increase of 0.7 per cent.

As with other variables, regional averages mask sharp differences by sub-groups of countries. The best-off group, the Gulf countries, suffered the greatest deterioration. Their GDP per capita, which grew at an average rate of 3 per cent between 1975 and 1980, turned sharply negative between 1980 and 1990 (-4.4 per cent) and remained negative (-1.7 per cent) between 1990 and 1998. The resulting rate for the quarter century as a whole is a neg-

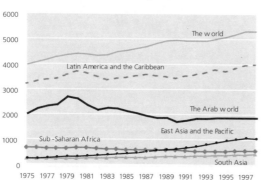

Figure 6-5
**Real GDP per capita,
the Arab world and selected regions, 1975-1998**

---

[8] Based on a comparison of mean years of education in a group of Arab countries which includes almost three-quarters of the total Arab population, according to population figures in the early 1990s.

ative -1.8 per cent. Low-income Arab countries did a little better but still had a negative rate of growth of GDP per capita over the period as a whole (-0.1 per cent), reflecting a deterioration between 1980 and 1990 (-1.4 per cent), followed by an improvement since 1990 (+1.9 per cent). Only middle-income countries registered a slight improvement throughout the period (+0.9 per cent), with a strong increase in 1975–1980 (5.8 per cent), followed by a decline   (-2.2 per cent) in 1980–1990 and a relative improvement (+1.5 per cent) in 1990–1998.

Out of the selected countries discussed here, seven have known a relatively significant improvement in average income: Egypt, Jordan, Morocco, Oman, Sudan, Syrian Arab Republic and Tunisia. Countries suffering declines included Comoros, Djibouti, Iraq (1975–1990), Kuwait, Mauritania, Saudi Arabia, United Arab Emirates and Yemen. Algeria and Bahrain saw effective stagnation.

Real GDP per capita (PPP)

Meaningful international comparisons of real GDP per capita need to be based on purchasing power parity (PPP). Figure 6.7 provides selected regional data on this basis, using OECD countries as the comparator. In 1975, real PPP GDP per capita in the Arab world (in the geographically selective sense used in this chapter) was 21.3 per cent, barely more than one fifth of the OECD level. By 1998, the real PPP income of the average Arab citizen had fallen to 13.9 per cent, or one seventh, of that of the average OECD citizen.

The figure graphically illustrates the pattern of brief initial Arab convergence in real PPP incomes with those of the OECD countries, followed by a long deterioration into increasing divergence. By contrast, East Asia and Pacific countries moved from a ratio of about 1:20 in 1975 to about 1:7 in 1998. South Asia, despite a heavy demographic burden, achieved some degree of modest convergence. Countries in Latin America and the Caribbean (and sub-Saharan Africa) suffered a deterioration of their relative position and substantial divergence from OECD averages.

Among Arab countries, only Egypt and to a lesser degree Jordan and Tunisia had a tendency towards convergence with OECD

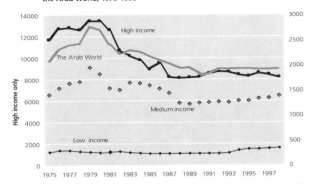

Figure 6-6
Real GDP per capita by levels of income, the Arab world, 1975-1998

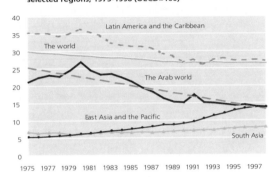

Figure 6-7
Real GDP per capita (PPP$), the Arab world and selected regions, 1975-1998 (OECD=100)

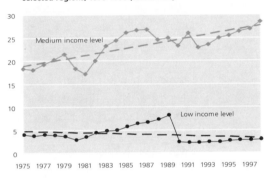

Figure 6-8
Real GDP per capita (PPP$), the Arab world and selected regions, 1975-1998 (OECD=100)

countries. All other countries, without exception, moved in the opposite direction.

Income convergence within the Arab region

Within the Arab world, the middle-income group has shown substantial convergence with the high-income (Gulf) countries. Figure 6.8, which equates the latter group's average income with 100, shows middle-income countries reducing the gap by 10 points, from 18.3 per cent in 1975 to 28.3 per cent in 1998. On the other hand, low-income countries, after having reduced the difference midway through the period, were actually in a slightly worse situation at its end than they were at its beginning, moving from a very low 4.11 per

By 1998, the real PPP income of the average Arab citizen had fallen to 13.9 per cent, or one seventh of that of the average OECD citizen.

cent in 1975 to only 3 per cent in 1998. This suggests that the pattern for the region as a whole is one of inter-country divergence rather than convergence.

INCOME DISTRIBUTION AND POVERTY

Income is the main determinant of the standard of living of an individual or a household and, at the macro level, of a population. Income distribution is a determinant of how a nation's wealth is shared among its citizens; it is thus an important indicator of inequalities in society.

Analysis of poverty and income-inequality issues in the Arab region is frustrated by lack of comprehensive and comparable data sets as well as by the reluctance of some official sources to share primary survey data with researchers. Moreover, United Nations agencies that try to collect and analyse poverty data often have different geographical coverage. Data for the World Bank's Middle East and North Africa (MENA) region, for example, do not include three Gulf countries classified as "high income" (Kuwait, Qatar and United Arab Emirates), or Comoros, Djibouti, Mauritania, Somalia or Sudan (all included in the Bank's sub-Saharan Africa region), and data are included on a non-Arab country, the Islamic Republic of Iran. ESCWA, on the other hand, covers the Asia-based Arab countries while the Africa-based ones are covered under the Economic Commission for Africa (ECA). Finally, the availability of reliable information is also limited by irregular patterns of data collection and publication at the level of the individual Arab country.

Nevertheless, attempts have been made to study income distribution patterns and policies in the Arab region and what they show about poverty. While acknowledging the difficulty of assessing poverty in the absence of good data on income distribution, recent studies have offered careful analyses and interesting, if not always identical, conclusions.

In their joint paper on poverty reduction in the World Bank's MENA region, 1970-2000,[9] Richard J. Adams, Jr. and John Page

MENA countries have had the lowest regional incidence of extreme poverty in recent years.

show that the MENA countries have had the lowest regional incidence of extreme poverty in recent years, with less than 2.5 per cent of the population living on or below the $1/day income level for dire poverty adopted for the Millennium Development Goals. They suggest that this has been due to essentially egalitarian income-distribution practices and to the ability of the region's poor to capitalize on periods of economic growth, particularly between 1970 and 1985.

On income distribution, their calculations suggest that the developing countries of the MENA region now have, on average, one of the most equal income distributions in the world, with an average Gini coefficient of 0.364 for the period 1995-1999, and that the average coefficient has been falling over time.[10] They attribute this to the relatively high share of income accruing to the bottom quintile of income distribution and its increasing rate over time, with the result that the MENA average income share going to this quintile over time is 7.2 per cent, the same as that of OECD and East Asia and Pacific countries.[11] The authors underline in particular the role of (a) migration and remittances, which "disproportionately benefited those at the bottom of the income ladder, either directly through transfers to poorer households or indirectly through their impact on the labor market"; and (b) government jobs, which cushioned the poor, especially in rural areas, from unemployment.

A UNDP analysis of the ratio of the income share of the richest to the poorest population groups in seven Arab countries for which data were obtained[12] confirms this picture of relatively low ratios of wealth to poverty by international standards and generally low inequality as measured by Gini coefficients. For example, by comparison with the richest/poorest 10 per cent ratios for Arab countries shown in table 6.1, Mexico's is 24.6, Kenya's is 19.3 and Turkey's is 14.2.

However, an ESCWA study on "Inflation in the ESCWA Region: Causes and Effects", published in 1999, offers a less positive picture, suggesting that income inequalities in

---

[9] Richard Adams, Jr. and John Page, "Holding the Line: Poverty Reduction in the Middle East and North Africa, 1970-2000", August 2001.

[10] Adams and Page, table 2.

[11] Adams and Page, table 4.

[12] HDR 2001.

Egypt, Iraq and Jordan increased in the last two decades. It estimates that in Egypt, between 1980/1981 and 1990/1991, the income share of the richest rose from 27 per cent to 28 per cent in urban areas and from 21 per cent to 28 per cent in rural areas. In Jordan, the share of the poorest 20 per cent decreased from 7.3 per cent in 1986/1987 to 6 per cent in 1992. In Iraq, the value of the Gini coefficient increased from 0.370 in 1993 to 0.508 in 1998. Implying that the gap between the higher and the lower income group had widened. The rural-urban divide is exemplified by Yemen, where the study shows that, in 1992, rural household income was less than two thirds (64 per cent) of that of urban residents.[13] Adams and Page also present a more nuanced picture from more detailed case studies of Egypt, Jordan, Morocco and Tunisia, with poverty during the 1990s falling in the latter two countries but rising in the former two. They conclude that "the mixed results from the country studies emphasize the diversity of contemporary experience with poverty reduction in MENA".

Could absolute poverty remain low while conventional measures of inequality rise? This question raises issues about the extent to which currently available data present the whole picture about income distribution in the region and, specifically, whether extreme poverty is alleviated by factors that are not captured in official reporting. Two such factors are briefly discussed below.

First, the Arab countries are marked by an unusually strong, cohesive system of social responsibility under which families provide sustenance to each other during hard times and income is redistributed through religious and charitable arrangements. The dual Islamic practices of *zakat* and *sadaqa* encourage the better-off to donate a percentage of their wealth to the poor. Under the *zakat,* the percentage is set at 2.5 per cent of annual cash earnings; the *sadaqa* is less rigid and more liberal with respect to the amount of sustenance provided, which can range from very minor to substantial sums. Charitable organizations have sprung up in all Arab countries to identify the poor, and to receive and distribute funds. There are no known figures for the vol-

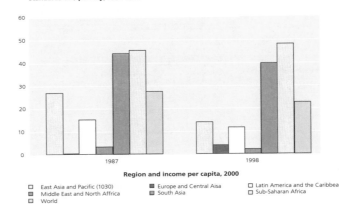

Figure 6-9
Incidence of poverty in the developing world, using international standards of $ per day, 1987-1998

Region and income per capita, 2000

☐ East Asia and Pacific (1030)   ■ Europe and Central Aisa   ☐ Latin America and the Caribbean
■ Middle East and North Affrica   ☐ South Asia   ☐ Sub-Saharan Africa
☐ World

ume of support involved, but it can be assumed to be enormous—and it may be that this parallel system of income is enabling large segments of the Arab population to escape visible poverty and need.

Second, many Arab countries provide subsidies, mainly to military and non-military government employees, that allow beneficiaries to obtain consumer goods and perishables at below-market prices. The value of subsidies to

TABLE 6.1
Income ratios of the richest to the poorest, selected Arab countries

Country	Richest 10% to Poorest 10%[a]	Richest 20% to Poorest 20%[a]	Gini index[b]
Jordan –1997	9.1	5.9	36.4
Tunisia – 1995	13.8	8.5	41.7
Algeria – 1995	9.6	6.1	35.3
Egypt – 1995	5.7	4.0	28.9
Morocco – 1998-99	11.7	7.2	39.5
Yemen – 1998	8.6	5.6	33.4
Mauritania – 1995	11.2	6.9	37.3

a. Data show the ratio of income or consumption share of the richest group to that of the poorest.
b. The Gini index measures inequality over the entire distribution of income or consumption.
A value of 0 represents perfect equality, and a value of 100, perfect inequality.

households is not readily calculated. Meanwhile, although beneficial to those who can take advantage of it, the system of subsidies does little to help the work force in the private sector or the self-employed in the organized or informal sector. In effect, subsidy regimes mask the real need for an equitable income-distribution policy that takes into account the interests of all workers.

These two factors may be playing a major role, in addition to more official mechanisms, in improving income distribution and lowering extreme poverty. Such phenomena merit

Subsidy regimes mask the real need for an equitable income-distribution policy.

13 ESCWA, "Inflation in the ESCWA Region: Causes and Effects", 1999.

more rigorous scrutiny through regular household surveys to measure unconventional sources of income and subsidies.

THE CHALLENGE OF FULL EMPLOYMENT

PATTERNS AND CAUSES OF UNEMPLOYMENT

As growth has either fallen or risen at slow immiserising rates in recent years, unemployment has been on the increase in almost all Arab countries. As with income distribution, consistent and comparable data on employment trends are hard to find; estimates of joblessness vary widely and come from a range of different sources (table 24, Statistical Annex). Thus a unified treatment of the topic on a region-wide basis is difficult, but it can safely be assumed that most countries suffer from double-digit unemployment and that regional hot spots, such as Algeria, Iraq and the occupied Palestinian territory, suffer from much higher rates (table 24 and Nader Fergany, 1998:480). Even in cases where official figures are considered to be underestimates (Nader Fergany, 1995), there is no disagreement that unemployment is a huge challenge.

Most (Arab) countries suffer from double-digit unemployment.

While slow or negative growth has affected employment across the region, other factors have had differential effects in different groupings of countries.[14]

• Gulf countries feature segmented labour markets with differential wages for nationals and non-nationals and among non-nationals as well. In the private sector, since nationals are generally unwilling to work at the same wage levels as non-nationals, employers tend to prefer expatriate labour, mostly male, unless prompted by national legislation enforcing the employment of a quota of nationals. Governments, on the other hand, have tended to absorb nationals in public-service employment for women, this has been of particular significance.[15] However, sluggish economic growth at 1.2 per cent and rapid population growth at 3.4 per cent during the period 1980-2000 have reduced governments' capacities to expand public-sector job opportunities via substantial new public investment, creating a rising problem of open unemployment of nationals in a number of these economies.

• Middle-income countries have been affected, to different degrees, by declines in labour exports to Gulf countries, which traditionally provided them with an employment cushion. This has coincided with the implementation of stabilization and structural-adjustment programmes by many of these countries. The short-term contractions resulting from such programmes along with the decline in labour exports have had a serious effect on employment in middle-income Arab countries. Over the long term, while the labour-export employment cushion may continue ameliorating domestic rates of unemployment and extreme poverty for perhaps another decade or so, signs of labour-market saturation in the Gulf indicate that exports of labour services from middle-income countries will face greater challenges and yield lower returns. The prospects for greater emigration to other destinations have been reduced since September 2001, with the probability of more stringent regulations being introduced by Europe and the United States. Declining prospects for remunerative emigration will be reflected in lower remittances to middle-income countries, creating strains on domestic economies and potentially adversely affecting poverty and perhaps reducing investment and consumption unless major international and national development programmes are put in place to accelerate productive investment and to reinvigorate growth.

• Countries affected by wars, protracted civil conflict, political instability, sanctions and occupation have experienced multiple shocks to stability that have exacerbated unemployment and poverty. Algeria, Djibouti, Iraq, Lebanon, the occupied Palestinian territory, Somalia and Sudan, for example, illustrate this point. In addition to hyperinflation and massive currency devaluations, factors such as conflict-torn governance structures, social fragmentation, destruction of productive assets and infrastructure, border closures

---

[14] This section on factors constraining employment is drawn from "Growth and Decline in Arab Economies: A Stock-Taking Study", Fadhil Madhi, 2001.

[15] As stated in CAWTAR 2001: "Of relevance here is the fact that expansion of the public sector became an important channel via which Arab women have entered the labour market." Ibid.:55.

and sanctions have all taken their toll on economic development and employment. As their economies have stagnated or declined, most of those affected have witnessed out-migration of agricultural workers and qualified labour along with mass unemployment, especially among the young. As in other Arab countries, migrant workers' remittances, while instrumental in buffering households against poverty, remain vulnerable to volatile oil markets and other external shocks.

In some cases, government policy mixes that have insufficiently emphasized agricultural development while favouring capital-intensive industrialization have created legacies of instability by prompting large-scale urban migration that has turned cities into centres of discontent as population, youth unemployment and poverty have increased over time.

More generally, there are important institutional impediments to employment generation in Arab countries. For example, labour markets are traditional, severely segmented and dysfunctional; labour-market intermediation, through employment exchanges, for example, is ineffective. Structural-adjustment packages have also played a role by paying insufficient attention to reforms that build competitive, efficient labour markets, an essential requirement for growth. This omission is sometimes glossed over by the claim that labour-market rigidities and high labour costs deter employers from hiring. An integrated labour-market reform package would certainly need to involve a degree of flexibility that improves efficiency while ensuring workers' rights and social cohesion. However, greater flexibility alone cannot bear the entire weight of employment-generation policy and might have adverse, unintended consequences by straining labour relations while hardly bringing Arab economies closer to full employment.

Reinvigorating growth that will generate productive, remunerative job opportunities provides the surest way forward. Yet to do this on a scale sufficient to reduce unemployment significantly and combat poverty effectively will require a complex policy package that goes far beyond, for example, labour codes that lead to a more flexible labour market, and addresses unemployment in its various forms.

The different faces of unemployment

Unemployment (underutilization of available labour) is often viewed narrowly in terms of open unemployment (in which job seekers cannot find work at all). This is not the only, or even the most pervasive, aspect of the underutilization of available labour in less developed countries. Understanding underemployment is also critical. Standard treatments of this subject, however, tend to stress visible underemployment (in which an employed person works less than a fixed time) and often fail to consider invisible underemployment, in which an employed person functions at low productivity, under-uses his or her capabilities, or earns less than enough to satisfy a defined set of basic needs. Each of these features of invisible underemployment is important. The first underpins low productivity at the level of the economy as a whole. The second results from poor articulation between the education and employment systems (noted in chapter 4) and reflects waste of resources. The third defines one sense of poverty. The concept is complex and its measurement problematic, but its importance cannot be overstated.

More generally, workers in less developed countries normally work under conditions that detract from their well-being. Hence, the unemployment problem in these countries needs to focus on aspects of the quality of employment—including humane working conditions, absence of discrimination, participation in decision-making and freedom of association (ensuring, among other things, the rights of unionization and collective bargaining)—as well as the simple availability of job opportunities.

Thus, full employment in this Report is taken to mean good jobs for all those available for work. This means jobs that are productive, in which the individual uses skills and fulfils his or her potential, under conditions consonant with human dignity, and through which enough is earned to avoid poverty and degradation.

Full employment ... means good jobs for all those available for work. This means jobs that are productive, in which the individual uses skills and fulfils his or her potential, under conditions consonant with human dignity.

UNEMPLOYMENT AND POVERTY

In a strict economic sense, unemployment

caused by stagnant or negative growth leads to poverty. However, poverty also aggravates unemployment. This is especially true with respect to the broad definition used in this Report. As explained in chapter 1, within the human-development paradigm, poverty is defined as a deprivation of human capability, of essential opportunities and choices needed for the well-being of an individual, a household or a community.

Thus, just as unemployment is not only about joblessness, poverty is not only about low income or expenditure, or even the failure to meet basic needs; most importantly, it is also about lack of human capability. From this perspective, poverty is almost synonymous with powerlessness. Powerlessness does manifest itself in income-expenditure deficiency and inadequate satisfaction of basic needs, but most critically, it denotes lack of access to, and control over, assets: human, physical, financial and social. This closes the vicious circle whereby poverty and unemployment reinforce each another.

On the level of the Arab region as a whole, many factors interact to shape this deprivation of human capability. Most fundamental is that of inadequate access to quality education. As noted in chapter 4, despite quantitative expansion in education, illiteracy is still high. As also noted earlier, the region's level of mean years of schooling is far below the level achieved in East Asia. The UNDP global Human Development Report illustrates the fact that, although Arab countries have made important strides in education, gaps remain by comparison with global averages. Thus, for example, they have an adult literacy rate of 62 per cent compared to a global average of 79 per cent; a combined school enrolment ratio of 60 per cent compared to 64 per cent; and average years of schooling of 5.2 compared to 6.7 years. In addition, the poor are deprived of education at higher-than-average rates, thus reducing their chances of good employment. Their access to the means of building human capabilities is also limited by the poor quality of health care, as noted in chapter 3. Finally, shortfalls in human capabilities also include the dearth of skills in the region, driven by the absence of a dynamic system of training, re-training and lifelong learning linked to the needs of labour markets and the demands of rapid economic transformation (chapter 4).

The poor also suffer from limited and in many ways diminishing access to physical assets, particularly land in rural areas, and financial assets. Furthermore, the poor are effectively excluded from social and political institutions, a key dimension of their powerlessness. The lack of effective, integrated support to small and micro enterprises is symbolic of these problems. This neglect also flies in the face of the fact that private economic activity in Arab countries, even in non-agricultural enterprises,[16] is overwhelmingly small-scale. Moreover, small/informal economic activity has proved relatively successful in job creation. Nevertheless, support for small and micro-enterprises is weak.

The challenge of attacking unemployment and poverty by creating productive and gainful jobs for today's openly unemployed plus those newly entering the labour force is enormous, but it is also critical for Arab countries (especially in environments where formal safety nets are ineffective)—and it must be addressed now because otherwise, the problem will only worsen. Assuming that new labour-market entrants create a modest annual increase in the labour force of 2-3 per cent a year, 50 million new jobs will be needed by 2010. If current rates of unemployment persist, the size of unemployment will almost double by then, to about 25 million. If unemployment is to be reduced to a manageable level by the year 2010, a minimum of five million jobs will have to be created every year.

THE WAY FORWARD

REVITALIZING ECONOMIC GROWTH

This chapter has illustrated the weak growth performance of Arab countries over most of the past two decades and it has suggested that reinvigorating economic growth is essential if unemployment and poverty are to be sustainably reduced. Stimulating growth requires ac-

If unemployment is to be reduced to a manageable level by the year 2010, a minimum of five million jobs will have to be created every year.

[16] Of 1.595 million private non-agricultural establishments in Egypt in 1996, 93 per cent employed less than 5 workers and 98 per cent (i.e., 1.566 million) employed less than 10. Establishments employing fewer than 5 workers accounted for nearly two thirds of employment (64 per cent) and those employing fewer than 10, for 77 per cent.

tion on multiple fronts, with individual country circumstances determining the appropriate combination of measures in each case. However, two key catalysts will be needed in all cases: mobilizing the private sector within an enabling, socially responsible policy and regulatory environment, and using the full productive capacities and human capital of all citizens. These are the keys to competitive economies based on high value-added and sustainable production.

Creating an enabling environment for the private sector

The private sector needs incentives conducive to its growth and willingness to invest and take risk. The fact that the public sector can no longer be relied on to generate large numbers of new jobs makes it all the more urgent to encourage the private sector to grow, to open opportunities, and to expand markets and networks.

Governments have a central role to play in creating a positive enabling environment for private sector growth. For example, fiscal policies need to focus on the consolidation of public finances, efficient and equitable mechanisms for the allocation of public expenditure, and the provision of adequate room for private initiative--in short, sound macroeconomic policies. More attention needs to be given to strengthening central banks and financial services and, in other areas, to economic incentives, efficient infrastructure, effective import/export facilities to enhance private investment, and to aspects of good governance such as reduced red tape and an effective rule of law that commands citizens' assent and trust.

Governance issues will be discussed in more detail in the next chapter, but it is important to note here that good governance practices play a key role in revitalizing private-sector-led economic growth. With respect to the rule of law, an equitable, well-functioning legal system, including an efficient and effective judiciary, is critical in the economic as well as the social sphere. Other aspects of good governance needed to establish stability and trust among private-sector partners in development include a strong commitment to public accountability; a regulatory system that is fair, transparent, effective and evenhandedly enforced (for example, in attacking public and private monopolies); and appropriate legislation (including, for example, protection of intellectual property rights).

Public-sector reform has become a major focus of attention in a number of Arab countries. Reforms need to be designed in terms of providing incentive structures to encourage private-sector investment and growth. In this respect, high transaction costs and unclear bureaucratic regulations and procedures are severe handicaps. Reform also needs to be undertaken from within, with the goal of motivating efficient public service through better incentive systems and organizational structures. Most critically of all, reform needs to focus on moving governments away from doing the work of the private sector and freeing them to concentrate on fostering free, open and competitive markets, which in turn create efficient mechanisms for economic exchange between buyers and sellers, producers and consumers, employers and workers, creditors and borrowers. The rewards of such reforms will be expanded participation by private firms in building the economy through innovation and entrepreneurship.

GENERATING AND USING KNOWLEDGE EFFECTIVELY

A theme running throughout this Report has been that the Arab region's existing and potential human capabilities represent an inadequately tapped asset. Strengthening and using these capabilities are as important for private-sector-led growth as they are for the overarching goals of human development. For example, a dependable, qualified work force is essential for ensuring competitiveness, attracting investors, and meeting the needs of a demanding private sector, both national and transnational. In the case of foreign direct investment (FDI), one of the main engines of globalization and a critical force for the transfer and development of new technologies,[17] the host country must be able to offer not only the right policy mix and supporting services but also competitive workforce skills and fixed

Governments have a central role to play in creating a positive enabling environment for private sector growth.

---

[17] See, for example, Sanjaya Lall, "Harnessing Technology for Human Development", background paper, HDR 2001, UNDP.

Partnerships with the private sector: breaking new ground in Morocco

A major financial and industrial holding in Morocco, BMCE Foundation, was established in 1995 by the President of the BMCE Bank to accomplish two specific missions: to fight illiteracy and preserve the environment.

medersat.com: A New Alliance to Promote Schooling in Rural Areas of Morocco

Displaying great foresight and social responsibility, BMCE Bank, through its Foundation, has launched a project "medersat.com", to build 1,001 rural community schools by 2010. The project is a concrete response to royal orientations establishing education and training as top national priorities. UNDP is a project partner.

This new partnership, the first of its kind in Morocco and the Arab region, shows that the private sector can emerge as a full-fledged stakeholder in the community development efforts of a nation.

The objective of medersat.com, built around the concept of the "school of life", is to promote schooling through integrated community development in the most disadvantaged rural areas of the country.

The Foundation undertakes the construction of rural community schools in a manner suited to the environment in each region. In order to preserve the local architectural heritage and the environment, medersat.com draws on knowledgeable construction enterprises and local materials as well as on labour and youth from the communities where schools are built on donated land.

medersat.com, "your school" in Arabic, is for children, parents and teachers and the community as a whole. The introduction of information technology as a medium helps medersat.com to build a new generation of students in rural areas while respecting the students' culture and mother tongues, whether Arabic or Berber.

Strategic alliances have been established with the Ministry of Education, integrating recommendations from the National Charter on Education and Training, and with foreign institutions such as the Sorbonne to capitalize on international expertise in illiteracy and training.

The backbone of medersat.com is the integrated community-development approach based on a successful UNDP pilot project in education linked to sustainable development activities.

assets.

The role of education and training strategies will be critical in this respect. These strategies need to achieve a better match than often exists today between the outputs of the education system and changing labour-market needs. To do this, the public sector needs to provide for quality educational facilities and curricula that meet job requirements in the market; it also needs to provide the regulatory environment and standards to permit private-sector facilities to fill key gaps through vocational training, on-the-job training and the development of other work-related skills.

Both growth and human-development will be enhanced if Arab countries take advantage of their intellectual capital to generate and apply knowledge. Acquiring knowledge through research centres, think tanks and consulting firms is only the beginning. Stimulating knowledge-driven growth depends on the productive application and use of knowledge

Both growth and human-development will be enhanced if Arab countries take advantage of their intellectual capital to generate and apply knowledge.

that promotes dynamic development and positive change. An environment for encouraging both knowledge acquisition and its efficient use through entrepreneurship can be provided by economic incentives supported by a strong institutional regime conducive to innovation and knowledge use.

Another source of knowledge for growth is the Arab expatriates, a dynamic component of knowledge networks outside the region where over 88 per cent of total R&D originates. These expatriates have gained a rich, varied experience working abroad and can provide technical know-how, innovative ideas and investment opportunities. Partnerships and knowledge transfer can be encouraged through targeted policies that provide financial incentives to attract both knowledge and follow-on economic investments. Developing Arab communities of learners to cross-fertilize experiences, technologies and methodologies will stimulate the economy and provide for a development environment receptive to innovation.

In addition to supporting private-sector development and the deployment of knowledge, broadly defined, as discussed above, Arab governments and societies might also consider some or all of the items discussed below when formulating strategies for revitalizing dynamic growth.

Region-wide economic integration

Most Arab economies are simply too small to be able individually to achieve rapid industrialization or diversified growth. A natural response to these limitations would be to pursue Arab regional economic and trade arrangements. Economic cooperation and freer trade among partner countries would provide mutual gains resulting from the internal and external economies of larger markets, from augmented bargaining strengths, from the pooling of resources, from inter- and intra-industry specialization, and from freer mobility of resources.

Regional economic integration is a powerful option. It can stimulate the economies of the region to work together, thereby positioning them better to participate effectively in the global economy. The Arab Free Trade Area (AFTA), which has a target date for completion in 2008, is a step in the right direction. As more Arab countries sign association agreements with Europe, the returns from such agreements can be multiplied if regional integration arrangements, including AFTA, are in place. It is therefore important to try to complete AFTA before association agreements come into force. Also, it is advisable to move beyond free trade towards levels of integration exemplified in a customs union or a common market. Forms of cooperation and integration that improve the region's productive capacity relative to others should be pursued wherever feasible. Meanwhile, existing regional associations that address economic cooperation need to be revitalized and supported. ICT offers a new and increasingly popular opportunity for increased growth-oriented and knowledge-based economic cooperation. Finally, effective regional and subregional economic agreements can form a basis of more sustainable association agreements with partners outside the region. Progress and options with respect to regional integration are discussed in chapter 8.

Growth triangles

Growth triangles provide a new means for sub-groups of countries within regions to cooperate and integrate. The growth-triangle concept is based on the proposition that the sum of factor endowments among compatible economic partners can be greater than the individual parts. In East Asia,[18] cross-border trade, investment, technology flows and enhanced cooperation in hard and soft infrastructure development fostered the electronics boom that propelled the region to the forefront of the industry and created vigorous industrial and economic linkages among collaborating countries. Growth triangles are built on flexible arrangements whereby the capital, labour and natural resources needed to enter regional and world markets can be shared among collaborating countries, with one contributing financial capital and technical know-how, for example, and another providing natural resources and cheap labour unavailable in the first. By combining the endowments of each country, partnerships

emerge that bring more growth and prosperity to partners as a group than any could have achieved alone.

Beyond comparative advantage, growth triangles can also help to create a competitive edge by focusing partner countries' joint resources, skills and knowledge on creating new products and services demanded by new markets, overcoming possible disadvantages that each may face individually. In addition, growth triangles can serve equity objectives; they can help to close the income and growth gap between economic centres and their peripheries by locating new industries in border regions of neighbouring countries (provided economic complementarities and adequate infrastructure are available). Since Arab countries' endowments vary greatly—e.g., the Gulf countries are richly endowed with capital while others such as Jordan, Lebanon and the Syrian Arab Republic are well endowed with labour—growth triangles could help them to combine their resources creatively to participate more effectively in global markets, making global forces work for, instead of against, their priorities.

Eliminating conflicts

Conflicts are not only human disasters and sources of volatility and political instability; they are also major constraints on high and sustained growth. Civil wars have impeded the growth of the mixed oil economies (Algeria, Iraq) relative to East Asia, and the growth of low-income Arab countries compared to the relatively stable middle-income countries of the region. The many recent regional and international conflicts have exacted significant costs. Resolving these conflicts would obviously require a just and comprehensive resolution of the Arab-Israeli question, which is at the core of the region's political crisis. In addition, resolution of other regional conflicts would require enhancing the Arab League's capacity to promote cooperation and conflict resolution among its Member States as well as between League members and other neighbours and partners. Addressing the damage wrought by civil wars, which remains a serious challenge for many Arab countries, would require a fundamental rethinking

It is therefore important to try to complete AFTA before association agreements come into force.

Conflicts are not only human disasters and sources of volatility and political instability; they are also major constraints on high and sustained growth.

[18] Examples of thriving growth triangles include the South China triangle comprising Fujina, Guangdong, Hong Kong, and Taiwan Province of China, and the SIJORI triangle made up of Singapore, Malaysia's Johore State and Indonesia's Riau Province.

of how to respond to, and reconcile, cultural and religious minorities in the Arab world. Recent evidence on the causes of civil wars suggests that they are essentially a response, usually by a social or cultural minority, to political repression and economic deprivation imposed by a dominant central state (Elbadawi and Sambanis, 2001).

Promoting social cohesion

The central role of social cohesion in the ability of an economy to sustain growth, especially following external shocks, has been demonstrated in countries round the world, perhaps most evidently (although with exceptions) in East Asia. Social cohesion can be high when a society is relatively homogenous (for example, because of religious and ethnic homogeneity or very low income or wealth inequalities). Social cohesion can also be high in socially diverse societies, provided that there are sufficiently strong institutions for mediating conflicts of interest among social groups. One aspect of social cohesion in Arab countries, the expression of solidarity with the poorest segments of society through social networks and charitable support, has already been noted, but persistent inequality, of income or of capabilities and opportunities, inevitably places strains on social cohesion in the long run.

Enhancing essential social cohesion in the Arab world will depend critically on improving political rights and political, social and economic participation and inclusion, as will be discussed in chapter 7. Moving in this direction will not only pay large positive dividends for societies and economies; it will also help them to be resilient in the face of the consequences of the increased economic shocks associated with globalization (which can be especially devastating for countries with low social cohesion). Moreover, it is reasonable to view civil wars as examples of the breakdown of social cohesion at the national level. Given the horrifying effects of such conflicts, enhancing political rights and inclusion should be a top priority for maintaining national integrity and peace.

Tapping the full potential of all

As noted earlier, economic growth relies on

human resources and capabilities. To be successful and liveable, societies need to do their best to mobilize these capabilities and seek to ensure their optimal deployment and fulfilment. However, significant gaps remain in the mobilization of human capabilities in Arab countries.

The most obvious of these gaps is that Arab women remain marginalized and underutilized in all arenas, notably in terms of their economic, intellectual and leadership potential. As women number half or more of any population, neglecting their capabilities is akin to crippling half the potential of a nation. This is exacerbated by the fact that even in those cases where some women are part of the economic arena, they suffer from extraordinary opportunity deficits, evident in employment status, wages, gender-based occupational segregation and other barriers. These factors block the full integration of women into the economic and intellectual life of their countries. Policies and regulations that can liberate half of the population of Arab countries will have a positive impact on economic growth and social cohesion.

Prospects for optimizing human capabilities over the medium term are deformed by the persistence of child labour. Child labour is both morally reprehensible and bad economics. This form of exploitation is first and foremost against the Rights of the Child as established by consensus in the international community; it also deprives the child of a skills-enhancing education, thereby automatically mortgaging his or her future potential in the work force. Policies should aim to correct the distorted incentive structure that forces Arab children to seek work rather than an education that benefits them and their societies in the medium term.

TOWARDS FULL EMPLOYMENT AND POVERTY REDUCTION

Conceptual and institutional context

The previous section has focused on ways to reinvigorate economic growth on the grounds that growth is essential for employment creation and that large-scale generation of productive and gainful job opportunities is both

Arab women remain marginalized and underutilized in all arenas, notably in terms of their economic, intellectual and leadership potential.

Policies should aim to correct the distorted incentive structure that forces Arab children to seek work rather than an education.

an essential objective in its own right and—along with other benefits from rapid, sustained and humane economic growth—also essential for poverty reduction, which must be at the heart of any human-development strategy. Hence, employment-creating and poverty-reducing growth must be one of the overarching objectives of human-development policies in Arab countries. In this context, however, it should be noted that past patterns of growth have not simply been erratic and insufficient, as demonstrated in earlier sections of this chapter; there are also indications that economic output is being increasingly unequally distributed in favour of capital, a development that does not augur well for the optimal job creation that is essential for poverty reduction .

Moreover, recalling this Report's broad definitions of both unemployment and poverty—which imply that moving towards truly full employment involves more than simply creating formal-sector jobs and that poverty reduction involves more than attacking income poverty, critical though both these objectives are—restoring GDP growth alone will not be enough. It needs to be accompanied by a range of wider initiatives to ensure employment that fully uses human capabilities and promotes human dignity and to address non-income aspects of poverty such as powerlessness and exclusion.

Moreover, development theory and practical experience now emphasize that these wider considerations are also critical for securing rapid and sustained economic growth. On this basis, there is no conflict between properly specified economic development and human-development policies and goals; rather, they should be seen as mutually reinforcing. Perceptions of conflict between them reflect factors such as analytical confusion of means with ends, the influence of outdated dogma and entrenched interests in some instances and, above all, inadequate understanding of the holistic nature of the development process.

This section therefore complements the preceding section and draws on findings from previous chapters to propose actions that will support moving towards full employment and poverty reduction in the broad sense in which these goals are understood in the human de-

velopment paradigm. However, it is contended here that these and other human-development-oriented initiatives designed to improve the use of human capabilities are also cornerstones of the effort to reverse the recent pattern of inadequate growth in Arab countries, which has been both a cause and a consequence of inadequate human development.

Finally, this section also briefly refers to some of the governance and institutional factors (discussed in more detail in the next chapter) that are needed to liberate human capabilities in order to enhance human well-being broadly defined. The primary responsibility for empowering the poor in less developed countries still lies with the state. More effective and responsive state institutions, based on public-service reform and governance reform, including the creation of representative and accountable local governance, will be essential components of efforts towards poverty eradication. However, just as growth alone cannot bear the whole weight of poverty reduction, the state alone cannot secure sustainable growth, full employment and elimination of the scourge of poverty. Arab countries' success in achieving these goals will be conditional on the evolution of a new social contract in which a synergy is generated between a revitalized and efficient government, a dynamic and socially responsible private sector, and a powerful and truly grass-roots civil society.

A policy package towards full employment

Arab States working towards full employment and poverty eradication will need to take action in three broad areas and on an integrated basis.

- *Monitoring of employment and poverty.* Any programme is only as good as the information on which it is based. Countries need to put in place an efficient, comprehensive system for monitoring employment and poverty. The system should include regular monitoring of basic parameters together with less frequent in-depth analyses of the characteristics and dynamics of employment and poverty. It should be complemented by bringing together currently dispersed data to provide an enhanced, regularly updated information base on human development, covering the state of human ca-

Employment-creating and poverty-reducing growth must be one of the overarching objectives of human-development policies in Arab countries.

pabilities, their use and their outputs in Arab countries.

• *Effective safety nets.* However determinedly implemented, policies take time to produce desired effects and may not be able to reach all citizens (for example, the elderly or the handicapped). Proactive policy therefore needs to be supported by an effective system of social protection. The social safety nets now in place in Arab countries are lacking in coverage and effectiveness. They need to be upgraded to provide for income transfers, indexed to inflation, that are sufficient to guarantee a minimum decent level of living to all in need; in particular, they should provide for adequate unemployment compensation.

• *Supportive development patterns.* Working towards full employment needs to be anchored in a pro-poor process of development based on labour-intensive growth that offers productive, gainful employment opportunities for all individuals available for work. As part of this process, the poor need to be equipped for employment opportunities through pro-poor human-capital accumulation provided through education, training and health-care systems. They also need to be enabled to help to create such employment opportunities through the creation and management of small and micro-enterprises. This entails ensuring easier access to, and firmer command of, other forms of capital, i.e., physical assets and finance, and because small and micro-enterprises are fragile economic entities, additional supportive services will be needed to guard against failure.

The crux of the process of poor-enabling development is major institutional reform that radically raises the share of the poor in the power structure of society. Institutional reform is the path to maximizing the societal capital of the poor. As such, it is institutional reform rather than economic growth per se that constitutes the heart of poor-enabling development. Without it, growth is likely to be slow. More importantly, growth is doomed, in the context of unregulated markets, to grossly favour the rich and penalize the poor.

Some specific dimensions of a policy package designed to attain full employment and eradicate poverty in Arab countries are out-lined below.[19] To realize its benefits, this package needs to be implemented as an integrated whole.

Building human capabilities

Education and training. A full-employment development policy should include the goal of providing universal, high-quality, development-relevant, basic education and ensuring that no beneficiary is excluded on account of poverty. In some cases, this means going beyond providing free education. For the poorest of the poor, some form of affirmative action in the shape of scholarships that provide for the direct and opportunity costs of education will be necessary. As with basic schooling, children from poor backgrounds should not be excluded from higher levels of education by lack of material means. In addition, redressing the gender gap in education and training must be a core element of the policy agenda.

Meanwhile, the quality of education, including its relevance to context-specific life skills and labour-market requirements, needs to be continuously improved at all levels. This is a demanding, complex societal endeavour that extends, as noted in chapter 4, beyond the confines of the education sector. For example, formal education is not the only vehicle for strengthening human resources for productive employment. Informal channels for effective, market-relevant skill acquisition may be more relevant for the poor, particularly in conditions of widespread joblessness. These sources of training would also be relevant for dropouts from the formal education system or graduates with limited skills.

Health care. Poverty should not deprive any individual of basic preventive and curative health care. The provision of health care for girls and women should be a priority. The issues raised in chapter 3 with respect to improving health care should be addressed without delay.

Employment and productivity

In addition to reducing joblessness to a level close to full employment—based on higher investment and labour-intensive growth that uses employment-intensive technology with-

The crux of the process of poor-enabling development is major institutional reform that radically raises the share of the poor in the power structure of society.

---

[19] This section closely follows the recommendations contained in the report on Poverty in the Arab Region, Bureau for Arab States, UNDP, 1997.

out sacrificing efficiency—the objective of a strategy should be to enhance the social welfare associated with higher employment by improving productivity so that real wages rise and disparities in the distribution of income and wealth fall. The goal should be to double productivity every few years and ensure adequate satisfaction of the basic needs of the working population. Barriers to the gainful employment of women must be lifted.

As well as raising levels of human-resource development, policies for enhancing productivity call for a favourable societal incentive system with positive rewards for education and high productivity. Moreover, a synergistic approach to technology development should be established by simultaneously raising the productivity of labour-intensive technologies in small and micro-enterprises while also strengthening modern technologies and reinforcing the linkages between the two.

Support for small enterprises. Development of informal small enterprises can contribute effectively to the strategic goal of poverty eradication through employment generation. Informal small enterprises are labour-intensive and capital-light, conditions that are perfectly suited to the national economies in which the vast majority of Arabs live. A major national effort needs to be put in place to promote them. The formulation and implementation of public policy should take into consideration the multifaceted nature of informal economic activity as well as current constraints to its development.

Small enterprises are notorious for high failure rates unless the economic and institutional environment in which they are set up is truly hospitable. Support for small enterprises needs to cover the entire spectrum of their needs: the legal and regulatory environment, finance, training, technical and management backstopping, and penetration of domestic and foreign markets. Ensuring easier access to, and firmer command over, physical assets, particularly land and water in rural areas, is also critical. Women, by virtue of their higher unemployment rates and proven ability to manage small enterprises and businesses, are prime candidates for programmes aimed at reinvigorating the small-enterprise sector.

This is not to say, however, that informal small enterprises can be the salvation of Arab economies. The appropriate approach is what the Chinese call "walking on two legs". No economy has developed without significant growth of enterprises of different sizes and, more importantly, without forging strong links between large and smaller enterprises. With wise policies, the promotion of small enterprises should lead, over time, to higher productivity and a process of growth and graduation into the formal sector.

Sustainable rural livelihoods. Unemployment and poverty are increasingly acquiring a rural character in Arab countries. Stimulating rural economies needs to be a central goal of policy. In this context, a key role for governments will be to improve rural infrastructure and farm-to-market linkages (domestic or international) and reform price structures in favour of producers. In addition, irrigation systems need to be rationalized, extension services improved, and off-farm employment opportunities promoted for the land-poor and the landless through industrial decentralization, micro-enterprises and public works. Women are a mainstay of agricultural communities; they should figure prominently in the design and implementation of rural-development policies and programmes.

Institutional reform

Labour-market reform. A full-employment policy needs to include ensuring that labour markets offer job seekers free access to information on employment opportunities and efficient employment exchanges. Labour markets also need to be deregulated gradually in order to increase flexibility within a competitive market framework while maintaining essential worker protections. This should be based on balancing the rights of employers with those of workers. As already noted, social safety nets need to provide for adequate unemployment compensation (which should be inflation-linked), and the prospects of productive employment for the jobless need to be improved, including through retraining if needed.

Reform of public services. Certain essential economic functions remain the unique domain of government. Nevertheless, governments in less developed countries are often notoriously inefficient, with implications

The goal should be to double productivity every few years and ensure adequate satisfaction of the basic needs of the working population.

for overall economic performance and specifically for the well-being of the poor in the critical areas of publicly provided health and education services.

Institutional reform in the health sector needs to focus on ensuring more efficient use of resources so that resources can be freed up to achieve wider social coverage. In addition to optimizing the allocation of health budgets, personnel and facilities, consideration should be given to providing health services through schemes that combine publicly owned clinical services, social and private insurance systems, and patient payments based on income. The financing of such schemes should have a positive bias in favour of the poorest segments of society. They could include targeted subsidies for transparently managed community health-insurance schemes in rural areas.

In the financing, management and oversight of education, institutional reform needs to emphasize increasingly modeling the role of the state not on ownership but on partnership. While publicly provided universal primary schooling remains a state responsibility, the state has no monopoly at other levels of education. All key stakeholders should be represented in the governance of education, particularly at the tertiary level where asymmetrical costs and returns require concerted action and independent quality assurance. The advent of privately funded universities should be welcomed in an environment of resource scarcity, but it will not serve Arab higher education to exchange government failure for market failure. The state must lead in building public-private partnerships in education and training systems that do not discriminate against the poor but instead actively promote their inclusion through scholarship schemes, vocational training grants and on-the-job training.

Public-sector reform, as an essential component of an institutional reform package, has many dimensions. For example, incentives for government workers need to be improved through transparent structures, adequate wages and removal of discrepancies among various sectors of government service. Appropriate arrangements for funding the equipment and operation and maintenance services necessary for efficient functioning

should be put in place. Sound public-administration practices that enhance productivity need to be instituted, including basing recruitment and advancement as well as termination of service on merit.

Development of civil society. Civil-society institutions have the potential to contribute significantly to poverty reduction and job creation. However, for this potential to materialize, civil-society institutions need to develop into a broad-based, inclusive, efficient and sustainable grass-roots vehicle for efficient, sustainable collective social action that effectively combats the powerlessness that lies at the heart of poverty. However, empowerment of the poor through inclusion in socially effective civil-society institutions can take place only through the full integration of women.

Governance reform. Encouraging the development of a vibrant, effective civil society needs to be part of a wider empowerment effort based on reform of governance, broadly defined. As already noted, the poor not only lack all forms of conventional capital—physical, 101 and human; they also have no voice in the affairs of society. Civil-society institutions alone cannot redress this state of affairs. For the poor to be heard and their interests recognized, government needs to be made truly representative and effectively accountable to all the people. Genuine local government, not simply decentralization, ensures more effective participation of people, especially the poor, in the difficult war on unemployment. Meaningful citizenship and political rights will emerge only once they are fully inclusive of women, in practice and not just in the letter of the law. The next chapter discusses key aspects of governance and governance reform in Arab countries in order to advance freedom— the full exercise of human capabilities—within a socially responsible and responsive institutional, legal and political environment. It thus completes the triad of actionable areas proposed in chapter 1 that has framed the structure of this report—building, using and liberating human capabilities as the basis for a human-development strategy for Arab countries.

For the poor to be heard and their interests recognized, government needs to be made truly representative and effectively accountable to all the people.

BOX 6.3

Poverty eradication and development from an Islamic perspective:
the case of the Arab world

At the start of the third millennium, the Arab countries find themselves in a state of structural underdevelopment and are suffering, in varying degrees, from poverty and dysfunctional economies.

On both the theoretical and practical levels, facts have clearly proved the inadequacy of the conventional economic approach to the problems of underdevelopment and the incapacity of such an approach to provide them with satisfactory solutions. On the other hand, as an untarnishable source of values, Islam advocates unity, brotherhood, solidarity, justice, peace, tolerance, equilibrium, order and discipline. Moreover, Islam encourages knowledge and all efforts aimed at promoting well-being and social justice. Within Islam, the material and spiritual aspects of life are inseparable. That is how Islam considers justice to be a fundamental principle, which should encompass all aspects of human activity.

Islam favours the global approach to the establishment of a society based on social justice by way of full employment (stressing the struggle against poverty), reduction of disparities through an adequate redistribution of wealth, and prohibiting the concentration of wealth and monopolies as well as illicit activities such as appropriation by extortion and usurpation, fraud, corruption, embezzlement of funds and property, hoarding (kenz), waste (tabthir), extravagant spending (israf), miserliness (bukhl) and usury (riba).

Thus, the struggle against poverty in the Arab world should be tackled within the framework of global policy. This means that national economies should be organized on the basis of full employment on one hand and organization of the economic integration of the Arab countries on the other.

At the domestic level, desirable and necessary measures for the establishment of a just, united society where solidarity prevails should be taken in four directions:

1. First of all to find ways and means to eradicate poverty by attacking the very roots of the problems through:

• The struggle against unemployment by means of a dynamic employment policy of social transfers for the benefit of the poor and the needy, particularly those who are physically incapable of working.

• The organization of social solidarity on the basis of an equitable policy of social transfers for the benefit of the poor and the needy, particularly those who are physically incapable of working.

In this context, we should call to mind that Islam makes justice of distribution a priority in an Islamic economy. Measures expressly advocated for such a purpose in the Quran and the Sunnah consist of voluntary contributions and mandatory actions such as the zakat.

2. It is imperative to increase development expenditure to benefit the sectors of education, health and scientific and technical research. In fact, giving the human factor its full value is imperative since development implies, first and foremost, the promotion of the human being and his/her active and responsible participation in the process of building a national economy, the fruits of which should benefit society as a whole.

3. Moreover, particular attention should be paid to the productive sectors (sectors that generate wealth, so as to ensure the sustainability of development), such as agriculture, small and medium industries, the construction sector and public works. In order to achieve such an objective, the private sector should be encouraged and public expenditure should be re-examined and rationalized.

Each Arab country is a unique case, but generally speaking, it may be said that military and prestige-related expenditures are very high in the Arab world and can be reduced to the benefit of productive activities and expenditure for development.

4. Finally, it is a matter of adopting institutional tools as frameworks for the economy, conducive to ensuring both social justice and economic growth in a dynamic perspective.

At the external level, the Arab countries have no choice, if they wish to avoid the deleterious effects of globalization but to establish their own regional economic space in an autonomous and viable manner and to position themselves as credible partners at the international level.

Within this framework, Arab regional integration should not be confined to a pseudo-liberalization of exchange of the common market type. It should be a global and coherent procedure implying in-depth and concerted actions among Arab countries, within a regional framework, in order to adapt the structures of industrial and agricultural production, the structures of the regional market and the regional financial space to the real and potential economic possibilities of the regional space in question. On the basis of a structural approach, the establishment of a regional economic space should be organized around common production, financial and exchange objectives in view of increasing inter-Arab real financial flow. The construction in stages of such an economic space necessitates organizing the coordination of economic policies of member countries and the implementation of a common regional policy of development of human resources to promote active solidarity in the Arab world.

The only way for Arab countries to emerge from poverty and structural underdevelopment is to promote economic efficiency, progress, welfare and social justice within a regional framework and from a perspective of unity.

Abdul Hamid Brahimi

CHAPTER 7

 # Liberating human capabilities: governance, human development and the Arab world

Previous chapters have discussed key aspects of building and using human capabilities. This chapter turns to important ways of liberating human capabilities by enhancing governance, broadly defined. It begins by reviewing the standard definition and characteristics of good governance as elaborated by UNDP and other international organizations and interprets that definition in the Arab context in order to identify needed reforms. In doing so, the chapter looks at questions of political participation, legislative representation and civil-society action as expressions of popular will, and at the state of judicial reform as an aspect of accountability. It next attempts to assess widely perceived deficits in popular freedoms and in the quality of Arab governance institutions by comparing these attributes with those of other regions using measurements based on the HDI and other internationally compiled data sets and indicators. Finally, the chapter proposes some key institutional reforms necessary to strengthen popular voice and freedoms and the accountability of states.

As the world emerges from the rapid and, at times turbulent, political developments of the twentieth century, the concept of good or democratic governance is approaching the status of a universal human aspiration and preoccupation. Democratic governance is now part of the United Nations consensus. The United Nations Millennium Declaration states that governments "... will spare no effort to promote democracy and strengthen the rule of law, as well as respect for all internationally recognized human rights and fundamental freedoms, including the right to development." Whether a nation succeeds or fails in its efforts to promote human development, or whether it even attempts to do so, is closely related to the character and quality of its governance.

DEFINITIONS AND CHARACTERISTICS

WHAT DOES GOVERNANCE MEAN?

What is meant by the concept of governance? And what is good governance? From a human-development perspective, good governance promotes, supports and sustains human well-being, based on expanding human capabilities, choices, opportunities and freedoms (economic and social as well as political), especially for the currently poorest and most marginalized members of society.

In this context, governance can be seen as the exercise of economic, political and administrative authority to manage a country's affairs at all levels. It comprises the mechanisms, processes and institutions through which citizens and groups articulate their interests, exercise their legal rights, meet their obligations and mediate their differences. Good governance is, among other things, participatory, transparent and accountable. It is also effective and equitable and it promotes the rule of law. Good governance ensures that political, social and economic priorities are based on broad consensus in society and that the voices of the poorest and the most vulnerable are heard in decision-making over the allocation of development resources.

Discussions of governance typically encompass state institutions and their operations but also include those of the private sector and civil-society organizations. Here, the state is defined to include political and public-sector institutions. The private sector covers private enterprises (manufacturing, trade, banking, cooperatives and so on) and the informal sector in the marketplace. Civil society, lying between the individual and the state, comprises groups

Whether a nation succeeds or fails in its efforts to promote human development, or whether it even attempts to do so, is closely related to the character and quality of its governance.

Characteristics of good governance according to UNDP

Participation. All men and women should have a voice in decision-making, either directly or through legitimate intermediate institutions that represent their interests. Such broad participation is built on freedom of association and speech as well as on capacities to participate constructively.

Rule of law. Legal frameworks should be fair and enforced impartially, particularly the laws on human rights.

Transparency. Transparency is built on the free flow of information. Processes, institutions and information are directly accessible to those concerned with them, and enough information is provided to understand and monitor them.

Responsiveness. Institutions and processes try to serve all stakeholders.

Consensus orientation. Good governance mediates between differing interests to reach a broad consensus on what is in the best interests of the group and, where possible, on policies and procedures.

Equity. All men and women have opportunities to improve or maintain their well-being.

Effectiveness and efficiency. Processes and institutions produce results that meet needs while making the best use of resources.

Accountability. Decision-makers in government, the private sector and civil-society organizations are accountable to the public as well as to institutional stakeholders. This accountability differs depending on the organization and whether the decision is internal or external to the organization.

Strategic vision. Leaders and the public have a broad and long-term perspective on good governance and human development, with a sense of what is needed for such development. There is also an understanding of the historical, cultural and social complexities in which that perspective is grounded.

Good governance is defined as a set of societal institutions that fully represent the people, interlinked by a solid network of institutional regulation and accountability (with ultimate accountability to the people), whose purpose is to achieve the welfare of all members of society.

(organized or unorganized) and individuals interacting socially, politically and economically and regulated by formal and informal rules and laws. Civil-society organizations (CSOs) are the host of associations around which society voluntarily organizes. They include trade unions; non-governmental organizations (NGOs); gender, language, cultural and religious groups; charities; business associations; social and sports clubs; cooperatives and community-development organizations; environmental groups; professional associations; academic and policy institutions; and media outlets. Political parties are also included although they straddle civil society and the state if they are represented in parliament.

THE CONTENT OF SYSTEMS OF GOVERNANCE

Types of governance vary greatly, but non-repressive (democratic) governance is currently taken to have certain essential characteristics, i.e., strong societal institutions, interacting in a well-articulated fashion through a solid network of regulation, checks and balances and accountability. The effectiveness of regulation is guaranteed by the transparency of governance, which in turn, facilitates accountability and ensures the primacy of respect for the public good.

Thus, good governance is defined as a set of societal institutions that fully represent the people, interlinked by a solid network of institutional regulation and accountability (with ultimate accountability to the people), whose purpose is to achieve the welfare of all members of society.

These core characteristics represent an ideal that no society has fully realized. Even if the ideal cannot be perfectly achieved, however, it is desirable that individual societies aim, through broad-based consensus-building, to define which of the core features are most important to them—for example, what is the appropriate balance between the state and the market, between authority and liberty, or how desirable progress is best achieved under different socio-cultural and economic conditions.

Finally, good governance regimes (those fully representative of the people at large and effectively accountable to them) strive to ensure the interests of all the people, i.e., by eradicating poverty and deprivation. They thus support people's aspirations towards pride and dignity and help to build human development and a high level of human welfare.

TERMINOLOGY AND MEANINGS

This chapter Arabizes the English term "governance" by using the Arabic word Al-hokm. This choice is discussed in box 7.2. It stands in contrast to a number of attempts at Arabization, such as "system of state management", that seek to avoid the political sensitivity surrounding the question of governance in many developing countries by using words or expressions that relegate the concept to the less controversial area of management. These efforts to avoid the political aspects of governance when discussing the question sometimes reflect fear of the expected or imagined consequences of dealing directly with the subject. However, restricting discussion of governance in this way does not serve the long-term interests of developing countries, many of which still face tremendous challenges in building good governance or in achieving the levels of human development that only good governance, including its political aspects, can ensure.

Poverty, in the broad sense used in this Report—deprivation of human capabilities—is the antithesis of human development. By contrast, good governance is fundamentally about liberating human capabilities As Kofi Annan, the UN Secretary-General said, "Good governance is perhaps the single most important factor in eradicating poverty and promoting development". The institutions of governance in the three domains (state, civil society and the private sector) must be designed to contribute to sustainable human development by establishing the political, legal, economic and social circumstances for liberating human capabilities in order to promote human welfare through, i.e., poverty reduction, job creation, environmental protection and the advancement of women.

In line with this concept of liberation, today's consensus is that the most effective way to eradicate poverty, i.e., to build human development, is to empower the poor to lift themselves out of poverty. However, the poor have no capital except their labour power and creative capabilities, which poverty suppresses. Empowering the poor, therefore, requires the state, the guardian of the interests of all citizens, to adopt policies and programmes that equip them with a range of capabilities and that give them a say in all decisions affecting them. As noted in chapter 6, building human capabilities--through education, training and health care--is critical for overcoming human poverty while financial capital is essential to give material expression to people's capabilities. That the state has the ultimate responsibility for empowering the poor does not mean that the state assumes the role of direct provider of economic goods and services. This approach has failed. The requirement is that the state guarantee the provision of different forms of capital to the poor through distributive measures; in fact, distributive justice is an essential element of the societal structure in all mature market economies.

In addition to government, civil society can be a critical social force for empowering the poor, provided that constraints on forming civil-society institutions and on their activities are lifted and that the sector's capacity to contribute effectively to poverty eradication is developed and strengthened.

BOX 7.2

Governance terminology in the Arabic language

The derivation of words relating to governance in the Arabic language is fascinating and instructive in that it embodies essentially all the elements of modern good governance.

Nearly all the names of modern governance institutions are derived from one three-letter root (حَكَـمَ) which corresponds to "govern". "Govern", in turn, means "to judge" between people.

The same root, with minor phonetic modification, leads to our preferred Arabization of "governance" (Al-hokm الحُكْـم). It also signifies "deep knowledge of the law and its interpretation", which determines criteria for judgement. Another phonetic modification results in "justice" as well as "wisdom", which pave the way for ethical considerations in judgement (mercy and public welfare, above justice?).

Another simple derivation from the root yields "court"--not so in English or French, for example.

Yet another simple derivation produces "government", which in the original Arabic usage literally means "lifting injustice"--a meaning that governments, especially in repressive regimes, would be well advised to contemplate.

Finally, a "ruler" is a "person appointed to judge among people". The other side of appointment is, naturally, the possibility of dismissal, which implies accountability of the ruler. "Tyranny" is another simple derivation from the root, and since justice is a supreme value in this (linguistic) governance system, tyranny must be grounds for dismissal.

BOX 7.3

Imam Ali bin abi Taleb: on governance

- He who has appointed himself an Imam of the people must begin by teaching himself before teaching others, his teaching of others must be first by setting an example rather than with words, for he who begins by teaching and educating himself is more worthy of respect than he who teaches and educates others.
- Your concern with developing the land should be greater than your concern with collecting taxes, for the latter can only be obtained by developing; whereas he who seeks revenue without development destroys the country and the people.
- Seek the company of the learned and the wise in search of solving the problems of your country and the righteousness of your people.
- No good can come in keeping silent as to government or in speaking out of ignorance.
- The righteous are men of virtue, whose logic is straightforward, whose dress is unostentatious, whose path is modest, whose actions are many and who are undeterred by difficulties.
- Choose the best among your people to administer justice among them. Choose someone who does not easily give up, who is unruffled by enmities, someone who will not persist in wrongdoing, who will not hesitate to pursue right once he knows it, someone whose heart knows no greed, who will not be satisfied with a minimum of explanation without seeking the maximum of understanding, who will be the most steadfast when doubt is cast, who will be the least impatient in correcting the opponent, the most patient in pursuing the truth, the most stern in meting out judgment; someone who is unaffected by flattery and not swayed by temptation and these are but few.

Source: Nahg El Balagha, interpreted by Imam Mohammad Abdou, Part I, Dar El Balagha, second edition, Beirut, 1985.

GOVERNANCE IN THE ARAB REGION: THE VOICE OF THE PEOPLE

Political participation is less advanced in the Arab world than in other developing regions.

Recent years have seen changes in how some Arab governments function. Political systems have begun to open up in ways that have seemed to herald a significant revival or introduction of democratic practices. These encouraging steps have taken various forms, whether through increased political participation and alteration of power within the governance institutions or through an increasingly active civil society working to enlarge the public space and defend basic freedoms. Reforms introduced in the 1980s and 1990s in countries from Morocco (box 7.4) to Bahrain (box 7.5)

have permitted more participation, elections have been organized more frequently, several human rights conventions have been ratified, more freedom has been offered to the press, freedom of association has gained some ground and the tight grip on civil society has been relaxed.

On closer observation, however, the picture is more complex. The process remains heavily regulated and partial; it has not been opened up to all citizens. Persisting inequities in the region—reflecting poverty, illiteracy, the urban/ rural divide and gender inequality—continue to exclude many from public discourse. As a result, the process of political liberalization has by-passed too many people. For example, in one country that has an elected national assembly, women are denied the right to hold office. In other countries, despite the legal equality of women and men in terms of political rights, women are greatly underrepresented in all political organizations. The proportion of women in Arab parliaments is low. According to UNDP (HDR, 2000) women occupy 3.5 per cent of all seats in parliaments of Arab countries compared to 4.2 per cent in East Asia (excluding China), 8.4 per cent in sub-Saharan Africa, 12.7 per cent in South-East Asia and the Pacific, 12.9 per cent in Latin American and Caribbean countries and 21.2 per cent in East Asia (including China).

BOX 7.4

Political alternation in Morocco

In 1996, a set of amendments was introduced into the Moroccan constitution taking the Kingdom further towards a "constitutional, democratic and social" monarchy. The constitution acknowledges the fundamental objective of continuity and the conception of Moroccan society as consisting of social groups with differing interests where parties and unions represent social interests and parliamentary institutions play a conciliatory role between the different interests. Successive changes have widened the different social groups' representation and strengthened parliament as the centre of control and initiative.

The government, a government of "Consensual Alternation" as it is called, reflects a large political coalition composed of seven parties; with the majority coming from the traditional opposition of the last twenty years.

The political representation of the Moroccan people has increased from 1.3 parliamentarians per 100,000 inhabitants in 1997 to 2.2 after the 1998 elections.

The creation of the second chamber increased the number of members of parliament from 333 to 595.

Source: country report prepared for the AHDR.

BOX 7.5

The National Action Charter of the Kingdom of Bahrain

Bahrain's new National Action Charter, approved by a 98.4 per cent majority in a national referendum, is a major step towards democracy in the State. The Charter establishes the new fundamentals of society. Among the key guarantees are:
• Personal freedoms and equality. Personal freedoms are guaranteed. Equality among citizens and justice and equality of opportunities are the fundamentals of society. It is the state's responsibility to guarantee these fundamentals to all citizens without discrimination.
• Freedom of belief. The state guarantees unrestricted freedom of belief. The state safeguards places of worship and guarantees freedom to perform religious rituals in keeping with the current customs of the country.
• Freedom of expression and publica-

tion. Every citizen has the right to express his/her opinion through speech, writing, or any other method of expressing opinion or personal creativity. By virtue of this principle, the freedom of scientific research, the freedom of expression and the freedom of the media, and publication are guaranteed within the limits set by the law.
• Activities of civil society. So that society may benefit from all civilian potential and activities, the state guarantees the freedom to form civil, scientific, cultural, and professional associations as well as labour unions, on a national basis, for legitimate purposes, and through proper means, within the conditions set by the law. No individual is to be coerced to join a society or a labour union or forced to maintain membership thereof.

Source: country report prepared for the AHDR.

POLITICAL PARTICIPATION

Political participation is less advanced in the Arab world than in other developing regions. In many countries in Latin America, East and South-East Asia, and sub-Saharan Africa, freedom of association is less restricted, governments change through the ballot box and people's groups have been encouraged to express themselves in various ways. Meanwhile, mass mobilization-type regimes still exist in a number of Arab countries, freedom of association is restricted in other cases, levels of political participation are uneven, and the transfer of power through the ballot box is not a common phenomenon in the Arab world.

Nevertheless, Arab countries have made progress. Citizens in two Gulf countries, Kuwait and Qatar, elect their representatives in national assemblies while citizens in two other Gulf countries, Bahrain and Oman, have been promised this right in the near future. There is a larger degree of freedom of expression and association in other Arab countries than was the case two decades ago. The mobilization type of political system is now limited to four Arab countries.

Although equality of political rights is ensured for all citizens in the constitutions of all Arab countries that recognize such rights, with no distinction as to race, ethnic origin, religion or language, some minorities claim that they are under-represented in the elected institutions of their countries. Where political participation is catered to constitutionally, changing official policies or incumbents in line with the will of the people is sometimes constrained by declarations of states of emergency. This limits the exercise of civil and political rights in some Arab countries and restricts freedom of expression[1] (Arab Organization of Human Rights, 2000:9).

Practical constraints of these kinds have had adverse effects on people's perceptions and actions, reflected in low turnout rates during national and local elections and in an aversion to participating in the activities of political parties. Voting rates in elections have been under 50 per cent in three countries that allow competitive legislative elections (Egypt, Jordan and Lebanon). In two other countries (Morocco and Yemen), the trend has been downward in recent elections. More recently, Egypt did, however, achieve a breakthrough when, for the first time, elections were conducted under the supervision of the judiciary, a move that restored some measure of public confidence in the electoral process. Disputes between governments and the opposition about fundamental arrangements for political participation, especially laws organizing parties and elections, have contributed to these generally low turnout rates. Electoral laws in Jordan and Lebanon were criticized by opposition parties and led the latter to boycott elections in the two countries.

CIVIL ASSOCIATIONS

Recent decades have witnessed a revival and renewal of Arab civil associations in terms of goals and objectives, modes of action, and financing. These positive changes reflect many associations' new approaches to their mission—involving less emphasis on traditional forms of assistance and more on mobilizing citizens in favour of important causes and proposing solutions for dealing with them. A case in point is that of civil associations seeking to promote the status of Arab women. However, Arab civil associations face many difficulties. These include external, mainly bureaucratic and state constraints; but they also include problems inherent in the organizations themselves, such as lack of internal democracy, dwindling voluntary work, the absence of a social base, and financial dependence on overseas partners.

Unlike other developing regions, the Arab world has an ancient civil tradition, based mainly on the *waqf* system. Since the end of the nineteenth century, this has taken the form of cultural associations and charities whose main activities were education and the provision of health care, together with social, religious and some political matters. These groupings, which were frustrated and even eliminated by some authoritarian states in the 1950s and 1960s, have revived their activities in recent years, more or less encouraged by public authorities needing their assistance in times of difficulty.

Civil-society actors encounter several external constraints in playing their role effectively. Bureaucratic constraints in the form of control of civic associations by public authorities present serious problems. The attitudes of Arab public authorities range from opposition to manipulation to freedom under surveillance. This explains why the question of the laws governing them has become an important rallying point for Arab civil associations. Although many active associations do not approach public authorities with confrontation in mind, the latter are not yet open to associations' positions on issues such as delegation, consultation and decentralization. Authorities are sometimes uncomfortable with the wide social bases established by large civil organizations, which can be mobilized by political parties outside government for their own goals.

Arab civil associations face many difficulties. These include external, mainly bureaucratic and state constraints; but they also include problems inherent in the organizations themselves.

[1] States of emergency existed, de jure or de facto, in seven Arab countries in 2000.

As already noted, Arab civic associations can also suffer from a number of dysfunctional internal characteristics. Some lack internal democracy, reflected in limited rotation of leadership, weak participation of women and youth in leading positions, and personalization of power and its concentration in the hands of a single individual, usually the historical head or founder of the association. As a result, leadership changes take place in an atmosphere of conflict that often leads to splits. Another internal constraint is a lack of transparency in decision-making and the fact that the rare internal debates often take place in a climate of tension since Arab NGOs have not yet found the institutional techniques for settling differences of opinion over issues. At the administrative level, some Arab NGOs find it difficult to respect clear-cut rules of management and accountability. These shortcomings have contributed to the problems many Arab NGOs encounter in financing their activities.

Civil associations active in social assistance tend to be more successful than others in maintaining financial independence because they enjoy relative credibility and legitimacy in society. Their missions are clear and their social impact is palpable because they satisfy immediate and sensitive needs of the population. Those that have a religious background can also obtain donations from the private sector in the form of *zakat* or *sadaqa*, as outlined in chapter 6. They can also achieve a degree of self-financing by providing certain services for a fee. Finally, their activities accord with traditional Arab, Muslim and Christian norms of civic action, which associate such action with welfare and charity work.

This is not the case with other, more advocacy-oriented types of civil-society organizations, whose functions are novel and often not well appreciated in society at large. That some of these organizations play what appears to be a more or less direct political role can provoke mistrust among private-sector donors, putting such organizations at odds with society as well as with public authorities and often leading them to resort to foreign and international financing. This in turn has serious negative effects. It deepens the hostility of the public authorities, which see their control of the associations diminishing; it also widens the communication gap between them and domestic society, to which they are not committed by voluntary work or financial contributions.

On the whole, however, the connection between Arab civil societies and what is currently known as international civil society is a desirable trend for developing countries (including Arab countries) facing the challenges of globalization. Global coalitions on issues such as poverty, women's empowerment, environment and debt have been effective in bringing about more constructive international attitudes and policies in these areas, also to the benefit of Arab countries. There has been an increase at the pan-Arab level in coordination, solidarity and communication among civil-society organizations on global issues, mainly in the establishment of networks and unified platforms at large international conferences. Even so, such common efforts face difficulties, owing partly to the heterogeneous nature of Arab civil associations and partly because of the mistrust of Arab public authorities.

MEASURING GOOD GOVERNANCE: FREEDOM AND THE INSTITUTIONAL CONSTITUENTS OF WELFARE

A broad understanding of some of the instrumental freedoms identified by Sen (1999) and discussed in chapter 1 would suggest that such freedoms have to do with the types of institutions available in a given society. A generally accepted definition of institutions is that they "are the rules of the game in a society or, more formally, are the humanly devised constraints that shape human interaction. In consequence, they structure incentives in human exchange, whether political, social, or economic. Institutional change shapes the way societies evolve through time and hence is the key to understanding historical change" (North, 1990:3-5). According to this understanding, institutions include any form of constraint that human beings devise to shape human interaction. These constraints could be formal (such as explicit rules devised by human beings) or informal (such as generally accepted conventions, codes or customs). Institutions affect the performance of the economy by their effect on

Arab NGOs have not yet found the institutional techniques for settling differences of opinion over issues.

the cost of production and exchange. Therefore, institutions affect the welfare of individuals in a given society directly and indirectly through what Sen (1999) has termed "transparency guarantees". This understanding of the role of institutions underpins the following discussion of the quality of governance institutions in the Arab world and its impact on the well-being of Arab citizens.

QUALITY OF INSTITUTIONS IN ARAB COUNTRIES

In a recent set of papers, Kaufmann et al. (1999a and b) report a method of constructing aggregate governance indicators based on a compilation of a large data set from 13 specialized agencies that monitor various aspects of institutions of governance covering 155 to 173 countries all over the world.[2] Defining governance as "the traditions and institutions by which authority in a country is exercised", the three major aspects of governance are identified. They are: (a) the process by which governments are selected, monitored and replaced; (b) the capacity of the government to effectively formulate and implement sound policies; and (c) the respect of citizens and the state for the institutions that govern economic and social interaction. A total of 31 indicators are organized in six clusters corresponding to these three major aspects of governance. The governance process has two clusters called "voice and accountability" and "political instability and violence"; government capacity has two clusters called "government effectiveness" and "regulatory burden"; and respect for the rule of law has two clusters called "rule of law" and "graft".

With respect to governance processes, the "voice and accountability" cluster includes a number of indicators measuring various aspects of the political process, civil liberties, political rights and independence of the media. It thus measures the extent to which the citizens of a country are able to participate in the se-

lection of governments and monitor, and hold accountable, those in authority. The "political instability and violence" cluster combines several indicators that measure perceptions of the likelihood of destabilization and overthrow of government by unconstitutional or violent means.

With respect to government capacity, the "government effectiveness" cluster combines indicators that measure the quality of public service, the quality of bureaucracy, the competence of civil servants, the independence of the civil service from political pressures and the credibility of the government's commitment to policies. All these indicators are based on perceptions. The "regulatory burden" cluster includes variables that measure the extent of government's imposed distortions as embodied in various policies.

With respect to citizen assent, the "rule of law" cluster includes indicators that measure the extent to which citizens have confidence in the rules devised by society and the extent to which they abide by such rules. The indicators include perceptions on the incidence of crime, the effectiveness and predictability of the judiciary and the enforceability of contracts. The cluster on "graft" measures perceptions of corruption in the sense of the exercise of public power for private gain.

Figure 7.1 shows the results of an econometric model that organizes the data on governance institutions from various sources.[3] It shows that Arab countries as a group fall below the world average on all indicators (the zero point on the scale) except that of the rule of law, where they only marginally exceed the average. Subdividing Arab countries on the basis of the UNDP HDI classification of high, medium and low human development, table 7.1 shows that the high human-development group of Arab countries enjoys above-average quality of institutions for all indicators except "voice and accountability". All the above-average indicators, however, are less than one standard deviation above the mean. The

Arab countries as a group fall below the world average on all indicators (of institutional quality) except that of the rule of law.

[2] The sources used are: Business Environment Risk Intelligence; Wall Street Journal; Standard and Poor's; European Bank for Reconstruction and Development; Economist Intelligence Unit; Freedom House; Gallup International; World Economic Forum; Heritage Foundation; Political Economic Risk Consultancy; Political Risk Services; Institute of Management Development; and the World Bank.

[3] The data from the various sources is reoriented so that higher values correspond to better outcomes (e.g., stronger rule of law and less corruption). Moreover, each indicator is re-scaled so that it is on a scale from zero to one. Using an econometric model to organize the data from the various sources and with an appropriate choice of measurement units, a standardization procedure is followed. In this, the estimate of the distribution of each governance indicator has a mean of zero (denoting the world average) and a standard deviation of one and ranges from about -2.5 to about 2.5, with higher values corresponding to better outcomes (Kaufmann et al., 1999a and b).

"voice and accountability" cluster, which incorporates political freedom, is about 0.6 standard deviation below the mean of the world distribution. Both the medium and low HDI groups of countries are below the mean with respect to all indicators of quality of institutions.

Table 7-1 gives the results of computing the averages for the six identified clusters for Arab countries into a composite index, shown in the table's last column. The table shows the positive relationship between high, medium and low human-development scores as measured by the HDI and institutional quality.

At the level of individual countries on "Voice and Accountability", Jordan does the best among Arab countries, with a score of 0.153, followed by Kuwait, whose score equals the mean of the world distribution. All other 19 Arab countries covered fall below the mean.

"Political stability"--in itself an indicator open to many interpretations since it may reward governments that are stable for the wrong reasons, e.g., by being oppressive-- shows an interesting pattern, with 8 out of 17 Arab countries covered having above-average scores. Qatar tops the list with an indicator of 1.383, followed by Oman (0.912), United Arab Emirates (0.825), Kuwait (0.684), Tunisia (0.661), Saudi Arabia (0.239), Morocco (0.090) and Syrian Arab Republic (0.083). All other countries have indicators below the mean, with the lowest score being 2.42 standard deviations below mean quality.

In terms of "government effectiveness", 8 Arab countries out of 20 scored above the mean. They are led by Oman with an indicator of 0.9, followed by Tunisia (0.633), Jordan (0.630) and Qatar (0.480). The remaining four are Morocco (0.267), Bahrain (0.235), Lebanon (0.174) and United Arab Emirates (0.138). All other Arab countries fall below the mean, with the lowest score being 1.883 standard deviations below the mean.

With respect to the "regulatory burden" variable, 9 out of 17 Arab countries covered have above-average indicators. The best performer is Bahrain, with a score of 0.752, followed by Tunisia (0.429), Jordan (0.417), Qatar (0.327), Oman (0.305), United Arab Emirates (0.296), Morocco (0.216), Egypt (0.118) and Lebanon (0.102). The worst-performing Arab countries are between 1.173 and 3.142 standard deviations below the mean.

In terms of the "rule of law", 11 Arab countries do better than the average. Qatar scores highest, with an indicator of 1.269 followed by Oman (1.077), Kuwait (0.907), United Arab Emirates (0.767), Jordan (0.708), Morocco (0.678), Bahrain (0.665), Tunisia (0.648), Saudi Arabia (0.494), Lebanon (0.262) and Egypt (0.128). The worst-performing Arab countries in this category are between 1.103 and 1.844 standard deviation below the mean; the remainder fall below the mean but by less than one standard deviation.

Lastly, judging the quality of institutions by looking at "graft", the data indicate that 7 Arab countries out of 17 have above-average scores, led by Kuwait with an indicator of 0.619, followed by Qatar (0.570), Oman (0.484), Lebanon (0.397), Jordan (0.139), Morocco (0.125) and Tunisia (0.020). The low cut-off point for the Arab countries is 1.265 standard deviations below the mean; again, the remainder have indicators below the mean but by less than one standard deviation.

GOVERNANCE AND WELFARE IN ARAB COUNTRIES IN A WORLD CONTEXT

This section provides the results of applying to Arab countries a composite welfare indicator that combines freedom, institutional and HDI values, and comparing it with world averages. The information shown in figure 7.2 was ob-

At the level of individual countries on "Voice and Accountability", Jordan does the best among Arab countries, with a score of 0.153, followed by Kuwait.

Figure 7-1
Quality of institutions in Arab countries by level of HDI

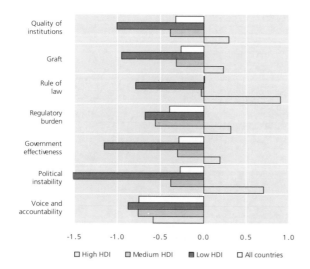

Quality of institutions in the Arab countries: standardized indicators

HDI Country Group	Voice and accountability	Political instability	Government effectiveness	Regulatory burden	Rule of law	Graft	Quality of institutions
High HDI	-0.589	0.704	0.198	0.321	0.902	0.237	0.296
Medium HDI	-0.761	-0.385	-0.305	-0.561	-0.032	-0.317	-0.394
Low HDI	-0.872	-1.602	-1.159	-0.680	-0.787	-0.953	-1.009
All	-0.749	-0.272	-0.287	-0.400	0.006	-0.262	-0.329

tained by using data for all countries for which all six institutional (governance) indicators plus HDI rankings were available. This yielded a sample of 147 countries, of which 17 are Arab countries. Without loss in generality and consistent with the established practice of the HDI, countries can be classified on the basis of the Borda rule as falling into the following categories: high human welfare (HHW) for countries with an aggregate composite score in excess of 0.8 of the maximum; medium human welfare (MHW) for countries with an aggregate score between 0.8 and 0.5 of the maximum; and low human welfare (LHW) for countries with an aggregate score of less than 0.5 of the maximum score.

On the basis described above, no Arab country enjoys high human welfare. Seven Arab countries, representing only 8.9 per cent of the population of the sample of 17, enjoy medium human welfare. The remaining 10 Arab countries, accounting for 91.1 per cent of the sample population, have low human welfare compared to the only 19.3 per cent who suffer from low human development as calculated by the HDI.

By the yardstick used in this section, the four Arab countries included in the HDI high human development category slip to the medium-human-welfare category, and only three of the 12 Arab countries that belonged to the medium HDI group retain their medium status. As noted above, on this broader basis for assessing welfare, less than 10 per cent of the population of the Arab sample can be considered as falling into the medium category. If development is understood as "a process of expanding the real freedoms that people enjoy", then the challenge of human development, calculated to include variables associated with various forms of instrumental freedom, remains a real one for over 90 per cent of the population of Arab

countries for which data are available.

MAJOR CIVIC AND POLITICAL RIGHTS AND FREEDOMS

Finally, another proxy indicator of the importance attached to various aspects of freedom is countries' records with respect to international treaties enshrining them. Table 7.2 shows that a number of Arab countries have yet to adopt some of the most important international instruments drawn up to safeguard human rights and freedoms. The gaps in the record of some Arab countries, including some that score relatively well on the HDI, are fairly clear from the table. (The table refers to ratifications rather than signatures because it is ratification, not signature, that in principle, although not always in practice, commits a country to implementation.)

GOVERNANCE REFORM: TOWARDS GOOD GOVERNANCE IN ARAB COUNTRIES

The preceding sections have indicated the need to improve key aspects of governance systems of Arab countries if they are to achieve higher levels of human development. While country circumstances and priorities will con-

...the challenge of human development, calculated to include variables associated with various forms of instrumental freedom, remains a real one for over 90 per cent of the population of Arab countries.

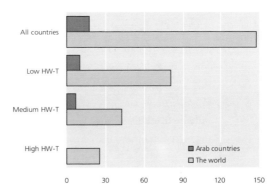

Figure 7-2
Human Well-Being in the World: Overall Borda Rule Ranking (HWB-T)

TABLE 7.2
Status of ratifications by Arab countries of the principal international human rights treaties

State	International Covenant on Civil and Political Rights	International Covenant on Economic, Social and Cultural Rights	The Convention on the Elimination of All Forms of Torture and Other Cruel, Inhuman or Degrading Treatment or Punishment	The International Convention on the Elimination of All Forms of Racial Discrimination	The Convention on the Elimination of All Forms of Discrimination against Women	The Convention on the Rights of the Child
Algeria	12 Sept. 1989	12 Sept. 1989	12 Sept. 1989	14 Feb. 1972	22 May 1996	16 Apr. 1993
Bahrain			06 Mar. 1998	27 Mar. 1990		13 Feb. 1992
Comoros			22 Sept. 2000	22 Sept. 2000	31 Oct. 1994	22 Jun. 1993
Djibouti					02 Dec. 1998	06 Dec. 1990
Egypt	14 Jan. 1982	14 Jan. 1982	25 Jun. 1986	01 May 1967	18 Sept. 1981	06 Jul. 1990
Iraq	25 Jan. 1971	25 Jan. 1971		14 Jan. 1970	13 Aug. 1986	15 Jun. 1994
Jordan	28 May 1975	28 May 1975	13 Nov. 1991	30 May 1974	01 Jul. 1992	24 May 1991
Kuwait	21 May 1996	21 May 1996	21 Mar. 1996	13 Oct. 1968	02 Sept. 1994	21 Oct. 1991
Lebanon	03 Nov. 1972	03 Nov. 1972	05 Oct. 2000	12 Nov. 1971	21 Apr. 1997	14 May 1991
Libyan Arab Jamahiriya	15 May 1970	15 May 1970	16 May 1989	03 Jul. 1968	16 May 1989	15 Apr. 1993
Mauritania				13 Dec. 1988		16 May 1991
Morocco	03 May 1979	03 May 1979	21 Jun. 1993	18 Dec. 1970	21 Jun. 1993	21 Jun. 1993
Oman						09 Dec. 1996
Qatar			11 Jan. 2000	22 Jul. 1976		03 Apr. 1995
Saudi Arabia			23 Sept. 1997	23 Sept. 1997	07 Sept. 2000	26 Jan. 1996
Somalia	24 Jan. 1990	24 Jan. 1990	24 Jan. 1990	26 Aug. 1975		
Sudan	18 Mar. 1976	18 Mar. 1986	04 Jun. 1986	21 Mar. 1977		03 Aug. 1990
Syrian Arab Republic	21 Apr. 1969	21 Apr. 1969		21 Apr. 1969		15 Jul. 1993
Tunisia	18 Mar. 1969	18 Mar. 1969	23 Sept. 1988	13 Jan. 1967	20 Sept. 1985	30 Jan. 1992
United Arab Emirates				20 Jun. 1974		03 Jan. 1997
Yemen	09 Feb. 1987	09 Feb. 1987	05 Nov. 1991	18 Oct. 1972	30 May 1984	01 May 1991
Total	13	13	15	19	13	20

dition what specific actions are appropriate in individual instances, what follows represents a broad set of areas and principles for reform designed to improve the enabling environment for human development. It must be stressed, however, that institutional and governance reform is complex and difficult. It involves understanding and addressing an exceptionally broad range of challenges, and it cannot be achieved simply by changing laws and regulations. Without the strong and sustained commitment of leaderships and the free assent of peoples, it will not deliver its benefits.

The twin pillars of governance reform are a competent state and an active civil society. Thus the reform agenda can be conceptualized as requiring:

(a) reform of the essence of governance: i.e state institutions; and

(b) activating the voice of the people.

REFORMING THE ESSENCE OF GOVERNANCE: STATE INSTITUTIONS

State institutions are the essential guarantors of fair, transparent and responsive public service. In the Arab world, the keys to institutional reform lie in improving political representation, civil-service capacity and the rule of law.

Representation and legislation

There can be no real prospects for reforming the system of governance, or for truly liberating human capabilities, in the absence of comprehensive political representation in effective legislatures based on free, honest, efficient and regular elections. If the people's preferences are to be properly expressed and their interests properly protected, governance must become truly representative and fully accountable.

The institution of representative legislative power is the basic link between the gover-

BOX 7.6

Fulfilling the promise of development: a focus on people and responsive governance

We entered the twentieth century calling for the eradication of poverty, ignorance and disease; and we left it still striving to combat poverty, ignorance and disease. More than ever today, as we enter the twenty-first century, we remain unprepared to face the rapid and dramatic pace of global change. Thus the gap is widening between the daily reality we see on the one hand, and our dreams of where and who we wanted to be by the end of the century on the other, exemplified by the gap between the Arab world and the advanced world.

What happened? Why do we find ourselves losing our way along the developmental path so many years after our region has achieved independence in all but one case: Palestine? Over the course of time, many regimes have assumed power under the banner of eliminating underdevelopment and surmounting obstacles to progress. Those regimes promulgated deeply encouraging developmental strategies, promising to better the quality of life in the Arab world.

There are many reasons for our faltering pace, not least the drastic regional and national changes that have occurred in our region since independence. These changes have had adverse repercussions on the political and socio-economic trends of our society and pushed us to an era of confusion in which our priorities were misarranged and our vision for the future lacked clarity. Thus, the nature of the age contributed to aborting development plans and their capacity for effectiveness.

Intellectual fashion has also contributed.

For example, the pivotal and fundamental concepts associated with the "human development" school of development thinking were all too often relegated to the sidelines of the development process and considered as outcomes rather than drivers of progress. Instead, expanding material resources was considered to be the goal of development. Accordingly, efforts were channelled into economic development out of a belief that it was the primary tool of renaissance, divorced from critical linkages with social development with its multiple ramifications, and delinked from human development, which has the capacity to become the engine of the development process and the driver of its success. Although many of our countries did much to support human-resources development, especially in education, policies remained conservative, programmes inflexible, and content disconnected from the needs of development.

As people's ways of life and expectations have diversified, formerly fashionable prescriptions for development are no longer sufficient for reaching desired human-welfare goals. In addition, Arab societies understand that the prerequisites for real progress have reached a level that transcends purely physical needs and relate to other types of needs and hopes, such as those for a "modern" state whose characteristics include respect for the role of the citizen as a person endowed with freedom, dignity and rights.

The essence of the modern state, which we have failed to establish to date, is what has come to be termed "good governance". A modern state is a state governed by the rule of law, and in which all citizens are equal before the law; it is a state where social coexistence prevails because it ensures equal opportunities to all citizens, providing them with options and enhancing their scope of knowledge.

It is no longer possible to delay the establishment of the pluralistic, democratic state in our Arab world because we need the benefits that such a state provides--good governance, marked by transparency, accountability and participation at the grass-roots level in the march of the nation. The democratic state is the guarantor of the protection and extension of human rights, and it is the form of government that best supports the flourishing of civil society and related institutions--key elements in a democracy. The democratic state encourages participation and serves as the catalyst for society's awareness, aspirations and hopes. It is the form of government that activates the role of women as recognized partners in the development process and seeks to ensure that no segment of society is marginalized by working to provide opportunity, empowerment and equality to all citizens. And it is the form of government that is best able to establish the kind of flexible and dynamic educational system that is essential for building, developing and empowering the individual of the new Arab age.

People now recognize that it is no longer satisfactory simply to be given fish to eat; they expect to be taught how to fish for themselves.

Leila Sharaf. Good Governance

---

nance regime and the people. In parliamentary (liberal) regimes, this link takes the form of freely elected representative legislatures that establish and refine the legal rules that govern different societal actors and, in particular, regulate control of government, or the executive power that is usually headed by the political party that obtained the confidence of the majority in the elections. This process of regulation is best guaranteed not only by the honesty and regularity of elections, as already noted, but also by the presence in legislatures of a free and effective party or parties of opposition to the party in charge of government.

Institutions that provide for a solid electoral system that permits the peaceful rotation of power, together with a legislature that transparently reflects the will of the people, are the best guarantors of the interests of the people—including the protection of fundamental human rights, freedoms and dignity and, in particular, ensuring respect for the International Bill of Human Rights, especially those elements embodied in binding covenants and conventions.

Public administration and services

The government is the executive mechanism that administers or manages the affairs of society (including implementation of laws passed by the legislature and decisions handed down by the judiciary). Ideally, the executive is composed of a permanent civil service of administrators and technicians. Its leadership, however, is often political, representing the people as a result of regular elections, which provide for accountability and legitimacy. Between general elections, the government is accountable to the representatives of the people, including the opposition to the political

It is no longer possible to delay the establishment of the pluralistic, democratic state in our Arab world.

party in government, through the legislature.

Governments—elected leaderships and permanent civil servants—need to perform their functions as providers of public services and enforcers of contracts in an effective, efficient and transparent manner. This calls for competent and well-functioning public administrations, which many Arab countries lack. Reforming public administration is thus a central and urgent task for these countries; it lies at the core of the wider agenda of institutional reform. The goals of reform include raising productivity and efficiency in public services and administration and establishing merit as the basis for appointment, promotion and termination of civil servants. There is also a need to reform the system of remuneration for civil servants by establishing a transparent salary structure, satisfactory wages and proper incentives. Finally, Arab countries have traditionally had higher proportions of public employees in the working population than other regions; reducing the numbers of these employees has now become a necessity. However, where reductions take place, it will be important to provide satisfactory compensatory measures such as end-of-service payments, re-employment and training schemes, and credit

and public works programmes to help cushion the shock of redundancy.

Public administration and services need to be financed by tax revenues. Both to pay for services and reduce budget deficits, public-administration reform needs to include tax reform that promotes both equity and efficiency—including the efficiency of tax collection from the wealthy. Meanwhile, public expenditure must be rationalized and pruned of extravagance at the expense of taxpayers.

Finally, and especially in economies committed to private-sector-led growth, governments have a critical role to play in guaranteeing market competition. This calls for an appropriate degree of regulation and measures to avoid monopolies through freedom of access to information and markets. Arab countries, like other countries, developed and developing, need to be constantly alert to regulatory reform designed to promote regulation that is effective but not onerous, with the objective of enhancing the efficiency of markets and the consequential benefits in terms of innovation, higher productive capacity and people-friendly market institutions.

The rule of law and the judiciary

Legal-system reform in Arab countries needs to focus on ensuring that the law and associated administrative procedures guarantee citizens' rights and are compatible with fundamental human rights, particularly the rights to freedom of expression and freedom of association for all, under the aegis of a truly independent judiciary that impartially enforces the rule of law. Where legal systems are weak or function inappropriately, reform is essential because the rule of law, embodied in legal and judicial institutions, is the foundation on which all other societal and governance institutions are built, including fair and honest political representation and effective and responsive public administration. (The very close linguistic link in Arabic between governance and the judiciary is relevant in this context.) The autonomy and effectiveness of legal and judicial institutions are basic conditions for good governance. Where these features are lacking, reform must be undertaken to ensure them. Legislatures and executives have the right and duty to propose and pass or

---

BOX 7.7

The Beirut Declaration for Justice

The provisions of the 1999 Beirut Declaration for Justice, adopted at the First Arab Conference on Justice, provide a substantial platform for action. For example:

Safeguards for the judiciary
• Arab countries should include the United Nations Basic Principles on the Independence of the Judiciary in Arab constitutions and laws, with penalties for interference in the work of the judiciary.
• States should guarantee independent budgets for the judiciary as a single item of the state budget.
• Judicial proceedings should be free from executive intervention.
• Judges should have the normal immunity associated with their jobs.

Election and appointment of judges
• The position of judge should be open, without discrimination, to all who meet the requirements of the profession. The higher councils of concerned judicial bodies should appoint judges.

Qualifications, training and preparation of judges

• States should try, through specialized centres, to provide judges with effective legal training to prepare them for their responsibilities. The judiciary should supervise these legal study and training courses.

Safeguards for the rights of defence and a fair trial
• Every defendant should be guaranteed an attorney of his or her choice. Where a defendant cannot afford the costs of an attorney, the judicial authority should appoint one to serve as counsel for the defence.
• Trials, civil or criminal, should be held within a reasonable time to secure a fair hearing and should be conducted with modern technical means to ensure efficiency and the accuracy of records.

Women judges
• No discrimination between qualified men and women should be permitted in the appointment of judges.
• Arab countries should pool experiences in supporting gender equality under the law in the practice of judicial work.

---

reject laws, but their intervention in the affairs of the judiciary needs to be confined to participation in selecting those who will occupy important posts, based on a past record of professional excellence and impartial administration of justice (box 7.7).

LIBERATING CAPABILITIES THROUGH VOICE AND PARTICIPATION

The second key area for governance reform listed earlier was that of activating the voice of the people. Reforms directed to this goal need first to secure core freedoms for all the people, in particular freedom of expression and freedom of association. Without these freedoms, authentic voice is suppressed and opportunities for creative citizen participation in governance at all levels are frustrated. Once these freedoms are in place, governance reform designed to enhance voice and participation in Arab countries can move productively forward in three critical areas: strengthening institutions of local governance; liberating civil-society organizations; and fostering free and responsible media. (Initiatives in these latter two could combine to promote informative and independent mass-media institutions that are both non-profit and non-governmental.)

Promoting local governance

True local governance involves far more than the mere decentralization of central-government control mechanisms, which is referred to in some Arab countries as local administration. Local governance is essential for good governance as a whole and for the wider goal of human development because it provides opportunities for more effective participation by the people, particularly the poor, in combating poverty broadly defined, notably through efficient, pro-poor provision of basic services such as education and health care. Effective local governance also complements good governance at the centre by fostering well-functioning local societal institutions and good relations among them. Vibrant local governance is especially important in larger countries. Small geographical size and population in principle enhance the potential for effective popular participation, but in larger countries, the possibility exists of neglecting the periph-

eries because of the centre's domination of society as a whole—a besetting defect of governance in developing countries. Finally, in democratic systems that encourage local governance, its institutions can catalyse effective participation at this level and also nurture individuals and groups capable of participating in governance at the centre.

REINVIGORATING CIVIL ACTION

There are two fundamental reform priorities with respect to dynamizing civil society in Arab countries. First, legal and administrative obstacles hampering the establishment and effective functioning of civil-society institutions need to be removed. Second, civil associations themselves need to be transformed into a widespread popular movement, undertaking sustainable collective action.

The obstacles hampering the development of Arab civil associations can be considered temporary and susceptible to redress through reforms that would enhance their performance and their contribution to building human development.

The first reform consists of reducing the burden of domination by the state. It should end the system of "authorization" of civil-soci-

The obstacles hampering the development of Arab civil associations can be considered temporary and susceptible to redress through reforms.

BOX 7.8

New forms of citizenship: the example of women's associations

New issue-oriented social groupings have arisen in Arab countries, aimed at raising the awareness of citizens and mobilizing them on behalf of various causes, such as protecting the environment, monitoring the interests of consumers, safeguarding heritage, combating administrative corruption and other campaigns.

Some of those groupings have concerns relating to political matters such as human rights and democracy. Consequently, they become privileged areas for experimenting with new forms of citizenship; they may have achieved a measure of success in their endeavours. These groups, for example, were highly influential in making human rights an established theme in Arab political debate.

The role of women's associations in questioning the inequality of the sexes and in promoting the status of Arab women is also noteworthy. Arab women have always played an important role in the civic sector although that role may

not be sufficiently recognized and even though they may rarely assume leading posts. In recent decades, some women's organizations have not hesitated to raise the problem of the status of women or to underline certain sensitive, and sometimes taboo, subjects concerning women.

In Lebanon, for instance, a group was set up in favour of a civil law option for marital status, calling for the establishment of civil marriage in that multi-confessional country. Similarly, in Egypt, women's associations have indirectly contributed to the recent reform of the personal-status law that facilitates women initiating divorce (khol'). Even if that reform was decided by the political powers, women's associations paved the way for the breakthrough by mobilizing public opinion earlier at international conferences, particularly at the International Conference on Population and Development held in Cairo in 1994.

---

ety organizations and introduce a system of "declaration", whereby the founders of associations would be required only to inform the public authorities about the intent and purposes of their association, its official address, its financial resources, and other practical matters. Basic state regulation would be maintained through the regular operation of the legal and judicial system—a necessary protection against, e.g., financial malpractice.

This reform would have a number of benefits. It would accord with the wishes of Arab civil society while removing the bias of administrative intervention and helping to end the client-like relationship that links a number of Arab civil associations to governments, which has given the former a quasi-public status. It might also encourage Arab civil associations to turn to their own supporters to provide the human and financial resources they lack and to develop a solid social base that would help to both democratize and regulate them without government interference. It would be of special importance to include in this reform revisions of laws and procedures with respect to the establishment and activities of civil-society organizations that would encourage youth and women to set up associations and play an effective role in their governance.

The second reform has to do with financing. It will be important to expand domestic financing of Arab civil-society organizations and thus to break the pattern of dependence on foreign (or public authority) resources. At the same time, it will be critical to ensure the financial and administrative accountability of

Any society is only as free as its media.

civil associations—perhaps by setting up independent NGOs at the national and pan-Arab levels to monitor and curb all forms of corruption and abuse.

Towards free and socially responsible mass media

Any society is only as free as its media. A few Arab countries have made important strides in promoting freedom of expression with respect to press coverage although state control over broadcast media that reach large segments of society, including the illiterate, remains widespread. In its Press Freedom Survey 2001, Freedom House reported that its ratings system for assessing press and other media independence showed that not a single Arab country had genuinely free media. Only three states, had media rated as partly free with the best of them being Kuwait; those in other Arab countries were rated as "not free".

It must be an important objective of institutional and governance reform for all Arab countries to work towards free mass media. At the same time, every country needs safeguards against abuse of rights. What is needed is a system of checks and balances that ensures that the media and society cooperate to preserve people's rights, including protecting individuals and institutions from irresponsible journalism or unfair media attacks. Effective libel laws, peer pressure from media competitors to ensure that professional ethics are upheld, and active civil-society scrutiny of media activities are essential accompaniments to freedom of expression. Reform should include a balanced package of legal, professional and social measures to improve both the freedom and the responsible quality of Arab media as an essential ingredient of furthering good governance in the region.

GOOD GOVERNANCE AND SOCIETAL INCENTIVES

At various points, this Report has touched on the importance of establishing proper incentives for human development, whether in modernizing education and health, in creating competent, people-oriented public services, in mobilizing the private sector as a partner in social and economic development or, more gen-

---

BOX 7.9

Slowly but steadily: recent advances towards gender equality in the Arab world

Dialogue between women's rights activists, policy-makers, and enlightened religious leaders in the Arab region has recently led to small, but significant, steps towards greater gender equality in a number of countries. Both Jordan Egypt made important amendments to the Family, Penal and Civil Status Laws in 2001. In Jordan, as of December 2001, the legal age of marriage was raised from 15 for women and 16 for men to 18 for both sexes. Legislative amendments to Article 340 of the Penal Code now stipulate that perpetrators of so called "honor crimes" are no longer exempt from the death penalty, a crucial first step by the

Government in recognizing honor crimes as a capital offense. In terms of Family Law, Jordanian women--for the first time--have legal recourse for divorce, subject to certain monetary compensation. Similarly, in Egypt, amendment Number 1 of 2001 to the Family Law challenges men's unilateral right to divorce for the first time in recent history. Known as "el-Khile" and based on a progressive interpretation of a religious Hadith, Egyptian women can now request, and be granted, a divorce, subject to forgoing certain financial rights in their marriage contract--rights to personal alimony (mutaa), dowry (mahr) and delayed payment (moakhar).

erally, in mobilizing people to use their productive talents and energies to the fullest extent. The norms, practices and behaviours that a society rewards or sanctions substantially influence the nature and extent of its citizens' contributions to it, together with wider levels of human well-being. These social incentive systems can be both formal and informal, explicit and tacit. In their explicit form they can include public declarations, prescriptions, value statements, economic and educational doctrines and laws. In their tacit form, they consist of signals, messages and directions communicated to people pervasively and continuously through the behaviour of dominant social groups and through the pursuit and reward of socially acceptable behaviours and activities. The extent to which social values and behaviours are shaped and directed by people's perceptions about social contribution and recognition bears directly on whether, in practice, policies designed to promote good governance achieve their objectives or are undermined.

The phenomenon is contextual, often subjective and related to levels of human capabilities. How far an individual is influenced by the subtext of a society's incentive structure varies by country (including, for example, country-specific factors such as the extent to which the education system is an effective force for change) and by other variables such as the strength or weakness of an individual's capabilities and social position. Measuring the impact of social incentives on individual behaviour poses considerable methodological challenges beyond the scope of this discussion, but some broad perceptions about the Arab system of societal incentives are held widely enough to be worth some brief comments.

In essence, these perceptions suggest that structural, social and economic factors deriving from the rentier character of some economies and the role of oil revenues in both oil and non-oil exporting economies have created at least four major dichotomies or conflicts in the system of societal incentives in Arab countries (box 7.11). These conflicts, which are closely linked to building and using human capabilities, affect a number of Arab societies in varying degrees and are presented in box 7.11 as tensions between perceived and ideal poles of value. On this basis, some social incentives in Arab countries are perceived as reinforcing the ideal or positive side of this tension, but many point society towards its negative aspects.

As a critical adjunct to formal and explicit policies directed at establishing good governance, Arab countries will need to re-examine and re-balance the tacit component of societal incentive structures so as to strengthen rather than undermine the fundamental values of human development. To the extent that dominant groups that pursue power, position and material affluence are seen as laudable and successful models, Arab citizens will have little encouragement to pursue such individual and societal values as freedom, a solid work ethic, the pursuit of knowledge and cooperative action—values on which the future of the Arab world will increasingly depend. The deepening of real democracy and the accompanying shift in power structures will help to bring about desirable change. However, change is

Arab countries will need to re-examine and re-balance the tacit component of societal incentive structures so as to strengthen rather than undermine the fundamental values of human development.

BOX 7.10

On diversity

In the course of many peoples' pursuit of independence, the concept of nationalism was an expression of their hopes for both freedom and progress. Nationalism served the cause of liberation from colonialism, which was only possible by appealing under its banner to the broad population without regard to religion and ethnic origin. The citizen, regardless of his or her beliefs or race, was the basis of, and driving force behind, the progress of nationalism. Many countries have recognized the importance of diversity and have opened their doors to creativity and social cohesion.

This direction is worth nurturing and cultivating until people reach their goals of progress within the framework of ethnic and ideological pluralism in order to strengthen creative movements and increase the variety and diversity of ideas.

There is no alternative to this effort until societies take pluralism to heart. Departure from this path will only lead to its opposite where nationalism becomes a secondary equation and people are judged by their ideologies and ethnicity, which will lead to polarized societies where discrimination, in all its forms, is widespread. This can only obstruct intellectual growth and lead to isolation. In this environment, participation in the growth and progress of the nation and the reaping of its rewards is transformed from a guaranteed right to an uncertain privilege. In addition, leadership and rule become the right of one ethnicity over another, and democracy loses its meaning as it becomes a means of control and exclusion. Moreover, culture is sacrificed to the demands and aims of autocracy instead of being the vessel of diverse opinions and ideas.

Regardless of strength, no such nation can withstand the negative impacts of globalization. Any state that has not strengthened its national base through pluralism and diversity, and which has created internal conflicts while facing external pressures, will face a difficult existence.

The pattern of globalization that we are witnessing today is fast accelerating and it is necessary to hold fast to these ideas to prevent current trends from placing divisive pressures on society instead of acting as drivers of equitable progress and human development.

Rather than being a call to discrimination, religious sectarianism and cultural elitism, nationalism, in this contemporary sense, becomes a force for human cooperation and integration.

Clovis Maksoud

BOX 7.11	
Conflicting societal incentives	
Perceived (-)	*Ideal (+)*
Authoritarianism	Freedom
Privilege and position	Work
Material possessions	Knowledge
Individualism	Collaboration

also one of the primary tasks of leadership at all levels of society, which must model the behaviours expected of the people under systems of good governance. Modelling these values will also help to liberate the human capabilities on which both sustainable growth and lasting advances in human development depend.

CHAPTER 8

Arab cooperation

This chapter concludes the Report with a discussion of the important issue of Arab cooperation. It summarizes the rationale for cooperation, including the enduring and new challenges countries face as they enter the twenty-first century, challenges that countries are poorly equipped to meet on their own. It describes the main institutions for Arab cooperation, examines the past history and current status of cooperation, suggests that achievements have been far from commensurate with the institutional and organizational structures elaborated over the past half century or more, and offers reasons for the lack of dramatic successes. However, it also notes some areas where progress has been made, including with respect to aspects of human development. The chapter concludes with a recapitulation of the external and internal challenges countries face, and argues that increased cooperation is both feasible (given the necessary commitment and political will) because the institutional base already exists and essential to strengthen the processes and meet the goals of human development.

THE RATIONALE FOR ARAB COOPERATION

Perhaps no other group of states in the world has been endowed with the same potential for cooperation, even integration, as have the Arab countries. Nevertheless, while much of the rest of the world is moving towards coming together in larger groupings—especially in today's world of globalization and increased international competition—Arab countries continue to face the outside world and the challenges posed by the region itself, individually and alone. By so doing, they are failing to capitalize on the benefits that close cooperation can yield in the fields of human development

and national security.

While many Arab regional institutions exist, they are characterized by fragility and ineffectiveness, and national considerations take precedence over wider regional ones, leading to disregard of wider Arab interests. Moreover, even if national interests were to converge rather than conflict, the fact that too many regimes cater to powerful entrenched interest groups means that there is no guarantee that they would serve the wider public good.

The international and economic environment of the twenty-first century will pose unprecedented challenges to Arab countries. International cooperation is intensifying and economic success is increasingly dependent on knowledge acquisition and ICT, as discussed in chapter 5. Meanwhile, the successive rounds of trade liberalization under the umbrella of the General Agreement on Tariffs and Trade (GATT) and WTO, burgeoning international investment flows, and rapid technological advances have together led to dramatic changes in global trade and capital flows. In addition, as the role of multinational corporations has grown, that of the state has declined. The last decades of the twentieth century also saw the rise of massive trading blocs such as the North American Free Trade Agreement (NAFTA), the expanding European Union and Asia-Pacific Economic Cooperation (APEC).

These developments are defining the factors on which the future of Arab countries will largely depend. These factors include their ability to (a) deal with structural problems and technological change; (b) meet the challenges of globalization (including its sometimes negative effects) and economic openness; and (c) generate effective collective action to face new developments and the challenges they pose to governments, businesses, investors, workers, political parties and institutions.

Arab countries continue to face the outside world, and the challenges posed by the region itself, individually and alone.

THE CURRENT STATUS OF JOINT ARAB ACTION

The argument for Arab cooperation revolves around the need for an economic and social group with a cooperative, innovative policy designed to fulfil a comprehensive agenda for broad-based social and economic renewal.

Since their independence, the subject of cooperation among the Arab States has been at the centre of discussion at various official and national levels, reflecting their common bonds in terms of language, civilization, history, geographic contiguity and ease of communication. Many formulas have been proposed and tried for Arab cooperation in the economic, political, social and cultural spheres. Likewise, various levels of cooperation have been proposed, including the bilateral, the multilateral on the basis of geographic proximity, the official, the national and the regional. A typical example of the latter is the League of Arab States, one of the earliest regional experiments in the world, which was set up in 1945, thus predating almost all other regional organizations, and which has spent more than half a century in uninterrupted efforts towards the realization of Arab cooperation. While the Arab League has been able to lay the foundations for joint Arab action through a large number of frameworks, institutions, covenants, agreements and resolutions, these efforts have remained only partially implemented. This explains the League's limited practical effectiveness in comparison to the European Union.

The League has facilitated the ratification of a number of agreements that have included all or some of the Arab States. Among the most important agreements are the Joint Defense and Economic Cooperation Agreement (1950) and the Economic Unity Agreement (1957). One of the League's objectives has been to ensure free movement of capital, goods and people, and to ensure the right of the latter to work and to own property. Other agreements include the resolution to form the Arab Common Market (1965), the Arab Cultural Unity Agreement (1964), the Strategy for Joint Arab Economic Action (1980), the Joint National Economic Action Covenant (1980), the Convention to Facilitate and Develop Trade Exchanges among the Arab States (1981), the Standard Convention for the Investment of Capital in the Arab States (1981), and the Arab Free Trade Area (1997).

These various efforts have been undertaken within an institutional structure that served as a framework for joint Arab action and comprised the Arab League Council, the Economic and Social Council, and the Council for Arab Economic Unity, in addition to a very large number of other governmental and non-governmental organs set up to manage the functional roles and operations involved in Arab cooperation. Too often, however, these efforts have failed to adopt a well-defined conceptual frame of reference for human development, relying instead on developing institutional frameworks. Nevertheless, the coverage of these frameworks encompasses an impressive range of areas relevant to human development, including health, education, culture, training, environment, jobs and the fight against unemployment and poverty--all of which are relevant to comprehensive economic and social development and to building the human capabilities and raising the standards of living of all Arabs.

THE INSTITUTIONAL FRAMEWORK FOR JOINT ARAB ACTION

The Arab States are well-supplied with joint institutions designed to secure and enhance

---

BOX 8.1

Working together: once a dream, today a necessity

No Arab country alone can adequately achieve dramatic social and economic progress based on diversification of sources of income and acquisition of competitive capabilities in the fields of accumulated knowledge and industry. However, by coming together, Arab countries can reap the benefits of size and scale, diversify their combined economies, and open up opportunities for investment that would be unavailable in the absence of coordinated efforts and cooperation. In addition, acting as a group will empower the Arabs and allows them to secure rights and legal claims in international agreements, which are inevitably affected by the negotiating powers of the parties concerned. More generally, Arab countries need to agree among themselves about what they need to do in order to take their place in the new World Order. To this end, they need to formulate a common perspective and to set up realistic common goals and effective institutions capable of attaining those goals so as to improve the outcomes of their economic and societal efforts along with their competitive edge in the world.

The argument for Arab cooperation revolves around the need for an economic and social group with a cooperative, innovative policy designed to fulfil a comprehensive agenda for broad-based social and economic renewal. This endeavour should go beyond setting up an efficacious economic programme, or even adopting a system of government programmes. It should also include working towards mutual understanding, assistance and cooperation, together with a clear strategy that allows all strata of society to work together as partners.

cooperation and coordination in the political, security, economic, social and cultural fields. Conceptually, these can be divided into governmental and non-governmental bodies.

The governmental institutional framework can in turn be subdivided into the political and the functional dimensions. The political dimension is represented by the summit conferences that have been held since 1964 on the basis of circumstances and need. It has recently been decided that these meetings would be held periodically at fixed dates and not be subject to political fluctuations. Resolutions taken at summit meetings are considered as authoritative guidance for the work of the Arab League Council and for its main organs. The functional dimension consists of the main organs within the Arab League: the Council of the League, the Council of Joint Arab Defence, the Economic and Social Council, the General Secretariat, the specialized ministerial councils, and the specialized Arab organizations and other control and judiciary systems (such as the administrative and the investments courts) that operate within the framework of the League.

The non-governmental institutional framework is embodied in vocational entities, including those that are relevant to a specific domain, entities in the business sector, the national societies and associations that exist in the Arab States, and joint investment projects--both public and private--in various productive sectors. Both the governmental and non-governmental institutional frameworks are described in more detail in the following sections.

THE GOVERNMENTAL INSTITUTIONAL FRAMEWORK

The governmental institutional framework is diverse. Its effectiveness can be gauged by examining three of its major constituent parts: the specialized ministerial councils, the specialized Arab organizations, and the Arab funds at both the regional and the individual country level.

The specialized ministerial councils

These councils, established within the framework of the Arab League, are composed of the

> BOX 8.2
> ### Cooperative institutions: a diverse set of actors
> In spite of the modest returns on Arab cooperation compared to the efforts spent and the hoped-for benefits, progress has been made through the establishment of specialized Arab economic organizations, specific vocational entities and national funds and financing institutions, and vocational training centres in a variety of fields. In addition, other regional bodies have been set up outside the purview of the Arab League. These include the Gulf Cooperation Council (1981), the Council of Arab Cooperation and the Arab Maghreb Union (1989). Again, however, the record has been mixed. For example, the Gulf Cooperation Council has all the ingredients for successful cooperation and coordination among the members (i.e., an abundance of financial resources and similar regimes and economic policies), but it has been unable to adopt unified industrialization programmes across its Member States. The other two initiatives have fared worse, with difficulties that caused the Arab Maghreb Union to stumble and the Arab Cooperation Council to freeze its activities one year after its inception, owing to differing political positions among the Member States.

ministers of information, interior, justice, housing, transport, social affairs, youth and sports, environmental affairs, communication, electricity and tourism. Each council convenes periodically to coordinate policies; propose unified policies, procedures and conventions; and meets prior to any international assemblies in order to reach a unified Arab position (as in the case of the Group of 77 and with respect to international conventions on the environment, including the United Nations Framework Convention on Climate Change, the Convention to Combat Desertification and other international conventions); and finally, to coordinate positions and discuss the candidacy of Arabs for high positions in international organizations and institutions.

Politics and fluctuating relations among Arab governments can limit the activity of these councils in spite of their importance. Another factor that has rendered the achievements of the councils relatively modest and has limited their effectiveness at coordination has been the extent to which they have been unable to take considered and unified positions on issues of international concern.

The specialized Arab organizations

These organizations operate in a range of areas, including education, culture, science, agriculture, industry, employment and technology. They have been set up in the same way as corresponding organizations in the United Nations and each has a developmental and coordinating role in its own field. The number of these organizations has grown randomly rather than on the basis of a compre-

The Gulf Cooperation Council has all the ingredients for successful cooperation and coordination among the members.

hensive perspective or well-defined plans to guide their work or to implement specific projects within a framework of political, financial and time commitments. This state of affairs necessitated the formation of a committee in 1974 whose function was to ensure coordination among these organizations.

These organizations continued to meet to provide for coordination, cooperation and discussion with respect to organizing conferences and training sessions and conducting field studies and surveys. These activities, however, carried little weight and were generally weak and ineffective. To remedy this situation, a committee was formed in the mid-1980s whose job was to evaluate the performance of Arab organizations. Proposals for improvement included restructuring some organizations, abolishing others, merging some with others, and changing activities and work programmes. Other procedural proposals included setting up work mechanisms, conducting specific studies, appropriating a yearly budget and establishing a common account in the Arab Monetary Fund along with certain controls and regulations pertaining to the management of this account.

Despite the importance of these modifications, they have not been implemented effectively, partly because of pressure from some Arab States to maintain the status quo of the organizations singled out for change and partly because of complex financial difficulties in the early 1990s that affected Arab governments and organizations, exemplified by budgetary deficits that have completely paralyzed some of them and severely limited the performance of others. The supreme coordinating committee has been unable to devise adequate solutions that would increase the organizations' financial resources and enhance their efficiency. One proposal to this end, which has been passed as a resolution, is to transform these organizations into expert institutions in their respective fields that would serve Arab public, private and non-governmental sectors.

Both the ministerial councils and the specialized organizations thus present a picture of weak performance. This has diluted the effectiveness of coordination efforts in general despite the work of a supreme coordinating committee entrusted with the task of coordinating the activities of the General Secretariat of the Arab League and the organizations concerned and despite the authority exercised by the Economic and Social Council over the specialized organizations' performance and work programmes. Other problems include the failure of Arab governments to pay their dues to the overall budgets of the specialized Arab organizations, the backlog of debt incurred by governments during past years, and the difficulty in covering current expenses of the specialized organizations, including salaries and administrative expenses, a state of affairs that contributes to their inefficiency and weak performance.

Arab development funds

Arab development funds are an important source of concessional financing. They have supported social and economic development in a number of Arab States, strengthened the productive sectors, and helped to develop the region's inadequate infrastructure in the fields of transportation, electric power, telephone and wireless communications, and other basic necessities such as clean water which millions of Arabs lack. Conceptually, they can be divided into regional, national and international funds. The regional funds consist of the Arab Fund for Social and Economic Development (1967) and the Arab Monetary Fund (1976). The national funds consist of the Kuwait Fund for Arab Economic Development (1961), the Abu Dhabi Fund for Development (1971) and the Saudi Development Fund (1974). Their participation in development has had a positive impact on Arab cooperation. The international funds consist of the Islamic Development Bank (1975), which is financed mostly by Arab countries, providing it with over 70 per cent of its financial resources, and the OPEC Development Fund (1976), which obtains about two thirds of its financial resources from seven Arab oil countries.

Perhaps the most important distinguishing characteristic of the Arab development funds is their ability to use their capital effectively without having to rely on yearly budgets that depend on whether or not contributing countries have paid their share. They also offer low interest rates and extended repayment periods. which brings the grant element up to 45

The most important distinguishing characteristic of the Arab development funds is their ability to use their capital effectively without having to rely on yearly (voluntary) budgets .

percent of financing, far above the percentage of other international sources. Another positive characteristic of these funds is their ability to mobilize additional resources from other private and public sources and use them to support Arab projects. They are thus active participants in the region and a counterweight to economic stagnation, quite apart from the contribution they make to building human and institutional capabilities in Arab countries.

THE NON-GOVERNMENTAL INSTITUTIONAL FRAMEWORK

This framework consists of trade and professional associations and joint private-investment projects. The importance of these various institutions lies in their connection to the private sector and their ability to function with greater flexibility than state bureaucracies.

Trade and professional associations

There are three types of trade and professional associations. The first consists of bodies that operate in services sectors such as air and sea transportation, insurance, banks, stock exchange, hotels, tourism, and real estate. Membership is limited to Arab companies in the above-mentioned sectors. There are also a number of associations in the services sectors whose membership is made up of Arab businessmen and investors from all Arab countries, for example the Union of Arab Investors, and the General Union of the Chambers of Commerce, Industry, and Agriculture of the Arab countries. These bodies are designed to strengthen bonds among their members and to protect their common interests.

The second type consists of professional groups whose membership is restricted to Arab citizens who work in such professions as medicine, law, accounting and teaching. Their objectives include deepening the roots of their common interests, skills development and defence of their professional rights.

The third type consists of groups whose activities are specific to a given manufacturing sector. Membership is limited to the companies and the establishments that work in a certain industry such as the steel industry or the iron industry or one of the following industries: textiles, chemical fertilizers, engineering, food, cement, paper, leather and sugar.

All these entities were formed in the 1970s in response to the interest of the Council for Arab Economic Unity in achieving coordination among the various sectors as an important first step towards Arab economic cooperation. This interest led to a search for appropriate organizational arrangements for building sector-specific databases, which could in turn help members of the relevant association to know their markets and relevant industrial conditions. Another objective was to facilitate the exchange of information and expertise and provide opportunities to discuss common problems and find solutions in order to foster better coordination of investment, production and marketing and promote Arab cooperation. Finally, associations were seen as being able to provide consultative services to ongoing projects at the technical and economic levels, to provide the tools and other requirements of production at competitive costs, resulting in the emergence of common interests with respect to these projects.

Over the past decades, a few of the manufacturing associations have been able to realize some important achievements. In the final analysis, however, they have been unable to develop relevant industrial activities and channel them into an integrated, comprehensive whole that creates common interests among the members and helps them to deal with the international market as a single unit that can make use of their combined resources. The limited outcome of the approach reflects three factors: lack of specialized, expert staff; restricted membership; and weak financial resources. For better results, Arab governments would need to enact legislation that would require public and private projects to become affiliated with the relevant association so as to expand membership and provide the additional financial resources needed for these bodies to play their role in enhancing Arab cooperation more effectively.

PRIVATE-INVESTMENT PROJECTS

During the last three decades, the Arab

The importance of (trade and professional associations) lies in their connection to the private sector.

States have worked to create an investment climate conducive to attracting Arab private investment. They have done this by enacting appropriate legislation, offering tax and monetary incentives, and providing Arab investors with insurance against possible political and trade risks. In addition, they have provided the necessary institutional frameworks and structural and administrative arrangements to facilitate the transfer of capital among Arab States.

These factors combined have enabled Arab investors in some States to launch a number of Arab projects that have in their turn contributed to the transfer of capital. These projects have been launched either by individuals or by a group of partners from different Arab countries interested in ensuring flows of goods and services across Arab borders, thus strengthening the bonds among Arab countries and enhancing mutual economic and trade relations.

Data on these private-investment projects are limited, so opinions differ about their size, sectoral orientation, geographic distribution, and the conditions under which they perform. However, estimates have put their number at around 3,000 projects, their nominal capital at around $35 billion dollars, and their invested capital at around $29 billion dollars.

In terms of sectoral distribution, the banking and finance sector comes first, followed by the industrial sector. Next come transportation and communications, hotels and tourism, then building, construction and contracting, agriculture, livestock and fisheries, services, business and stock in trade, mining and extraction, in that order.

It is estimated that the joint private-investment projects—i.e., those that are shared by two or more Arab parties—account for 25 per cent of the total number of projects. Made up of holding companies, along with banks, hotels and tourist establishments, they are considered to have an important role in promoting joint Arab action; they represent a form of Arab cooperation, using Arab capital for investments in Arab countries other than those to which the investors belong.

Despite the importance of private Arab investments, they remain relatively small and limited in number. Most projects involve simple services and small industries with limited capital and impact on development. Few are in the important agricultural or industrial sectors, both of which need to be developed in view of their respective links to food security and other major industries. They can also run into obstacles that cause some of them to stumble and others to close down, with consequent large losses. Other limitations on private investment include the instability of investment regimes in some Arab countries, the depreciation of local currencies, the multiplicity of government agencies that oversee investments, and the complexity of licensing regulations, together with the deterrent effect of political instability and security concerns in some Arab States.

WHAT HAS BEEN ACHIEVED?

Much has changed with respect to the framework for Arab cooperation over the past 50 years, and some successes have been achieved. However, the end result has been far from commensurate with the massive institutional superstructure that has been erected and the expectations and aspirations that have surrounded the cooperation effort over five decades of field work. The performance in practice of cooperation organizations, including the Arab League and the Council for Arab Economic Unity, has been limited by attention to political considerations and issues of regional balance so that their role has been confined to mediation and weak coordination. This state of affairs has led Arab governments to fail to honour their commitments to the various cooperative agreements that have been produced. It has also detracted from the value of joint Arab action and has minimized its effect, not only among Arab countries but also on their relations with the outside world.

The most striking evidence of the lack of economic integration among Arab countries is the fact that inter-Arab trade accounts for no more than 7 per cent to 10 per cent of total Arab foreign trade, a figure that has not changed since the 1950s. Another example is the limited flow of capital among Arab countries. Investment capital has instead flowed to the industrial countries, making inter-Arab flows far lower than flows of Arab money to

The most striking evidence of the lack of economic integration among Arab countries is the fact that inter-Arab trade accounts for no more than 7 per cent to 10 per cent of total Arab foreign trade.

foreign markets.

Other examples of the limited nature of Arab cooperation include the unfulfilled ambitions reflected in joint resolutions at the Economic Summit Meeting held in Amman in 1980, such as the resolutions of the Charter for Arab Economic Action and of the Strategy for Arab Economic Action and also the Arab Development Contract.

The failure to achieve comprehensive, coherent, integrated Arab development and the consequent reliance on limited domestic markets or integration with foreign markets have adversely affected Arab economic and social development. National efforts to promote social and economic transformation, including institution-building and raising literacy rates, have done little to ease the situation. Meanwhile, the productive sectors have been unable to deliver rapid growth in national incomes or new job opportunities. Other problems have included acute water scarcity, problems of food security, widening social and economic disparities, and the inability of social services to expand to meet demand resulting from rapid population growth, leading to quality shortfalls in education and health services discussed in earlier chapters.

SOME POSITIVE OUTCOMES

Arab cooperation has nevertheless had some positive outcomes, whose impact has been dulled by the slow pace of achievement, the ambitious expectations that Arab peoples and leaders have had for cooperation, and the meagerness of what has been achieved by comparison with other multinational groupings, especially the European Union. Nevertheless, cooperative Arab achievements do exist. They include:
• the establishment of important economic institutions that continue to play a prominent role in joint Arab action. Among them are the Arab Fund for Economic and Social Development, the Arab Monetary Fund, the Arab funds discussed earlier, the Arab Foundation for the Insurance of Investments and a large number of joint Arab production, financial and banking companies. Arab development funds have been able to attain a degree of success and to establish a presence for

themselves in both the Arab and international arenas. These positive outcomes have been brought about fundamentally by an effort on the part of those funds to base their operations on the needs of the beneficiary states and to develop close cooperation with the governments of those countries to promote their interests. Likewise, joint Arab institutions and companies have been able to finance a number of projects in the Arab countries that have yielded concrete results in terms of helping to promote economic and social development. Finally, a number of organizations exist that have done important work in developing information databases and undertaking studies directly relevant to the development of the Arab economy and cooperation in a variety of fields;
• the growing interest in joint Arab projects and shared economic interests that have the potential to stimulate large investments that can obtain the benefits of mass production, advanced technologies, international competitiveness and human-resource development. There have also been projects that have supported the natural unity of Arab countries—for example, those supported by the Arab Fund for Economic and Social Development with respect to connecting the electricity networks in most Arab countries along with road and communications networks. Connecting the electricity networks alone has reduced electricity-sector investment requirements, increased usage and cut costs. Extending the network to all Arab States could create an Arab electricity market similar to those of Europe and North and South America. Likewise, connecting the roads and highways will tend to increase the flow of goods among Arab countries and promote inter-Arab trade. Future similar cooperative efforts could be envisaged with respect to natural gas pipelines;
• the successful efforts of a number of Arab States (the Member States of the Arab Maghreb and the Member States of the Gulf Cooperation Council), which have done much to achieve freedom of movement of their citizens among the countries concerned, their right to work in various professions and businesses, and coordination and unification of legislation and capital transfer arrangements;
• the continuity of inter-Arab communica-

Arab cooperation has nevertheless had some positive outcomes, whose impact has been dulled by the slow pace of achievement.

Contributions to human development

Joint Arab action has focused mainly on economic aspects of development, but it has also contributed to human development. Examples include the following:

• The Arab Organization for Education, Culture, and Science has worked on a range of educational issues, including the development of curricula and educational technologies, programmes to eradicate illiteracy, and adult education. It has also worked to promote the use of computers, especially with respect to Arabization, and to encourage scientific research at the pan-Arab level (although its achievements in this domain remain few in number and limited in scope).

• The Arab Council of Ministers Responsible for the Environment has worked towards developing solutions to environmental problems and to improve environmental conditions at the pan-Arab level. The Council has organized training sessions and specialized and technical seminars and conducted studies and research projects on environment problems and the status of biodiversity in Arab countries. It has undertaken efforts with respect to desertification, green belts, and industrial pollution in the Arab world. In addition, the Council has formed national committees to gather and use information about the Arab environment and has created an Arab network for environmentally sustainable development. It has set up the latter as an Arab organization for promot-

ing coordination and cooperation among concerned NGOs operating in the Arab countries. Finally, the Council has invited Arab environment experts to a number of meetings to prepare coordinated positions for international conferences and conventions such as the United Nations Framework Convention on Climate and international conventions and protocols concerned with environment and sustainable development.

The Arab Labour Organization and the Arab Funds have worked on improving working conditions and raising productivity standards, on improving transport networks to enhance labour mobility, and on upgrading labour qualifications and skills to allow workers to participate in the process of comprehensive social and economic development. Efforts towards these ends include increasing education and training resources, raising skills standards, promoting a work ethic, and fighting illiteracy. The purpose of all these efforts is to enable Arab labour forces to use and absorb modern technologies. As noted in chapter 6, productivity is a major issue for the region, and despite efforts by countries in the areas of health, education and caloric intake (and consequential improvements in social indicators), much still remains to be done if Arab countries are to raise productivity even to the levels achieved in many developing countries, let alone developed ones.

Even if outcomes have not yet come up to expectations, the continued existence of so many levels and forms of regional dialogue is a hopeful sign.

tion through a range of governmental and non-governmental levels already discussed, including summit conferences, the activities of the General Secretariat of the Arab League and its organizations, ministerial councils, or private-sector entities types of services, professions or manufacturing industries. Even if outcomes have not yet come up to expectations, the continued existence of so many levels and forms of regional dialogue is a hopeful sign of deeper future cooperation;

• the growing role of CSOs and the emergence of joint Arab CSOs that are normally accompanied by such new elements as openness, plurality and expressed public opinion. This phenomenon should help to promote the expansion of political participation and the formation of political parties and organizations, all of which are considered to be the basis of civil society and an effective, vital force behind economic and human development. CSOs

have often acted earlier and more quickly than governments in responding to the needs of marginalized social groups.

OBSTACLES TO ARAB COOPERATION

In spite of the positive elements noted above, major obstacles to Arab cooperation remain. They include:

• *trying to imitate other economic groupings* such as the European Union without taking into account Arab conditions and whether other groupings' initiatives are suitable to Arab countries' resources and conditions. An example is the gradual introduction of the principle of free trade in the hope of achieving Arab economic integration, without taking into account the inadequacy of Arab countries' production capacity or their similar production patterns that detract from the benefits achievable by complementarity;

• *the differences in the political systems and types of Arab regimes,* which can lead to differences between countries with respect to social and economic priorities and attitudes towards the means and ends of cooperation. The consequences have been that political goals have lacked clarity and specificity; that the modalities of joint Arab action have remained subject to fluctuations and change over the past decade; and that real commitment to adopt joint Arab action has remained weak. A case in point is that of the Arab common market which, despite having been ratified, was actually joined by no more than seven Arab States with divergent economic systems and policies; this in turn produced conflicting interests and negligible achievements;

• *the strongly negative effect of inter-country differences* noted above on the performance of the various institutions and arrangements set up to promote cooperation. These did not originate and do not operate in a vacuum; they reflect developments within and among Arab countries, including their disputes and relationships with one another. They are therefore equally affected by both positive and negative developments that take place in countries;

• *the sometimes overly ambitious and overly*

idealistic goals set for common action and the tendency to consider cooperation a failure when these goals are not met. This reflects poor articulation between goals and the prerequisites for meeting them. What is required is to identify achievable goals, determine the nature of the effort needed to achieve them and commit to transparent implementation. The Convention of the Council for Arab Economic Unity, ratified in 1957, is one example of failure to meet what turned out to be unrealistic goals, which included freedom of employment, trade, mobility and ownership. Council membership remains limited to a small number of States that have failed, even after 40 years, to realize any of the set goals. A second example is provided by the resolutions of the 1980 Amman Economic Summit, which were never implemented, despite being ratified, because they lacked credibility and failed to attract commitment;

• *the limited effectiveness of ratified agreements* and the bodies charged with their implementation. In addition to the inter-country differences already noted and the tendency of governments to be preoccupied with domestic problems and pressures, this weakness reflects poor follow-up by country-level implementing agencies, sometimes compounded by conflicts of interest. Guarding against this problem entails careful evaluation of country-level factors, including social composition, political system and vested interest groups, political parties, and factors relating to households and even individuals. Effectiveness in the economic sphere, and especially in the field of trade, has also been undermined, as noted earlier, by the similarity of countries' production and export systems and structures along with the legacy of 1960s-style protectionism. Meanwhile, labour mobility and investment have been hampered by domestic tensions and economic and social instability in some countries. Finally, reflecting unclear or conflicting national and social and economic policies, not all States have acceded to all agreements and joint Arab projects have not emerged from coordinated production policies;

• *the limitations on effective cooperation imposed by State inaction.* One example in this regard concerns the Arab Organization for Economic Development, which is supposed to achieve, through its constituent bodies and its ministerial council, a reasonable degree of industrial coordination at least with respect to important industrial projects requiring substantial investment, advanced technological skills and a large market. Putting these factors in place would ensure the success of these projects and their benefits in Arab and foreign markets. This end, however, has not been achieved. Similarly, the Arab Economic Council, the Arab Monetary Fund and the Council of Presidents of Arab Banks have been unable to ensure freedom with respect to Arab money transfers among Arab countries, even among those that enjoy relatively close relations with each other such as the GCC Member States, which could have taken steps towards monetary union along the lines of the European Union's introduction of the Euro but have not done so;

Finally, a number of broad contextual factors that have tended to put obstacles in the way of Arab cooperation. These include the oil effect; the vast social differences, which, in certain cases, are accentuated by discrepancies in income and standard of living; and the far-reaching political and social implications of integration despite its huge potentially positive impact on economies and people.

ARAB COOPERATION: LOOKING TO THE FUTURE

Today's Arab world faces substantial internal and external challenges to its habitat and its people's livelihoods. Awareness of these challenges has driven Arab countries to take a greater interest in all forms of cooperation.

Externally, the likely defining feature of the new millennium is the rapid trend towards globalization, which is transforming all aspects of economic and financial activity, notably trade, along with associated economic, financial and legal structures and institutions. Other effects of globalization include developments already discussed in this and other chapters of this Report. These include the expanding role of powerful new groupings of countries in the world economy; new developments in transportation and ICT, which have not only permeated all areas of cultural, social

What is required is to identify achievable goals, determine the nature of the effort needed to achieve them and commit to transparent implementation.

and economic life but have also increased the intensity of international competition; unprecedented rates of technological change and new production systems based on just-in-time methods and outsourcing, transcending national barriers; the increased global integration of financial markets; the redefinition of traditional attributes of production in favour of technical and organizational knowledge that requires labour forces with advanced technological expertise and skills; the changing role of the state, in which it becomes a referee, not a player, in production and markets, concerned particularly with ensuring balanced and fair competition and preventing monopolies that distort pricing mechanisms and detract from the efficiency of markets; and finally, the growing demand for human development and for the freedom and dignity of individuals.

Arab countries have not been, and cannot be, immune to these and other new developments at the outset of the 21st century. The implication of such developments is that Arab cooperation or Arab integration is increasingly becoming a prerequisite for a decent life, a better future, and the preservation of an appropriate Arab status in the world community. Such cooperation or integration is needed as globalization changes the way the global economy works, helps to eliminate obstacles posed by geographic location and distance, remakes traditional economic concepts, integrates economic activities that link all parts of the world, and reinforces the market power of multinational corporations and economic coalitions of states worldwide.

The establishment of WTO is itself symbolic of a new world of reduced trade barriers, increased international competition, and transformation of the world trading system. This new world poses risks to Arab countries individually and offers another reason for their working to coordinate and cooperate with one another--in this case in the context of WTO negotiations so as to develop a strong negotiating position in areas such as textiles, agriculture, petrochemicals and cultural property.

Moreover, it is not only economics that presents compelling arguments for greater Arab cooperation. International political relations are also being transformed by the rise of a supranationalism exemplified by the formation of giant coalitions with their own institutions and systems that take precedence over national authorities in the member states. The ability of small entities such as almost all Arab countries to deal individually with the emergence of these coalitions, which include the most important economically advanced states, is highly doubtful.

All these developments suggest the need for Arab countries to deepen cooperation among themselves at all levels--economic, political and social--and to consider their national interest in terms of a wider Arab interest. Much of this chapter has focused on institutions of Arab cooperation because these institutions, properly reinvigorated, form a strong foundation and a comprehensive structure that can help Arab countries to work together and move forward into the global arena as a coherent, unified force with common mutual interests—provided, of course, that the finance and the political will are present to implement existing agreements, strengthen existing structures and mechanisms, and improve working procedures and performance.

In addition to external challenges, however, Arab countries face serious internal challenges that threaten their future economic and social development. Among the most important are poverty, unemployment and mounting environmental problems, including depletion and degradation of natural resources such as water and land. The seriousness of these challenges is heightened by a weak production base and deteriorating education systems in the Arab world. As noted in previous chapters, these challenges put a special premium on reinvigorating Arab education, training, research systems and institutions region-wide, based on the re-evaluation of the content and the objectives of education and scientific research and development and of the structure of the corresponding institutions, together with improving region-wide economic performance and management to improve international competitiveness.

The future of the Arab States is to a large extent contingent on the responsiveness and the will of their governments, their business-

Arab integration is increasingly becoming a prerequisite for a decent life, a better future, and the preservation of an appropriate Arab status in the world community.

men and their investors to initiate effective collective action to meet global challenges, especially those stemming from increased economic openness, and to deal with internal structural problems and technological challenges so as together to reap the benefits of globalization.

The need is to deepen Arab political, social and economic cooperation in coming years, based on mutual understanding and support and a clear strategy that enables all classes of society to work together as partners. Achieving such cooperation means going beyond lifting trade restrictions and enlarging trade through the Arab Free Trade Area to embrace other key priorities. These include building human, technological and productive capabilities across the Arab region and establishing what can be called "a zone of Arab citizenship" that guarantees the freedom of movement of factors of production, including labour, capital, goods and services. This will require an institutional structure able to work towards these goals in ways that secure widespread popular assent and participation in line with the theme running throughout this Report, namely, that the human being must be at the centre of development processes and goals.

The dignity and the freedom of the Arab people demand that countries join together to provide human services: health, education and training, particularly for girls and women and people living in rural areas, along with strong efforts to abolish illiteracy, especially in the less developed Arab countries. Cooperation in financing and implementing such programmes (whether at the regional or the individual country level) is in essence the true basis of all other forms of cooperation. It deserves to be given priority in joint Arab action because such initiatives are at the heart of human development—and human development is at the heart of securing a freer, more secure and more fulfilled future for every citizen of all the Arab States.

The future of the Arab States is to a large extent contingent on the responsiveness and the will of their governments, their businessmen and their investors to initiate effective collective action.

References

English References

Abdel-Azeem, F., S. Farid and A. Khalifa (eds.), 1993. "Egypt Maternal and Child Health Survey 1991". Central Agency for Public Mobilization and Statistics and PAPCHILD/League of Arab States, Cairo.

ACSAD, 1997. "Water Resources and their Utilization in the Arab World". Second Water Resources Seminar, Kuwait, 8-10 March 1997.

Adams, Richard, Jr. and John Page, "Holding the Line: Poverty Reduction in the Middle East and North Africa, 1970-2000", August 2001.

Al-Hamad, A., 2000. "The Dilemmas of Development in the Arab World", Paper presented at Arab World 2000 Symposium: Transformations and Challenges, Center for Contemporary Arab Studies, Washington, D.C., 30-31 March 2000.

AOHR, 2000. The State of Human Rights in Arab Countries.

Bangemann, 1994. "Europe and the Global Information Society: Recommendations to the European Council."

Centre for Ageing Studies, 1991. "Ageing in the Eastern Mediterranean Region: A Four-country Study". Intermediate Report, Flinders University of South Australia, Adelaide, June 1991.

Chen, S. and M. Ravillion, 2000. How Did the World's Poorest Fare in the 1990s?. World Bank, Washington, D.C.

Cole, S. and T. Phelan, 1999. "The Scientific Productivity of Nations". Minerva, vol. 37, no.1, pp. 1-23.

Dasgupta, P., 1993. An Inquiry into Welfare and Destitution. Clarendon Press, Oxford.

Datt, G., D. Jolliffe and M. Sharma, 1998. "A Profile of Poverty in Egypt: 1997". FCND discussion paper no. 49, IFPRI, Washington, D.C.

Dewachi, A., 2000. "Information and Communications Infrastructures of the ESCWA Region". ESCWA, Beirut, 15-16 May 2000.

Dhonte, P., R. Bhattacharya and T. Yousef, 2000. "Demographic Transition in the Middle East: Implications for Growth, Employment and Housing". IMF Working Papers, WP/00/41, International Monetary Fund, Washington, D.C.

Doraid, M., 2000. "Human Development and Poverty in the Arab States". Paper presented at the Third Mediterranean Development Forum: Voices for Change, Partners for Prosperity, Cairo, 5-8 March 2000.

Earl, P. The Economic Imagination: Towards a Behavioural Analysis of Choice. M.E. Sharp, Inc., New York, 1983.

Egyptian Committee for Industrial Technology, 2001. "Towards E-Development: Closing the Digital Divide." Country paper presented to Group of Fifteen, Federation of Chambers of Commerce, Industry and Services (15 FCCIS), Cairo, May 2001.

Elbadawi, I. and N. Sambanis, 2001. "How Much War Will We See? Estimation of the Incidence of Civil War in 161 Countries." Policy Research Working Paper, Development Research Group, World Bank, Washington, D.C. (forthcoming) Journal of Conflict Resolution.

El-Tawila, S., 1997. "Child Well-being in Egypt: Results of Egypt's Multiple Indicator Cluster Survey 1995". Social Research Centre, American University, Cairo.

ESCWA, 2000. "Report of the Expert Panel on Information Technology and Development Priorities: Competing in a Knowledge-based Global Economy". Beirut, 15-16 May 2000.

-------, 1999. "Inflation in the ESCWA Region: Causes and Effects", 1999.

FAO, 2001. Statistics Database on web site, http://www.fao.org.

Fergany, N., 1998a. "Dynamics of Employment Creation and Destruction in Egypt, 1990-1995." Almishkat, Research Notes, no. 11, Cairo, January 1998.

-------, 1998b. "Human Capital and Economic Performance in Egypt". Almishkat, Cairo, August 1998.

-------, 1995. "Recent Trends in Participation in Economic Activity and Open Unemployment in Egypt". Almishkat, September 1995.

-------, 1991. "Overview and General Features of Employment in the Domestic Economy: Final Report. CAPMAS, Labour Information System Project, Cairo, April 1991.

Freedom House, 1999. "Annual Survey of Freedom, Country Scores 1972-1973 to 1998-1999." Freedom House web site, visited on 11 February 1999.

Harbison, F., 1973. Human Resources as the Wealth of Nations. New York and London: Oxford University Press.

ILO, 1998. "World Employment Report 1998-1999: Employability in the Global Economy: How Training Matters". France.

Kaufmann, D., A. Kraay and P. Zoido-Lobaton, 1999a. "Governance Matters". Working Paper no. 2195, World Bank, Washington, D.C.

-------, 1999b. "Aggregating Governance Indicators", mimeo, World Bank, Washington, D.C.

Kazancigil, A., 1998. "Governance and Science: Market-like Modes of Managing Society and Producing Knowledge". International Social Science Journal, UNESCO, Vol. 155, pp. 69-79.

League of Arab States, Arab Fund for Economic and Social Development, Arab Monetary Fund and OAPEC, 2000. "Unified Arab Economic Report". Cairo.

Mrayati, M., 2000. "Knowledge-based Economy: Arabization of Information Technology". Expert Panel on Information Technology and Development Priorities: Competing in a Knowledge-based Global Economy, ESCWA, Beirut, 15-16 May 2000.

Page, J., 1995. "Economic Prospects and the Role of Regional Development Finance Institutions". Regional Economic Development in the Middle East: Opportunities and Risk, Centre for Policy Analysis on Palestine, Washington, D.C.

Population Reference Bureau, Arab World Region, 1996. "Arab World Population: Selected Demographic and Reproductive Health Indicators". International Planned Parenthood Federation.

Pritchett, L. and L. Summers, 1996. "Healthier is Wealthier". Journal of Human Resources, vol. 31, no. 4, pp. 841-868.

Richards, A. and J. Waterbury, 1996. A Political Economy of the Middle East. Boulder and Oxford: Westview Press.

Sen, A.K., 2000. "Culture and Development". Paper presented at the World Bank Meeting, Tokyo, December 2000.

Sen, A. K., 1999. Development as Freedom. London: Anchor Books.

Tzannatos, Z., 2000. "Social Protection in the Middle East and North Africa: A Review". Paper presented at the Mediterranean Development Forum, Cairo, March 2000.

United Nations, Department of Economic and Social Affairs, Population Division, 2000. "The World Population Prospects: The 2000 Revision Highlights". February 2001.

UNDP, 2001. Human Development Report 2001. New York and Oxford: Oxford University Press.

-------, 2000. Human Development Report 2000. New York and Oxford: Oxford University Press.

-------, 1997a. "Preventing and Eradicating Poverty: Main Elements of a Strategy to Eradicate Poverty in the Arab States." New York, May 1997.

-------, 1997b. Human Development Report 1997. New York and

Oxford: Oxford University Press.

------, 1995. Human Development Report 1995. New York and Oxford: Oxford University Press.

------, 1994. Human Development Report 1994. New York and Oxford: Oxford University Press.

------, 1993. Human Development Report 1993. New York and Oxford: Oxford University Press.

------, 1990. Human Development Report 1990. New York and Oxford: Oxford University Press.

UNESCO, 1998a. 1998 World Education Report: Teachers and Teaching in a Changing World. Darantière, France.

------, 1998b. 1998 World Science Report. Elsevier, France.

------, 1996. 1996 Statistical Yearbook. UNESCO Publishing and Bernan Press.

UNICEF, 1998. Situation Analysis of Children and Women in Iraq, 30 April 1998.

UNIDO, 1992/1993. Industry and Development: Global Report, 1992/1993.

United States Energy Information, 2000.
Web site: http://www.eio.doe.gov/emeu/eio/tableh1.html.

WHO, 2000. The World Health Report 2000. Health Systems: Improving Performance. Geneva.

World Bank, 2001. "World Development Indicators."

------, 2000. World Development Report 2000/2001: Attacking Poverty. New York and Oxford: Oxford University Press.

------, 1998. World Development Report 1998/1999: Knowledge for Development. New York and Oxford: Oxford University Press.

------, 1997. World Development Report 1997: The State in a Changing World. New York and Oxford: Oxford University Press.

------, 1995a. "Will Arab Workers Prosper or be Left Out in the Twenty-first Century?" Regional Perspectives on World Development Report 1995. August 1995.

------, 1995b. World Development Report 1995: Workers in an Integrating World. Oxford and New York: Oxford University Press.

WRI, UNDP, UNEP and World Bank, 1998. World Resources 1998-1999: A Guide to the Global Environment, Environmental Change and Human Health. New York and Oxford: Oxford University Press.

Yount, K., E. Agree and C. Rebellon, 2001. "Gender, Health and Use of Formal Care among the Elderly in Egypt and Tunisia". Paper presented at the Population Association of America (PPA) meeting, Washington, D.C., 29-31 March 2001.

Yousif, T., 1997. "Demography, Capital Dependency and Globalization in MENA". Presented at ERF conference on "Globalization: Challenges and Opportunities for Development in the ERF region", Cairo.

Arabic References

Ali, N., 2001. "Arab Culture and the Age of Information". A'alam Al-Maa'refa, Kuwait, no. 265, January 2001.

AEUC, 2001. "Joint Investment and Development Memorandum." Submitted to the Arab Summit, Amman, 27-28 March 2001.

ALECSO, 1998. "A Vision for the Future of Education in the Arab Homeland". Tunisia, June 1998.

Fakhro, M., 1999. "The Position of Feminist Movements in Civil-society Institutions in Bahrain, Kuwait and UAE". A'alam al-Fikr, Kuwait, Vol. 27, no. 3, January/March 1999.

Fergany, N., 1998. "Unemployment in the Arab Homeland, Revisited". In Organizing and Modelling Labour Markets: Dynamics of Manpower in Arab Countries, Part II, Arab Planning Institute, Kuwait, and Arab Labour Office, pp. 459-490.

------, 1988. "On Human Beings and Development in the Arab Homeland". Arab Future, Beirut, July 1988.

------, 1980. "Human Resources Development in the Arab countries (1960-1975): An Attempt at Measurement of Progress and Classification". In Patterns of Development in the Arab Homeland, Part I, Chapter 5, Arab Planning Institute, Kuwait.

Galal, S., 1999. Translation in the Arab Homeland: Reality and Challenge. Higher Council for Culture, Cairo.

Higher Committee for Coordination of Joint Arab Action, 1998. "General Secretariat Paper." Meeting of Higher Committee for Coordination of Joint Arab Action, Cairo, 29-30 March 1998.

Madhi, Fadhil, 2001. "Growth and Decline in Arab Economies: A Stock-Taking Study", 2001.

Rached, R., 1999. The History of Arab Mathematics: between Algebra and Arithmetic (in Arabic), Centre for Arab Unity Studies, Beirut, April, 1989.

Taleb, Ali bin abi, Nahj Al-Balagha, interpreted by Imam Muhammad Abdu, Vol. 1, Dar-Al-Balagha, Beirut, 2nd edition, 1985.

Tulba, M. K. et al, 2001. Future of Environmental Work in the Arab World, UNEP, Regional Bureau for Western Asia, Bahrain.

Yamani, M., 2001. Changing Identities: The Challenge of the New Generation in Saudi Arabia. Riyad el-Rayes Publishing.

Zahlan, A., 1999. Arabs and the Challenges of Science and Technology: Progress without Change. Centre for Arab Unity Studies (CAUS), Beirut, March 1999.

------, 1994. "Arabs and the Technological Challenge: A World without Borders". Arab Future, Beirut, year 16, no. 180, February 1994, pp. 98-112.

Annex 1: List of Background Papers

ANNEX 1: LIST OF BACKGROUND PAPERS
(AUTHOR, TITLE, NO. OF PAGES)

IN ARABIC

* F. Allaghi, Reinvigorating civil society, 42.
* F. Sarkis, Education of mathematics and sciences, 26.
* G. Corm, Towards a more equitable distribution of income and wealth, 16.
* M. A. Faris, Employment and productivity in the Arab countries, 41.
* M. A. Nassar, Benefiting from globalisation in the Arab region, 45.
* M. Dewidar, Globalisation: scientific category or ideological position, 21.
* M. G. Reda, Arab education in the arena of social conflict, 17.
* N. Ali, Making ICT available to all, 28.
* N. Fergany,
* Human development in the Arab countries, the institutional context and knowledge acquisition perspective, 24.
* Education and learning, 8.
* The societal incentive system, 4.
* Governance and human development in the Arab countries, 29.
* Educational reform, 15.
* Cultivation of talent in early childhood, 5.
* N. Mosa'ad, Joint Arab Action, 25.
* O. El-Kholy, Towards a safe and giving environment, 27.
* T. Kana'an, Arab co-operation and human development, 18.

IN ENGLISH

* A. A. Ali,
* Human Well-Being in the Arab Countries, 23.
* International poverty estimates for the Arab region: A preliminary scrutiny, 15.
* A. El-Bayoumi, Research and Development, 20.
* A. Zahlan, Knowledge Acquisition, 19.
* F. El-Zanaty, Arab population profile, 20.
* H. Rashad, State of health, 20.
* I. Elbadawi, Reviving growth in the Arab world, 28.
* M. Abido, State of environment in the Arab region, 31.
* M. Al-Khalidi - H. Zurayk, Ensuring survival and good health, 19.
* M. K. El-Sayed, Political participation in Arab countries, 38.
* M. Za'alouk, Innovation in basic education, 15.
* N. Fergany, The challenge of full employment in Arab countries, 21.
* S. Morsy, Opportunities for girls and women, 22.

IN FRENCH

* A. Mahjoub, Growth and distribution in the Arab world, 32.

* S. Ben Nefissa, Civil Society, 6.

Annex 2: Youth Questionnaire

Annex 2: Youth Questionnaire
(country: ....)

PLEASE CIRCLE CORRECT ANSWER OR WRITE ANSWER BRIEFLY AND LEGIBLY IN THE SPACE PROVIDED

(1) Name (OPTIONAL): ....

(2) Gender: Young woman   Young man

(3) Age: .... years

(4) Educational attainment: ....

(5) Does your family own one or more private car(s)?   None   One   More

(6) (One car or more)

    Make of car (the more expensive if more than one): ....

Choose from the following topics, the one that you consider the most important and comment on it in the case of your country
(Education, health care, the environment, accountability of job opportunities, participation in political life, extent of poverty, discrepancy in the distribution of income and wealth)

(7) Chosen topic: ....

(8) Characterisation of topic at present in your country: ....
....

(9) Reasons for the present situation: ....
....

(10) How can the situation be improved in your opinion? ....
....

(11) What is the most difficult problem facing youth in your opinion? ....
....

(12) How can it be solved in your opinion? ....
....

(13) Do you entertain the idea of emigrating outside the Arab countries?   Yes   No

(14) (if yes) Why?

....

....

(15) Where would you like to emigrate (specify country): ....

(16) Any additional observations on youth and the future:

....

....

Statistical Annex

This statistical annex consists of tables containing information on human development collected and consulted during the preparation of the Report. The tables are preceded by notes on the measurement of human welfare and the governance indicators used in the Report.

1. MEASUREMENT OF HUMAN WELFARE: THE FREEDOM APPROACH

The UNDP human development index (HDI) represents a partial application of the "capability" approach to welfare. The index measures achievements in three types of freedom: freedom to enjoy a decent level of living, proxied by real per capita income; freedom to live longer or to live a life free from avoidable diseases and premature death, proxied by life expectancy at birth; and freedom to have adequate knowledge, proxied by various education indicators. These are indeed generally agreed upon fundamental freedoms. Morris' (1979) physical quality of life index (PQLI) and the HDI are considered to be the most explicit attempts at international comparisons of welfare. However, given the methodology of aggregation, they are judged to be devoid of normative significance (see, for example, Dasgupta, 1993).

A possible method of aggregation that has normative significance is the Borda rule. "This rule provides a method of rank-order scoring, the procedure being to award each alternative (here, a country) a point equal to its rank in each criterion of ranking, adding each alternative's scores to obtain its aggregate score, and then ranking alternatives on the basis of their aggregate score. The rule invariably yields a complete ordering of alternatives. It can be viewed as a 'social welfare function'" (Dasgupta, 1993). Here, Dasgupta is followed

by looking at welfare on the basis of Borda rankings derived using a number of conventional determinants of welfare and a set of freedom and institutional constituents of welfare.

FREEDOM AND INSTITUTIONAL CONSTITUENTS OF WELFARE

Standardized variables of indicators of freedom and institutions are used in an econometric model to see the effect of governance on development outcome indicators: per capita GDP, infant mortality rate and adult literacy rate. Each governance indicator was found to be a significant determinant of these development outcomes.

For our purposes, the standardized governance indicators are used as proxies for transparency guarantees in the sense of the quality of institutions. Given the normalization and standardized procedures used and the dominant methodology of using the simple average of indicators as a composite index for the phenomenon under analysis, an overall index for the quality of institutions is also computed. Table 1 summarizes the evidence for the Arab countries.

From the table, it is perhaps clear that there is a positive relationship between human-development achievements as reflected by the HDI and the quality of institutions. The group of countries with high human development enjoys above-average quality of institutions for all indicators except that of voice and accountability. All of these above-average indicators, however, are less than one standard deviation above the mean. The voice and accountability cluster, which incorporates aspects of political freedom, is about 0.6 standard deviation below the mean. Both the medium and low HDI groups of countries have quality of institutions below the mean. Overall, for all three groups, and ex-

Quality of institutions in the Arab countries: standardized indicators

HDI country group	Voice and accountability	Political instability	Government effectiveness	Regulatory burden	Rule of law	Graft	Quality of institutions
High HDI	-0.589	0.704	0.198	0.321	0.902	0.237	0.296
Medium HDI	-0.761	-0.385	-0.305	-0.561	-0.032	-0.317	-0.394
Low HD	-0.872	-1.602	-1.159	-0.680	-0.787	-0.953	-1.009
All	-0.749	-0.272	-0.287	-0.400	0.006	-0.262	-0.329

cept for the rule-of-law indicator, the Arab countries suffer below mean quality of transparency guarantees. The indicator for rule of law is marginally better than the mean quality.

HUMAN WELFARE OF THE ARAB COUNTRIES IN A WORLD CONTEXT

One possible way of aggregating the above indicators is to use the Borda rule, which could be interpreted as a social welfare function. To organize the data for the world, the sample consists of countries for which all six institutional (governance) indicators and HDI rankings are reported. This requirement results in a sample of 147 countries, of which 17 are Arab countries. Without loss in generality and consistent with the established practice of HDI, countries can be classified into three groups on the basis of this ranking rule: those with high human welfare (HHW), which comprises those with an aggregate score in excess of 0.8 of the maximum score; those with medium human welfare (MHW), which consists of countries with an aggregate score between 0.8 and 0.5 of the maximum score; and those with low human welfare (LHW), that is, countries with an aggregate score of less than 0.5 of the maximum score. While this is an arbitrary procedure, it has analytical value.

With a sample of 147 countries, the maximum possible score for the best-performing country is 882 points. On this basis, the lower cut-off point for the high human-welfare group (HHW-F) is 705.6 points, which in our sample is attained by Hungary, with an aggregate score of 711 points. The lower cut-off point for the medium human-welfare group (MHW-F) is 441 points, with Mexico achieving an aggregate score of 442 points. Table 2 summarizes the results for the distribution of welfare in the world.

In terms of the freedom and institutional constituents of human welfare, none of the Arab countries enjoys high human welfare, compared to 2.4 per cent of the population of the Arab countries that have a high human-development ranking. Eight Arab countries, representing 20.6 per cent of the population of the Arab countries, enjoy medium human welfare, compared to 78.3 per cent in the high-human-development group. The remaining nine Arab countries, representing 79.4 per cent of the sample population, have low human welfare compared to 19.3 per cent with low human development.

POPULATION

1. Estimates of total population, 1950 and 2000; annual growth rate, sex ratio, total fertility rate, life expectancy, and percentage of urban population, by Arab country/territory, around 2000.
2. Life expectancy, by gender, by Arab country/territory, 1950-1955 and 1990-1995
3. Estimates of total population (based on two different projection scenarios), population ages 0-14, population ages 65+, dependency ratio, and median age, by Arab country/territory, 2000, 2010 and 2020.

Human welfare in the world: Borda rule ranking on freedoms and institutions (HW-F)

Country group	Number of countries	Maximum score achieved (country)	Minimum score achieved (country)	Number of Arab countries
HHW-F	26	856 (Switzerland)	711 (Costa Rica)	0
MHW-F	42	705 (Chile)	442 (Mexico)	8
LHW-F	79	439 (Gambia)	13 (Iraq)	9
All	147	856 (Switzerland)	13 (Iraq)	17

selected Arab countries and Republic of Korea, 1991-1996 (1990=100).

POLITICAL PARTICIPATION

27. Constitutions in force, by Arab country/territory.
28. Voter participation, by Arab country/territory.
29. Major and banned political parties, by Arab country/territory.
30. Status of freedom of associations, by Arab country/territory.
31. Accession to major international human rights conventions, by Arab country/territory, 2000.

ECONOMIC OUTPUT

32. Microeconomic environment, by Arab country/territory, selected countries and regions.
33. Location and geography, by Arab country/territory, selected countries and regions.

HUMAN WELFARE

34. HDI, by Arab country/territory and selected regions, 1998.
35. Freedom and institutional constituents of well-being: standardized indicators, by Arab country/territory, 1997/1998.

AHDI

36. Ranking of 111 countries on HDI and AHDI.
37. GDP per capita, by Arab country/territory, 1999.

1 Population

ESTIMATES OF TOTAL POPULATION, 1950 AND 2000, ANNUAL GROWTH RATE, SEX RATIO, TOTAL FERTILITY RATE, LIFE EXPECTANCY, AND PERCENTAGE OF URBAN POPULATION, BY ARAB COUNTRY/TERRITORY, AROUND 2000

	Population (thousands)				"Annual growth rate (%)"	"Sex ratio (%)"	"Total fertility rate (%)"	"Life expectancy (years)"	"Percentage of urban population, 1996
	1995	Males	Females	Both					
Algeria	8753	15364	14945	30309	1.82	103	3.25	68.9	50
Bahrain	116	368	272	640	2.21	135	2.63	72.9	88
Comoros	173	354	352	706	2.95	100	5.40	58.8	29
Djibouti	62	297	335	632	2.96	89	6.10	45.5	77
Egypt	21834	34364	33521	67885	1.82	103	3.40	66.3	44
Iraq	5158	11666	11280	22946	2.70	103	5.25	58.7	70
Jordan	472	2554	2359	4913	2.90	108	4.69	69.7	78
Kuwait	152	1115	800	1915	2.48	139	2.89	75.9	96
Lebanon	1443	1711	1786	3497	1.97	96	2.29	72.6	86
Libyan Arab Jamahiriya	1029	2741	2549	5290	2.13	108	3.80	70.0	85
Mauritania	825	1321	1344	2665	3.16	98	6.00	50.5	39
Morocco	8953	14964	14914	29878	1.87	100	3.40	66.6	47
Oman	456	1347	1191	2538	3.29	113	5.85	70.5	12
Occupied Palestinian territory	-	-	-	3100	4.78	-	-	-	-
Qatar	25	366	199	565	1.99	184	3.70	68.9	91
Saudi Arabia	3201	10872	9474	20346	3.49	115	6.15	70.9	79
Somalia	2264	4358	4420	8778	3.56	99	7.25	46.9	24
Sudan	9190	15639	15457	31096	2.13	101	4.90	55.0	27
Syrian Arab Republic	3495	8200	7988	16188	2.59	103	4.00	70.5	51
Tunisia	3530	4776	4682	9458	1.12	102	2.31	69.5	60
United Arab Emirates	70	1722	884	2606	2.05	195	3.17	74.6	82
Yemen	4316	9142	9207	18349	4.17	99	7.60	59.4	23
Arab region	75517	143241	137959	284300		104			50

Sources:

"United Nations, Department of Economic and Social Affairs, Population Division, 2001, " "World Population Prospects: The 2000 Revision"", February 2001. Except for occupied Palestinian territory (West Bank and Gaza Strip) and percentage of urban population: Population Reference Bureau, Arab World Region, 1996. Arab World Population: Selected Demographic and Reproductive Health Indicators", International Planned Parenthood Federation.

2 Population

LIFE EXPECTANCY, BY GENDER, BY ARAB COUNTRY/ TERRITORY, 1950-1955 AND 1990-1995"

	Life expectancy (years)				Achievement (%)	
	1950-1955		1990-1995		(1990-1995)/(1950-1955)	
	Males	Females	Males	Females	Males	Females
Algeria	42.1	44.2	66.0	68.3	156.8	154.5
Bahrain	49.6	52.5	69.8	74.1	140.7	141.1
Comoros	39.5	40.5	55.0	56.0	139.2	138.3
Djibouti	31.5	34.5	46.7	50.0	148.3	144.9
Egypt	41.2	43.6	62.4	64.8	151.5	148.6
Iraq	43.1	44.9	77.4*	78.2*	179.7	174.2
Jordan	42.2	44.3	66.2	69.8	156.9	157.6
Kuwait	54.1	57.5	73.3	77.2	135.5	134.3
Lebanon	54.3	57.7	66.6	70.5	122.7	122.2
Libyan Arab Jamahiriya	41.9	43.9	61.6	65.0	147.0	148.1
Mauritania	34.0	37.1	49.9	53.1	146.8	143.1
Morocco	41.9	43.9	62.8	66.2	149.9	150.8
Oman	35.8	37.0	67.7	71.8	189.1	194.1
Occupied Palestinian territory	-	-	-	-	-	-
Qatar	46.7	49.3	68.8	74.2	147.3	150.5
Saudi Arabia	39.1	40.7	68.4	71.4	174.9	175.4
Somalia	31.5	34.5	45.4	48.6	144.1	140.9
Sudan	36.3	39.1	49.6	52.4	136.6	134.0
Syrian Arab Republic	44.8	47.2	65.2	69.2	145.5	146.6
Tunisia	44.1	45.1	66.9	68.7	151.7	152.3
United Arab Emirates	46.7	49.3	72.9	75.3	156.1	152.7
Yemen	32.0	32.3	54.9	55.9	171.6	173.1
Arab region	40.5	42.6	62.6	65.2	154.5	152.8

* Data for 1990.

Source:

United Nations, Department of Economic and Social Affairs, Population Division, 2001. "World Population Prospects: The 2000 Revision", February 2001.

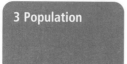

3 Population

ESTIMATES OF TOTAL POPULATION (BASED ON TWO DIFFERENT PROJECTION SCENARIOS), POPULATION AGES 0-14, POPULATION AGES (65+), DEPENDENCY RATIO, AND MEDIAN AGE, BY ARAB COUNTRY/TERRITORY, 2000, 2010 AND 2020"

| | Total population (millions) | | | | | | "Population aged (0-14) (millions, based on second scenario)" | | |
| | Scenario (1)* | | | Scenario (2)** | | | | | |
	2000	2010	2020	2000	2010	2020	2000	2010	2020
Algeria	30.31	36.21	43.18	30.31	35.23	40.63	11.87	10.44	10.27
Bahrain	0.64	0.74	0.83	0.64	0.73	0.83	0.20	0.19	0.18
Comoros	0.71	0.91	1.23	0.71	0.89	1.07	2.99	2.89	3.00
Djibouti	0.63	0.77	0.90	0.63	0.77	0.90	0.28	0.33	0.40
Egypt	67.89	83.53	102.46	67.89	78.73	90.88	26.43	23.39	22.60
Iraq	22.95	30.59	41.07	22.95	29.60	35.20	10.21	11.70	10.49
Jordan	4.91	6.60	8.73	4.91	6.37	7.47	2.03	2.38	2.19
Kuwait	1.91	2.27	2.63	1.92	2.22	2.49	0.57	0.56	0.53
Lebanon	3.50	4.01	4.76	3.50	3.98	4.67	1.52	1.12	1.19
Libyan Arab Jamahiriya	5.29	6.51	8.36	5.29	6.29	7.53	2.64	2.26	2.00
Mauritania	2.66	3.48	4.62	2.66	3.46	4.09	1.17	1.51	1.35
Morocco	29.88	36.36	43.49	29.88	35.38	40.53	10.85	10.71	10.20
Oman	2.54	3.66	4.87	2.54	3.55	4.15	0.80	1.40	1.23
Occupied Pales tinian territory	-	-	-	-	-	-	-	-	-
Qatar	0.56	0.66	0.77	0.56	0.65	0.72	0.16	0.16	0.14
Saudi Arabia	20.35	29.44	39.36	20.35	28.31	32.89	6.43	11.02	9.43
Somalia	8.78	11.93	16.33	8.78	11.98	14.96	3.86	5.63	5.81
Sudan	31.10	38.95	49.36	31.10	38.32	44.48	13.36	14.40	12.61
Syrian ArabRepublic	16.19	20.81	27.11	16.19	20.03	24.25	7.24	6.84	7.07
Tunisia	9.46	10.85	12.38	9.46	10.75	12.30	3.29	2.86	3.08
United Arab Emirates	2.61	3.01	3.36	2.61	2.95	3.21	0.52	0.60	0.60
Yemen	18.35	28.66	43.43	18.35	28.18	36.98	8.74	14.17	15.26
Arab region	281.22	359.95	459.23	281.23	348.37	410.23	115.16	124.55	119.63

* Scenario (1):   Under the assumption that total fertility rate and life expectancy at birth remain constant at their estimates in the year 2000.

** Scenario (2):   Using the total fertility rate and life expectancy at birth as estimated by the United Nations for every year during the period (2000-2020).

3 Population

| | Population ages (65+) (millions, based on second scenario) | | | Dependency ratio (%) (based on second scenario) | | | Median age (years) (based on second scenario) | | |
	2000	2010	2020	2000	2010	2020	2000	2010	2020
Algeria	1.19	1.59	2.06	0.76	0.52	0.44	20	24	29
Bahrain	0.01	0.03	0.04	0.50	0.41	0.36	26	31	33
Comoros	0.00	0.02	0.02	1.07	0.74	0.55	16	19	24
Djibouti	0.04	0.03	0.02	1.01	0.86	0.57	18	19	22
Egypt	2.21	3.81	5.88	0.73	0.53	0.46	20	24	29
Iraq	0.78	0.98	1.37	0.92	0.75	0.51	17	20	24
Jordan	0.12	0.20	0.30	0.78	0.68	0.50	19	21	25
Kuwait	0.03	0.06	0.14	0.45	0.39	0.37	27	32	34
Lebanon	0.00	0.02	0.02	0.88	0.51	0.47	18	23	28
Libyan ArabJamahiriya	0.12	0.20	0.32	1.09	0.64	0.45	15	20	25
Mauritania	0.00	0.02	0.02	1.01	0.89	0.57	18	18	22
Morocco	1.40	1.86	2.31	0.69	0.55	0.45	21	25	29
Oman	0.06	0.10	0.17	0.51	0.73	0.51	26	22	24
Occupied Palestinian territory	-	-	-	-	-	-	-	-	-
Qatar	0.01	0.01	0.04	0.41	0.38	0.33	27	33	36
Saudi Arabia	0.45	0.79	1.38	0.51	0.72	0.49	26	23	25
Somalia	0.55	0.39	0.44	1.01	1.01	0.72	18	17	19
Sudan	0.82	1.25	1.98	0.84	0.69	0.49	19	20	25
Syrian Arab Republic	0.49	0.72	1.04	0.91	0.61	0.50	17	21	26
Tunisia	0.51	0.68	0.82	0.67	0.49	0.46	22	26	30
United Arab Emirates	0.07	0.13	0.28	0.29	0.33	0.38	30	36	41
Yemen	0.40	0.63	1.00	0.99	1.11	0.79	16	15	18
Arab region	9.26	13.51	19.66						

Source: United Nations, Department of Economic and Social Affairs, Population Division, 2001. "World Population Prospects: The 2000 Revision", February 2001."

4 Health

LIFE EXPECTANCY, DISABILITY-ADJUSTED EXPECTANCY AT BIRTH, AND RELATED MEASURES,
BY GENDER, BY ARAB COUNTRY.TERRITORY, ESTIMATES FOR 1999"

	"Life expectancy (years)		People not expected to survive to age 40 (%), 1998	Disability-adjusted expectancy at birth (years)		Expectation ofdisability years at birth		
	Males	Females		Males	Females	Males	Females	Both**
Algeria	68.2	68.8	8.8	62.5	60.7	5.7	8.1	6.9
Bahrain	70.6	73.6	4.6	63.9	64.9	6.8	8.7	7.8
Comoros	56.0	58.1	20.1	46.1	47.5	9.9	10.6	10.3
Djibouti	45.0	45.0	32.8	37.7	38.1	7.3	7.0	7.2
Egypt	64.2	65.8	9.9	58.6	58.3	5.6	5.7	5.7
Iraq	61.8	62.8	15.8	55.4	55.1	7.5	8.7	8.1
Jordan	66.3	67.5	6.9	60.7	59.3	5.6	8.2	6.9
Kuwait	71.9	75.2	2.8	63.0	63.4	8.9	11.9	10.4
Lebanon	66.2	67.3	7.3	61.2	60.1	5.1	7.2	6.2
Libyan Arab Jamahiriya	65.0	67.0	6.3	59.7	58.9	5.3	8.1	6.7
Mauritania	49.5	53.0	28.7	40.2	47.5	9.3	10.5	9.9
Morocco	65.0	66.8	11.3	58.7	59.4	6.4	7.4	6.9
Oman	70.4	73.8	6.2	61.8	64.1	8.6	9.7	9.2
Occupied Palestinian territory*	70.3	73.4	-	-	-	-	-	-
Qatar	71.6	74.6	4.8	64.2	62.8	7.4	11.8	9.6
Saudi Arabia	71.0	72.6	5.6	65.1	5.8	8.7	7.3	
Somalia	44.0	44.7	-	35.9	36.9	8.2	7.8	8.0
Sudan	53.1	54.7	26.6	42.6	43.5	10.5	11.2	10.9
Syrian Arab Republic	64.6	67.1	8.2	58.8	58.9	5.8	8.2	7.0
Tunisia	67.0	67.9	7.5	62.0	60.7	5.0	7.2	6.1
United Arab Emirates	72.2	75.6	3.0	65.0	65.8	7.3	9.8	8.6
Yemen	57.3	58.0	21.2	49.7	49.7	7.6	8.3	8.0

* Estimates for year 2000.

** Calculated as a simple average.

Sources:

WHO, 2000, The World Health Report 2000: Health Systems: Improving Performance, table (2), (5), pp. 156, 176. Except for people not expected to survive to age 40 (%): UNDP, 2000, Human Development Report 2000, and occupied Palestinian territory: Palestinian Central Bureau of Statistics, 1998, ""Population in the Palestinian Territory 1997-2025.

5.1 Health

INFANT MORTALITY RATE FOR THE 10-YEAR PERIOD PRECEDING THE LATEST AVAILABLE SURVEY, BY GENDER
AND RESIDENCE, BY ARAB COUNTRY/TERRITORY

	Survey		Infant mortality rate (per thousand)				
	Year	Males	Females	Urban	Rural	Total*
Algeria	1992	61.8	45.5	41.1	64.1	43.7
Bahrain	1995	15.1	13.2	-	-	13.6
Comoros		-	-	-	-	-
Djibouti		-	-	-	-	-
Egypt	2000	55.0	54.5	43.1	61.8	43.5
Iraq		-	-	-	-	-
Jordan	1997	34.3	23.4	26.7	39.1	28.5
Kuwait	1996	11.9	10.6	-	-	11.6
Lebanon	1996	33.4	33.7	-	-	27.9
Libyan Arab Jamahiriya	1995	33.3	28.4	27.7	38.3	24.4
Mauritania		-	-	-	-	-
Morocco*	1997	39.1	34.0	23.8	46.1	36.6
Oman	1995	21.4	19.2	18.4	23.6	14.3
Occupied Palestinian territory	2000	25.3	25.6	-	-	25.3
Qatar*	1998	10.2	8.2	-	-	10.2
Saudi Arabia*	1996	21.1	21.8	18.3	27.9	21.4
Somalia		-	-	-	-	-
Sudan	1993	84.6	69.2	75.2	78.0	69.5
Syrian Arab Republic	1993	34.9	29.9	30.3	34.6	34.6
Tunisia	1994	45.6	42.0	31.3	58.9	35.3
United Arab Emirates	1995	14.5	10.5	11.3	14.5	10.8
Yemen	1997	98.4	80.0	75.4	93.6	75.3

* Figure for the five-year period preceding the survey.

UNDER-FIVE MORTALITY RATE FOR THE 10-YEAR PERIOD PRECEDING THE LATEST AVAILABLE SURVEY, BY GENDER AND RESIDENCE, BY ARAB COUNTRY/TERRITORY

	Survey		Under-five mortality rate (per thousand)			
	Year	Males	Females	Urban	Rural	Total*
Algeria	1992	67.7	54.8	47.4	72.8	48.6
Bahrain	1995	18.9	15.5	-	-	16.7
Comoros		-	-	-	-	-
Djibouti		-	-	-	-	-
Egypt	2000	68.8	69.7	52.8	79.2	54.3
Iraq		-	-	-	-	-
Jordan	1997	37.9	29.9	31.3	45.7	34.2
Kuwait	1996	17.3	16.0	-	-	17.2
Lebanon	1996	36.4	36.6	-	-	32.2
Libyan Arab Jamahiriya	1995	38.9	34.8	33.9	43.7	30.1
Mauritania		-	-	-	-	-
Morocco*	1997	47.1	44.5	29.9	61.1	45.8
Oman	1995	27.3	25.4	23.8	30.8	20.0
Occupied Palestinian territory	2000	29.1	28.3	-	-	-
Qatar*	1998	-	-	-	-	15.2
Saudi Arabia*	1996	30.1	26.8	26.0	35.2	29.0
Somalia		-	-	-	-	-
Sudan	1993	135.6	113.6	109.5	132.9	112.7
Syrian Arab Republic	1993	42.4	36.9	38.8	40.6	41.7
Tunisia	1994	54.3	51.3	36.8	72.2	43.6
United Arab Emirates	1995	17.7	13.1	13.2	19.1	13.0
Yemen	1997	128.1	113.5	95.8	128.2	104.8

* Figure for the five-year period preceding the survey.

5 Childhood mortality

Sources (according to the sort of countries in the table):

National Office of Statistics (Algiers) and PAPCHILD/League of Arab States, 1994,

"Algeria Maternal and Child Health Survey 1992", Cairo.

Naseeb, T. and S. M. Farid, 2000, ""Bahrain Family Health Survey 1995:

Principal Report"", Ministry of Health, Manama.

El-Zanaty, F. and A. A. Way, 2001, ""Egypt Demographic and Health

Survey 2000"". Ministry of Health and Population, National Population Council, Cairo,and Macro International, Inc., Calverton, Maryland.

Department of Statistics, Jordan, and Macro International, Inc., Calverton, Maryland, 1998, "Jordan Population and Family Health Survey 1997".

Yousef, A., R. H. Al-Rashoud and S. M. Farid, 2000, "Kuwait Family Health Survey 1996: Principal Report", Ministry of Health, Kuwait.

Ministry of Health, Beirut, and PAPCHILD/League of Arab States, Cairo, 1996,

"Lebanon Maternal and Child Health Survey 1996" and PAPCHILD/League of Arab States, Cairo.

General Committee for Health and Social Security, Tripoli, and PAPCHILD/League of Arab States, Cairo, 1997, "Libya Maternal and Child Health Survey 1995".

Azlamat M., and A. Abdel Moneim, 2000, "Morocco Maternal and Child Health Survey, 1996-97". National Office of Statistics and PAPCHILD/League of Arab States, Cairo.

"Suleiman, M., A. A. Al-Riyami and S. Farid. (eds.), 2000, "Oman Family Health Survey 1995, Ministry of Health", Muscat.

Palestinian Central Bureau of Statistics, 2000, "Health Survey-2000: Main Findings", Ramallah. Al-Jaber, K. A. and S. M. Farid, 2000, "Qatar Family Health Survey 1998: Principal Report", Ministry of Health, Doha.

Khoja, T. A. and S. M. Farid, 2000, "Saudi Arabia Family Health Survey 1996: Principal Report", Ministry of Health, Riyadh.

Federal Ministry of Health, Khartoum, and PAPCHILD/League of Arab States, Cairo,1995, "Sudan Maternal and Child Health Survey 1993".

Central Bureau of Statistics, Damascus, and PAPCHILD/League of Arab States, Cairo, 1995, "Syria Maternal and Child Health Survey 1993".

Ministry of Health, Tunisia, and PAPCHILD/League of Arab States, Cairo, 1996,"Tunisia Maternal and Child Health Survey 1994/1995".

Fikri, M. and S. M. Farid, 2000, "UAE Family Health Survey 1995: Principal Report", Ministry of Health, Abu Dhabi.

Central Statistical Organization and Macro International, Inc., Calverton, Maryland, 1998,"Yemen Demographic and Maternal and Child Health Survey 1997".

MALNUTRITION IN INFANTS, 1990-1997*, AND IN CHILDREN UNDER FIVE YEARS OF AGE, 1995-2000*, BY ARAB COUNTRY/TERRITORY

	Infants with low birth weight (%)	Percentage of under-five children suffering from:			
		Underweight		Wasting	Stunting
		Moderat & severe	severe	Moderate & severe	Moderate & severe
Algeria	9.0	13.0	3.0	9.0	18.0
Bahrain	6.0	9.0	2.0	5.0	10.0
Comoros	8.0	26.0	8.0	8.0	34.0
Egypt	10.0	12.0	3.0	6.0	25.0
Iraq	15.0	23.0	6.0	10.0	31.0
Jordan	10.0	5.0	1.0	2.0	8.0
Kuwait	7.0	10.0	3.0	11.0	24.0
Lebanon	10.0	3.0	0.0	3.0	12.0
Libyan Arab Jamahiriya	7.0	5.0	1.0	3.0	15.0
Mauritania	11.0	23.0	9.0	7.0	44.0
Morocco	9.0	10.0	2.0	4.0	23.0
Oman	8.0	24.0	4.0	13.0	23.0
Occupied Palestinian territory**	8.6	2.7	6.2	1.7	9.1
Qatar	-	6.0	-	2.0	8.0
Saudi Arabia	7.0	14.0	3.0	11.0	20.0
Somalia	16.0	26.0	7.0	12.0	14.0
Sudan	15.0	34.0x	11.0x	13.0ˣ	33.0ˣ
Syrian Arab Republic	7.0	13.0	4.0	9.0	21.0
Tunisia	8.0	4.0	0.0	1.0	8.0
United Arab Emirates	6.0	14.0	3.0	15.0	17.0
Yemen	19.0	46.0	15.0	13.0	52.0

* Figure for the five-year period preceding the survey.

* Data refer to the most recent year available during the period specified.

** Data for year 2000.

x Data refer to a year or period other than those specified in the column heading, or differ from the standard definition, or refer to only a part of the country.

6 Anthropometrical measures

Sources:

UNICEF, 2001, The State of the World's Children 2001, Oxford University Press. Except for Palestine: Palestinian Central Bureau of Statistics, 2000, "Health Survey 2000: Main Findings", Ramallah; infants with low birth weight:

UNICEF, 2000, The State of the World's Children 2000, Oxford University Press; and percentage of under-five children suffering from underweight, wasting or stunting in Bahrain, Kuwait,

- Naseeb, T. and S. M. Farid, 2000, "Bahrain Family Health Survey 1995: " Principal Report", Ministry of Health, Manama.

- Yousef, A., R. H. Al-Rashoud and S. M. Farid, 2000, "Kuwait Family Health Survey 1996:Principal Report", Ministry of Health, Kuwait.

Azlamat M., and A. Abdel Moneim, 2000,"Morocco Maternal and Child Health Survey, 1996-1997", National Office of Statistics and PAPCHILD/League of Arab States, Cairo.

- Suleiman, M., A. A. Al-Riyami and S. Farid. (eds.), 2000, "Oman Family Health Survey 1995", Ministry of Health, Muscat.

- Khoja, T. A. and S. M. Farid, 2000, ""Saudi Arabia Family Health Survey 1996:Principal Report", Ministry of Health, Riyadh.

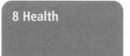

7 Health

	Maternal mortality ratio (per 100,000 live births) 1990-1998	Percentage of pregnant women with anemia, 1975-1991*
Algeria	220	42
Bahrain	46	-
Comoros	500	-
Djibouti	-	-
Egypt	170	24
Iraq	310	18
Jordan	41	50
Kuwait	5	40
Lebanon	100	49
Libyan Arab Jamahiriya	75	-
Mauritania	550	24
Morocco	230	45
Oman	19	54
Occupied Palestinian Territory**	70-80	-
Qatar	10	-
Saudi Arabia	18	-
Somalia	-	-
Sudan	550	36
Syrian Arab Republic	110	-
Tunisia	70	38
United Arab Emirates	3	-
Yemen	350	-

* Data refer to the most recent year available during the period specified

** Data for year 1995.

Sources:

UNDP, 2000, Human Development Report 2000. Except for Palestine: Palestinian Central Bureau of Statistics, 2000, ""Health Survey 2000: Main Findings"", Ramallah, and maternal mortality ratio in Iraq and Saudi Arabia: World Bank, 1999. "The Long-term Consequences of Reproductive Health Issues: A Reproductive Health Review of the Middle East and North Africa Region", draft report prepared by Human Development Group, Middle East and North Africa Region.

8 Health

	Percentage of 1-year-old children fully immunized, 1997-1999		Percentage of population without access to:		
	TB	Measles	Safe water 1990-1998	Health services 1990-1993	Sanitation 1990-1998
Algeria	97	78	10	-	9
Bahrain	72	100	6	0	3
Comoros	84	67	47	18	77
Djibouti	26	23	32	0	-
Egypt	99	97	13	1	12
Iraq	85	94	19	2	25
Jordan	-	83	3	10	1
Kuwait	-	96	-	0	-
Lebanon	-	81	6	5	37
Libyan Arab Jamahiriya	100	92	3	0	2
Mauritania	76	56	63	70	43
Morocco	90	93	35	38	42
Oman	98	99	15	11	22
Occupied Palestinian territory	73	93	-	-	-
Qatar	100	90	0*	0	3
Saudi Arabia	92	92	5ˣ	2	14ˣ
Somalia	39	26	-	-	-
Sudan	100	88	27	30	49
Syrian Arab Republic	100	97	14	1	3
Tunisia	99	93	2	10	20
United Arab Emirates	98	95	3	10	8
Yemen	78	74	39	84	34

* Data refer to the urban population without access to safe water.

x Data refer to a year or period other than that specified in the column heading or differ from the standard definition, or refer to only part of the country.

Sources:

UNICEF, 2001, The State of the World's Children 2001". Except for "Percentage of population without access to ...": UNDP, 2000, Human Development Report 2000.

SELECTED NATIONAL HEALTH-ACCOUNTS INDICATORS, BY ARAB COUNTRY/TERRITORY, ESTIMATES FOR 1997

	Health expenditure (%)				Per capita health expenditure (in international dollars)	
	Total expenditure as % of GDP	Public expenditure as % of total expenditure on health	Out-of-pocket expenditure as % of total expenditure	Total expenditure	Public expenditure	Out-of-pocket expenditure
Algeria	3.1	50.8	49.2	122	62	60
Bahrain	4.4	58.5	37.7	539	315	204
Comoros	4.5	68.2	31.8	47	32	15
Djibouti	2.8	72.9	27.1	48	35	13
Egypt	3.7	27.0	73.1	118	32	86
Iraq	4.2	58.9	41.1	110	65	45
Jordan	5.2	67.2	32.8	178	119	58
Kuwait	3.3	87.4	12.6	605	529	76
Lebanon	10.1	29.6	53.8	563	167	303
Libyan Arab Jamahiriya	3.4	54.2	45.8	221	120	102
Mauritania	5.6	30.3	69.7	73	22	51
Morocco	5.3	40.7	59.3	159	65	95
Oman	3.9	54.5	35.9	334	182	120
Occupied Palestinianterritory	-	-	-	-	-	-
Qatar	6.5	57.5	42.5	1105	635	470
Saudi Arabia	3.5	80.2	6.3	332	297	35
Somalia	1.5	71.4	28.6	11	8	3
Sudan	3.5	20.9	79.1	43	9	34
Syrian Arab Republic	2.5	33.6	66.4	109	37	72
Tunisia	5.4	41.7	53.0	239	100	127
United Arab Emirates	4.2	35.4	3.8	816	262	38
Yemen	3.4	37.9	62.1	33	12	20

Source:

WHO, 2000, The World Health Report 2000: Health Systems: Improving Performance.

RESPONSIVENESS AND FAIRNESS OF HEALTH SYSTEMS, AND RELATED MEASURES, BY ARAB COUNTRY/TERRITORY

	Responsiveness			Fairness		
	Index	Ranking among Arab countries	World ranking	Index	Ranking among Arab countries	World ranking
Algeria	5.19	11	90-91	0.94	11	74-75
Bahrain	5.82	4	43-44	0.95	9	61
Comoros	4.46	16	157-160	0.94	12	79-81
Djibouti	4.28	19	170	0.98	1	3-5
Egypt	5.06	13	102	0.92	14-15	125-127
Iraq	5.05	14	103-104	0.95	7-8	56-57
Jordan	5.25	10	84-86	0.96	6	49-50
Kuwait	6.34	2	29	0.97	4	30-32
Lebanon	5.61	5	55	-	-	-
Libyan Arab Jamahiriya	5.53	6	57-58	0.98	2	12-15
Mauritania	4.33	18	165-167	0.89	19	153
Morocco	4.58	15	151-153	0.92	14-15	125-127
Oman	5.27	9	83	0.95	7-8	56-57
Occupied Palestinian territory	-	-	-	-	-	
Qatar	6.51	1	26-27	0.94	10	70
Saudi Arabia	5.40	7	67	0.97	5	37
Somalia	3.69	21	191	0.91	17	136-137
Sudan	4.34	17	164	0.88	20	160-161
Syrian Arab Republic	5.37	8	69-72	0.90	18	142-143
Tunisia	5.15	12	94	0.93	13	108-111
United Arab Emirates	6.33	3	30	0.97	3	20-22
Yemen	3.98	20	180	0.91	16	135

Source:

WHO, 2000, The World Health Report 2000: Health Systems: Improving Performance.

CULTIVATED AREA AND CULTIVATED AREA PER CAPITA, 1970 AND 1998, AND
THE ANNUAL CHANGE RATE IN TOTAL FOREST AREA, 1990-1995, BY ARAB COUNTRY/TERRITORY

| | Cultivated area (1,000 ha) | | Cultivated area per capita (ha) | | Land area (1000 ha) | Forest area | |
| | | | | | | Percentage to land area,1995 | Annual change rate,1990-1995 (%) |
	1970	1998	1970	1998			
Algeria	6800	8173	0.490	0.270	238174	0.78	-1.2
Bahrain	3	6	0.010	0.010	69	0.00	0.0
Comoros	90	118	0.330	0.180	223	4.04	-5.0
Djibouti	-	-	-	-	2318	0.95	0.0
Egypt	2843	3300	0.080	0.050	99545	0.03	0.0
Iraq	4993	5540	0.530	0.250	43737	0.19	0.0
Jordan	314	390	0.210	0.080	8893	0.51	-2.4
Kuwait	1	7	0.001	0.004	1782	0.28	0.0
Lebanon	325	308	0.130	0.100	1023	5.08	-6.7
Libyan Arab Jamahiriya	2025	2115	1.000	0.400	175954	0.23	0.0
Mauritania	283	500	0.230	0.200	102522	0.54	0.0
Morocco	7505	9976	0.490	0.360	44630	8.59	-0.3
Oman	32	63	0.04	0.030	21246	0.00	0.0
Occupied Palestinian territory							
Gaza Strip	21	25	0.060	0.020	-	-	-
West Bank	186	209	0.230	0.130	-	-	-
Qatar	1	17	0.009	0.030	1100	0.00	0.0
Saudi Arabia	1420	3830	0.250	0.190	214969	0.10	-0.8
Somalia	950	1062	0.260	0.11	62734	1.20	-0.2
Sudan	11745	16900	0.850	0.110	237600	17.51	-0.8
Syrian Arab Republic	5909	5484	0.940	0.360	18378	1.19	-2.1
Tunisia	4480	4900	0.870	0.520	15536	3.57	-0.5
United Arab Emirates	12	81	0.050	0.030	8360	0.72	0.0
Yemen	1418	1613	0.220	0.100	52797	0.02	0.0
Arab region	51356	64617	0.410	0.240	1351590	3.72	-0.8

Sources:

FAO, 1997, "State of the World's Forests", Rome.

FAO, 1999, "State of the World's Forests". Rome.

Except for cultivated area: FAO, 2001, Statistics Database on web site, http://www.fao.org.

RENEWABLE WATER RESOURCES, ANNUAL WATER WITHDRAWAL AND WATER BALANCE, BY ARAB COUNTRY/TERRITORY

(in cubic metres)

	Renewable water resources (per capita), 1995	Annual water withdrawal (per capita)	Water balance (per capita)
Algeria	512	180	332
Bahrain	206	465	-259
Comoros	-	-	-
Djibouti	520	20	500
Egypt	926	913	13
Iraq	3688	2367	1321
Jordan	161	246	-85
Kuwait	13	348	-335
Lebanon	1465	444	1021
Libyan Arab Jamahiriya	111	880	-769
Mauritania	5013	923	4090
Morocco	1110	436	674
Oman	455	728	-273
Occupied Palestinian territory	-	-	-
Qatar	96	528	-432
Saudi Arabia	134	1040	-906
Somalia	1702	99	1603
Sudan	3150	633	2517
Syrian Arab Republic	1791	1017	774
Tunisia	463	382	81
United Arab Emirates	79	1107	-1028
Yemen	283	251	32

Source:

FAO, 1997, "Water Resources of the Near East Region: a Review"

PRIMARY ENERGY PRODUCTION AND CONSUMPTION, AND CARBON DIOXIDE EMISSIONS FROM THE CONSUMPTION AND FLARING OF FOSSIL FUELS, BY ARAB COUNTRY/TERRITORY, 1980 AND 1999

	Energy production (quadrillion btu)		Energy consumption		Carbon dioxide emissions (million metric tons of carbon equivalent)	
	1980	1999	1980	1999	1980	1999
Algeria	2.80	6.06	0.80	1.31	16.44	23.42
Bahrain	0.22	0.41	0.14	0.37	2.13	5.52
Comoros	0.00	0.00	0.00	0.00	0.01	0.02
Djibouti	0.00	0.00	0.02	0.02	0.45	0.49
Egypt	1.45	2.72	0.71	2.02	11.71	33.49
Iraq	5.45	5.48	0.52	1.16	13.95	21.66
Jordan	0.00	0.01	0.08	0.22	1.48	3.98
Kuwait	3.99	4.58	0.48	0.68	8.54	12.27
Lebanon	0.01	0.01	0.11	0.23	1.83	4.22
Libyan Arab Jamahiriya	4.03	3.10	0.40	0.58	8.80	11.33
Mauritania	0.00	0.00	0.01	0.05	0.16	0.85
Morocco	0.04	0.02	0.23	0.41	4.22	7.61
Oman	0.64	2.12	0.06	0.30	1.06	5.48
Occupied Palestinian territory	-	-	-	-	-	-
Qatar	1.20	2.44	0.21	0.70	3.78	9.96
Saudi Arabia	22.43	19.64	1.66	4.34	48.76	73.93
Somalia	0.00	0.00	0.02	0.01	0.29	0.16
Sudan	0.01	0.13	0.05	0.07	0.90	1.22
Syrian Arab Republic	0.41	1.51	0.27	0.81	4.67	13.02
Tunisia	0.24	0.25	0.13	0.29	2.34	5.06
United Arab Emirates	3.89	6.25	0.27	1.88	8.21	32.19
Yemen	0.00	0.85	0.10	0.14	1.92	2.52
Arab region	46.82	55.57	6.27	15.59	141.65	268.40

Sources:

United States Energy Information, 2000, web site: http://www.eio.doe.gov/emeu/eio/tableh1.html Except for carbon dioxide emissions: WRI, UNDP, UNEP and WB, 1998, World Resources 1998-1999: A Guide to the Global Environment, Environmental Change and Human Health.

TOTAL NUMBER OF ADULT ILLITERATES, ADULT ILLITERACY RATE BY GENDER, 1999, AND MEAN YEARS OF SCHOOLING, 1970, 1992 AND 2000, POPULATION AGE 15 YEARS OR OLDER, BY ARAB COUNTRY/TERRITORY AND WORLD REGION

	Number of adult illiterates (million)	Adult illiteracy rate (%), 1999			Mean years of schooling		
		Males	Females	Both	1970	1992	2000
Algeria	6.4	22.6	44.3	33.4	1.6	2.8	5.4
Bahrain	0.1	9.5	17.8	12.9	2.8	4.3	6.1
Comoros	0.2	33.7	47.9	40.8			1.0
Djibouti	0.1	25.1	47.2	36.6	-	0.4	-
Egypt	19.4	33.9	57.2	45.4	-	3.0	5.5
Iraq	-	-	-	-	-		5.0
Jordan	0.3	5.5	16.6	10.8	3.3	5.0	6.9
Kuwait	0.2	16.0	20.6	18.1	3.1	5.5	6.2
Lebanon	0.3	8.2	20.2	14.4	-	4.4	-
Libyan Arab Jamahiriya	0.7	9.8	33.1	20.9	-	3.5	-
Mauritania	0.8	47.8	68.6	58.4	-	0.4	-
Morocco	9.9	38.9	64.9	52.0	-	3.0	-
Oman	0.4	20.9	40.4	29.7	-	0.9	-
Occupied Palestinian territory	-	-	-	-	-	-	-
Qatar	0.1	19.9	17.4	19.2	-	5.8	-
Saudi Arabia	2.7	16.5	34.1	23.9	-	3.9	-
Somalia	-	-	-	-	-	0.3	-
Sudan	7.8	31.1	55.1	43.1	0.6	0.8	2.1
Syrian Arab Republic	2.4	12.3	40.7	26.4	2.2	4.2	5.8
Tunisia	2.0	19.6	40.7	30.1	1.5	2.1	5.0
United Arab Emirates	0.5	26.2	22.0	24.9	-	5.6	-
Yemen	4.9	33.4	76.1	54.8	-	0.9	-
Developing countries	835.8	19.4	34.7	27.1	-	3.9	-
Least developed countries	167.4	38.4	58.1	48.4	-	1.6	-
Arab region	57.7	26.9	51.0	38.7	-	3.4	-
East Asia and the Pacific	196.6	8.5	21.3	14.7	-	5.2*	-
Latin America and the Caribbean	40.8	11.3	13.1	12.2	3.8	5.4	6.1
South Asia	399.0	33.5	56.8	44.9	2.1	2.3	4.7
Sub-Saharan Africa	132.1	31.7	47.4	40.4	-	1.6	-
Eastern Europe and the CIS	4.4	0.8	1.8	1.4	-	8.8	-
OECD	-	-	-	-	7.3	11.1	9.6
World	-	-	-	-	-	5.2	-

* East Asia only.

Sources:

UNDP, 2001, Human Development Report 2001. Except for 1992: UNDP, 1994, Human Development Report 1994.

GROSS ENROLMENT RATE, BY LEVEL OF EDUCATION AND GENDER, BY
ARAB COUNTRY/TERRITORY, HONG KONG, REPUBLIC OF KOREA AND WORLD REGIONS, 1980 AND 1995

| | Pre-primary | | | | | | Primary | | | | | |
| | 1980 | | | 1995 | | | 1980 | | | 1995 | | |
	Males	Females	Both	Males	Females	Both	Males	Females	Both	Males	Females	Both
Algeria	-	-	-	2.0	2.0	2.0	108.0	81.0	94.0	112.0	100.0	107.0
Bahrain	15.0	14.0	15.0	34.0	33.0	33.0	111.0	97.0	104.0	107.0	109.0	108.0
Comoros	-	-	-	-	-	-	-	-	-	85.0	71.0	78.0
Djibouti	-	-	-	0.0	0.0	0.0	-	-	-	44.0	33.0	38.0
Egypt	3.0	3.0	3.0	8.0	8.0	8.0	84.0	61.0	73.0	107.0	93.0	100.0
Iraq	9.0	9.0	9.0	8.0	7.0	8.0	119.0	107.0	113.0	-	-	-
Jordan	14.0	11.0	12.0	27.0	24.0	25.0	105.0	102.0	104.0	94.0	95.0	94.0
Kuwait	38.0	36.0	37.0	52.0	51.0	52.0	105.0	100.0	102.0	73.0	72.0	73.0
Lebanon	-	-	59.0	76.0	73.0	74.0	-	-	111.0	111.0	108.0	109.0
Libyan Arab Jamahiriya	5.0	4.0	4.0	-	-	-	129.0	120.0	125.0	107.0	104.0	106.0
Mauritania	-	-	-	0.0	0.0	0.0	47.0	26.0	37.0	85.0	72.0	78.0
Morocco	74.0	25.0	50.0	85.0	40.0	63.0	102.0	63.0	83.0	94.0	71.0	83.0
Oman	1.0	0.5	1.0	4.0	3.0	3.0	69.0	36.0	52.0	82.0	78.0	80.0
Occupied Palestinian territory	-	-	-	-	-	-	-	-	-	-	-	-
Qatar	26.0	23.0	25.0	32.0	29.0	31.0	108.0	103.0	105.0	92.0	87.0	89.0
Saudi Arabia	5.0	4.0	5.0	-	-	8.0	74.0	49.0	61.0	79.0	76.0	78.0
Somalia	0.5	0.5	0.5	-	-	-	24.0	14.0	19.0	-	-	-
Sudan	-	-	13.0	42.0	33.0	37.0	59.0	41.0	50.0	59.0	48.0	54.0
Syrian Arab Republic	4.0	3.0	4.0	7.0	6.0	7.0	111.0	88.0	100.0	106.0	95.0	101.0
Tunisia	-	-	-	11.0	11.0	11.0	118.0	88.0	103.0	119.0	112.0	116.0
United Arab Emirates	40.0	35.0	37.0	59.0	56.0	57.0	90.0	88.0	89.0	96.0	92.0	94.0
Yemen	1.0	1.0	1.0	1.0	1.0	1.0	-	-	-	113.0	45.0	79.0
Hong Kong	81.0	81.0	81.0	83.0	84.0	84.0	107.0	106.0	107.0	95.0	97.0	96.0
Republic of Korea	8.0	7.0	8.0	85.0	85.0	85.0	109.0	111.0	110.0	100.0	101.0	101.0
Developing countries*	-	-	-	23.5	22.6	23.1	104.0	85.4	94.7	105.0	92.9	99.1
Least developed countries	-	-	-	11.9	9.8	10.8	-	-	-	78.2	60.7	69.5
Arab region	-	-	-	17.7	12.9	15.4	91.7	66.7	79.5	91.7	75.6	83.8
Sub-Saharan Africa	-	-	-	9.7	8.7	9.2	-	-	-	80.7	67.1	73.9
Latin America/Caribbean	-	-	-	50.7	51.5	51.1	-	-	-	112.0	108.8	110.4
East Asia/Oceania	-	-	-	29.0	28.8	28.9	-	-	-	115.8	113.0	114.5
South Asia	-	-	-	10.6	9.0	9.8	-	-	-	105.5	82.1	94.2
More developed countries	-	-	-	70.5	69.3	69.9	104.0	103.0	104.0	104.8	104.2	104.5
North America	-	-	-	69.5	66.6	68.1	-	-	-	103.8	102.7	103.3
Asia/Oceania	-	-	-	52.9	53.8	53.3	-	-	-	102.8	103.0	102.9
Europe	-	-	-	77.4	77.2	77.3	-	-	-	106.9	106.4	106.7
World	-	-	-	30.6	29.5	30.1	104.0	88.2	96.1	104.8	94.2	99.6

* Figures in 1980 are for all developing countries

	Secondary						Tertiary					
	1980			**1995**			**1980**			**1995**		
	Males	Females	Both	Males	Females	Both	Males	Females	Both	Males	Females	Both
Algeria	40.0	26.0	33.0	66.0	59.0	62.0	8.5	3.1	5.9	12.8	8.9	10.9
Bahrain	70.0	58.0	64.0	97.0	100.0	99.0	5.3	4.8	5.0	-	-	-
Comoros	-	-	-	21.0	17.0	19.0	-	-	-	0.6	0.3	0.5
Djibouti	-	-	-	15.0	11.0	13.0	-	-	-	0.2	0.2	0.2
Egypt	61.0	39.0	50.0	80.0	68.0	74.0	21.4	10.6	16.1	22.1	13.7	18.1
Iraq	76.0	38.0	57.0	-	-	-	11.6	5.6	8.7	-	-	-
Jordan	79.0	73.0	75.0	-	-	-	28.9	24.2	26.6	-	-	-
Kuwait	84.0	76.0	80.0	64.0	64.0	64.0	8.6	14.8	11.3	22.4	28.3	25.4
Lebanon	-	-	59.0	77.0	84.0	81.0	40.5	20.6	30.1	27.2	26.8	27.0
Libyan Arab Jamahiriya	88.0	63.0	76.0	-	-	97.0	11.2	4.1	7.8	-	-	-
Mauritania	17.0	4.0	11.0	19.0	11.0	15.0	-	-	-	6.8	1.4	4.1
Morocco	32.0	20.0	26.0	44.0	33.0	39.0	9.0	2.7	5.9	13.0	9.4	11.3
Oman	19.0	6.0	12.0	68.0	64.0	66.0	0.0	-	0.0	4.7	4.6	4.7
Occupied Palestinian territory	-	-	-	-	-	-	-	-	-	-	-	-
Qatar	64.0	68.0	66.0	83.0	84.0	83.0	6.3	17.1	10.4	14.7	42.1	27.4
Saudi Arabia	36.0	23.0	29.0	62.0	54.0	58.0	9.0	4.6	7.1	15.9	14.7	15.3
Somalia	11.0	4.0	8.0	-	-	-	-	-	-	-	-	-
Sudan	20.0	12.0	16.0	14.0	12.0	13.0	2.5	0.9	1.7	-	-	-
Syrian Arab Republic	57.0	35.0	46.0	47.0	40.0	44.0	23.4	10.1	16.9	21.4	14.3	17.9
Tunisia	34.0	20.0	27.0	63.0	59.0	61.0	6.7	3.0	4.9	14.2	11.5	12.9
United Arab Emirates	55.0	49.0	52.0	76.0	84.0	80.0	2.4	4.6	3.1	4.7	14.1	8.8
Yemen	-	-	-	36.0	8.0	23.0	-	-	-	-	-	-
Hong Kong	63.0	65.0	64.0	73.0	77.0	75.0	13.8	6.6	10.3	23.9	19.7	21.9
Republic of Korea	82.0	74.0	78.0	101.0	101.0	101.0	21.3	7.5	14.7	65.6	37.6	52.0
Developing countries*	42.0	28.7	35.5	53.9	43.6	48.8	6.6	3.7	5.2	10.3	7.3	8.8
Least developing countries	-	-	-	22.5	14.1	18.4	-	-	-	4.6	1.7	3.2
Arab region	42.4	30.5	36.6	58.4	48.8	53.7	12.5	5.9	9.2	14.5	10.5	12.5
Sub-Saharan Africa	-	-	-	26.9	21.6	24.3	-	-	-	4.6	2.5	3.5
Latin America/Caribbean	-	-	-	53.9	59.3	56.6	-	-	-	17.6	17.0	17.3
East Asia/Oceania	-	-	-	64.5	58.3	61.5	-	-	-	10.5	7.2	8.9
South Asia	-	-	-	53.4	35.0	44.5	-	-	-	8.2	4.6	6.5
More developed countries	86.1	87.0	86.5	104.8	106.9	105.8	35.9	36.2	36.1	56.0	63.3	59.6
North America	-	-	-	96.5	97.4	97.0	-	-	-	74.6	93.8	84.0
Asia/Oceania	-	-	-	107.3	108.3	107.8	-	-	-	47.9	42.6	45.3
Europe	-	-	-	109.8	113.1	111.4	-	-	-	45.9	49.8	47.8
World	51.3	41.1	46.3	62.5	53.4	58.1	13.2	11.1	12.2	16.8	15.6	16.2

* Figures in 1980 are for all developing countries.

Sources:

UNESCO, 1998, 1998 World Education Report: Teachers and Teaching in a Changing World.

Except for 1980: UNESCO, 1996, 1996 Statistical Yearbook

16 EDUCATION

PERCENTAGE OF GIRLS AMONG PUPILS, BY LEVEL OF EDUCATION, BY
ARAB COUNTRY/TERRITORY, HONG KONG AND REPUBLIC OF KOREA, LATEST AVAILABLE YEAR

	Pre-primary 1994/1995	Primary 1995/1996	Secondary 1995/1996	Tertiary 1995/1996
Algeria	48	39	54	40
Bahrain	47	50	67	-
Comoros	-	-	-	-
Djibouti	-	-	-	-
Egypt	48	47	46	36
Iraq	49	-	-	-
Jordan	46**	-	-	-
Kuwait	49	-	-	57
Lebanon	48	66	59	50
Libyan Arab Jamahiriya	-	33	-	-
Mauritania	-	50	37	17
Morocco	30	41	38	39
Oman	44	49	48	-
Occupied Palestinian territory	-	-	-	-
Qatar	47	59	-	71
Saudi Arabia	54**	32	47	48
Somalia	-	-	-	-
Sudan	47*	40	46	-
Syrian Arab Republic	46	43	39	39
Tunisia	-	41	48	43
United Arab Emirates	47**	49	53	70
Yemen	47**	28	16	-
Hong Kong	48	51	51	43
Korea	47	-	-	35

* Data for 1991/1992.

** Data for 1993/1994.

Sources:

UNESCO, 1998, 1998 World Education Report: Teachers and Teaching in a Changing World. Except for pre-primary: UNESCO, 1996, 1996 Statistical Yearbook.

17 EDUCATION

NUMBER OF PUPILS PER TEACHER, BY LEVEL OF EDUCATION, BY ARAB COUNTRY/TERRITORY, HONG KONG AND
REPUBLIC OF KOREA, 1980, 1985 AND 1995

	Pre-primary			Primary			Secondary		
	1980	1985	1995	1980	1985	1995	1980	1985	1995
Algeria	-	-	26	35	28	27	25	22	17
Bahrain	-	30	27	19	21	18	22	16	14
Comoros	-	29	29	-	35	42	-	32	25
Djibouti	-	59	41	-	44	36	-	23	23
Egypt	-	40	28	-	30	24	24	21	20
Iraq	24	17	19	28	24	22	31	30	20
Jordan	27	21	23	32	31	21	21	18	20
Kuwait	18	17	16	19	18	15	12	13	11
Lebanon	19	25	-	18	16	12	-	-	-
Libyan Arab Jamahiriya	17	14	-	18	16	-	12	14	-
Mauritania	-	-	-	41	51	52	-	24	24
Morocco	20(2)	21	21	38	28	28	22	19	16
Oman	36	23	20	23	27	26	-	13	17
Occupied Palestinian territory	-	-	31	-	-	42	-	-	7
Qatar	-	20	22	15	13	9	10	9	10
Saudi Arabia	25	17	13	18	16	13	13	14	11
Somalia	15	12	-	33	19	-	21	18	-
Sudan	47	42	-	34	35	36	20	25	23(3)
Syrian Arab Republic	31	31	22	28	26	24	-	18	17
Tunisia	-	29	-	39	32	25	20	-	18(4)
United Arab Emirates	48(1)	22	16	16(1)	18	17	-	13	13
Yemen	18	-	18	35	-	-	44	-	-
Hong Kong	38	30	21	30	27	24	29	23	20
Republic of Korea	20	34	21	48	38	32	39	37	24

(1) General education only.
(2) Teachers of religious schools only.
(3) Data for 1992/1993.
(4) Data for 1994/1995.

Sources:

UNESCO, 1998, 1998 World Education Report: Teachers and Teaching in a Changing World. Except for 1980: UNESCO, 1996, 1996 Statistical Yearbook.

PERCENTAGE OF VOCATIONAL EDUCATION IN SECONDARY EDUCATION, BY
ARAB COUNTRY/TERRITORY, HONG KONG AND REPUBLIC OF KOREA, 1980/1981, 1990/1991 AND 1994/1995

Percentage of vocational education

	1980/1981	1990/1991	1994/1995
Algeria	1.41	7.05	5.52
Bahrain	10.59	13.25	12.69
Comoros	-	-	-
Djibouti	-	-	-
Egypt	21.64	18.63	32.34
Iraq	5.51	-	11.38[2]
Jordan	5.26	24.80	24.27[3]
Kuwait	0.23	0.62[2]	0.69
Lebanon	10.86	-	-
Libyan Arab Jamahiriya	5.40	25.50	38.18[2]
Mauritania	4.54	2.12[5]	2.46[3]
Morocco[4]	1.27	1.50	1.44
Oman	6.04	2.79	1.41[3]
Occupied Palestinian territory	-	-	-
Qatar	2.77	2.92	1.78
Saudi Arabia	1.46	2.78	2.34[3]
Somalia	17.57	-	-
Sudan	4.05	4.15	4.04[1]
Syrian Arab Republic	4.33	7.27	9.36
Tunisia	27.34	6.52	2.16
United Arab Emirates	1.30	0.71	1.41
Yemen	7.45	2.71	
Hong Kong	6.61	-	-
Republic of Korea	20.56	18.08	18.64

(1) Data for 1991/1992.
(2) Data for 199219/93.
(3) Data for 1993/1994.
(4) Does not include technician schools.
(5) Does not include health programs.

Source:
UNESCO, 1996, 1996 Statistical Yearbook.

PERCENTAGE DISTRIBUTION OF TERTIARY EDUCATION STUDENTS, BY FIELD OF STUDY, BY
ARAB COUNTRY/TERRITORY, HONG KONG AND REPUBLIC OF KOREA, 1995

	Field of study				
	Education	Humanities	Law and social sciences	Natural sciences, engineering and agriculture	Medical sciences
Algeria	0	13	23	52	10
Bahrain	26	**	22	39	13
Comoros	-	-	-	-	-
Djibouti	28	—	72	—	—
Egypt*	17	18	40	15	8
Iraq	-	-	-	-	-
Jordan	10	17	32	28	12
Kuwait	31	8	34	23	4
Lebanon	0	26	52	17	3
Libyan Arab Jamahiriya	-	-	-	-	-
Mauritania	11	26	55	8	—
Morocco	0	30	37	29	3
Oman	-	-	-	-	-
Occupied Palestinian territory					
Gaza	28	29	15	19	5
West Bank	9	30	27	28	6
Qatar	-	-	-	-	-
Saudi Arabia	47	27	7	14	4
Somalia	-	-	-	-	-
Sudan	-	-	-	-	-
Syrian ArabRepublic	2	21	35	29	11
Tunisia	3	25	39	24	9
United Arab Emirates	-	-	-	-	-
Yemen	-	-	-	-	-
Hong Kong	7	8	25	36	4
Republic of Korea	7	18	29	39	6

* Universities only.
"** "Humanities"" was added to "Education".

Source
UNESCO, 1998, 1998 World Education Report: Teachers and Teaching in a Changing World.

RESEARCH OUTPUT, BY ARAB COUNTRY/TERRITORY,
1970-1975 AND 1990-1995

Arab science and technology output, papers published in refereed international journals (number of publications)

	1970-1975	1990-1995
Algeria	338	1431
Bahrain	-	453
Comoros	-	-
Djibouti	-	-
Egypt	3261	12072
Iraq	380	931
Jordan	61	1472
Kuwait	148	1936
Lebanon	743	500
Libyan Arab Jamahiriya	96	348
Mauritania	-	27
Morocco	96	2418
Oman	1	466
Occupied Palestinian territory	-	51
Qatar	-	377
Saudi Arabia	126	8306
Somalia	1	79
Sudan	426	690
Syrian Arab Republic	38	471
Tunisia	145	1832
United Arab Emirates	1	579
Yemen	4	155
Arab region	5865	34594

Source:

Zahlan, A., 1999. Arabs and the Challenges of Science and Technology: Progress without Change.

HDI AND THE DIGITAL DIVIDE, BY ARAB COUNTRY/TERRITORY AND SELECTED REGIONS

	HDI, 1998	Number of telephones mainline (per 1,000 people), 1999	Number of PCs (per 1,000 people), 1999	Number of web sites (per 10,000 people), 2000	Total number of Internet users (in thousands)
Algeria	0.69	52	6	0	0
Bahrain	0.82	249	140	17	62
Comoros	-	-	-	-	-
Djibouti	0.45	14	10	0	0
Egypt	0.63	75	12	1	7
Iraq	0.58	30	0	0	0
Jordan	0.71	87	14	1	14
Kuwait	0.83	240	121	23	53
Lebanon	0.73	201	46	12	70
Libyan Arab Jamahiriya	0.75	101	0	0	1
Mauritania	0.45	6	27	0	0
Morocco	0.58	53	11	0	2
Oman	0.72	90	26	3	20
Occupied Palestinian territory	-	-	-	-	-
Qatar	0.81	263	136	1	76
Saudi Arabia	0.74	129	57	2	14
Somalia	-	-	-	-	-
Sudan	0.47	9	3	0	0
Syrian Arab Republic	0.65	99	14	0	1
Tunisia	0.71	90	15	0	12
United Arab Emirates	0.80	332	102	92	167
Yemen	0.45	17	2	0	1
Arab region	0.64	88	19	2	1525
South Asia	0.56	23	3	2	3034
Sub-Saharan Africa	0.46	14	8	3	2357
South East Asia and the Pacific	0.69	82	17	4	23593
Latin America and the Caribbean	0.76	130	38	30	10184

Sources:

World Bank, 2001, "World Development Indicators".Except for HDI: UNDP, 2000, Human Development Report, and number of Internet users: ESCWA, 2000. "Report of the Expert Panel on Information Technology and Development Priorities: Competing in a Knowledge-based Global Economy",Beirut, 15-16 May 2000.

22 ICT

TECHNOLOGY ACHIEVEMENT INDEX (TAI), BY ARAB COUNTRY/TERRITORY AND SELECTED TOP-RANKING COUNTRIES

	(TAI) Rank	(TAI) Value	S&T status	Technology creation Patents granted to residents (per million people), 1998	Diffusion of recent innovations High and medium-technology exports (as % of total goods exports) 1999	Diffusion of old innovations Telephones mainline & cellular (per 1,000 people), 1999
Algeria	58	0.221	(2)	-	1.0	54
Bahrain	-	-	-	-	5.7**	453
Comoros	-	-	-	-	-	10
Djibouti	-	-	-	-	-	14
Egypt	57	0.236	(2)	(.)	8.8	77
Iraq	-	-	-	-	-	-
Jordan	-	-	-	-	-	105
Kuwait	-	-	-	-	6.8	398
Lebanon	-	-	-	-	-	-
Libyan Arab Jamahiriya	-	-	-	-	1.8**	-
Mauritania	-	-	-	-	-	6
Morocco	-	-	-	3	12.4**	66
Oman	-	-	-	-	13.2	139
Occupied Palestinian territory	-	-	-	-	-	-
Qatar	-	-	-	-	-	406
Saudi Arabia	-	-	-	(.)	5.2**	170
Somalia	-	-	-	-	-	-
Sudan	71	0.071	(3)	-	0.4**	9
Syrian Arab Republic	56	0.240	(2)	-	1.2	102
Tunisia	51	0.255	(2)	-	19.7	96
United Arab Emirates	-	-	-	-	-	754
Yemen	-	-	-	-	-	18
Finland	1	0.744	(1)	187	50.7	1203[x]
United States	2	0.733	(1)	289	66.2	993[x]
Japan	4	0.698	(1)	994	80.8	1007[x]
Republic of Korea	5	0.666	(1)	779	66.7	938[x]
Israel	18	0.514	(1)	74	45.0	918[x]
Brazil	43	0.311	(2)	2	32.9	238

"* To calculate the TAI, a value of zero was used for countries for which data were not available.

** Data refer to 1998.

[x] To calculate the TAI, the value "901" was used as a weighted average value for OECD countries.

Science and technology (S&T) status: (1) Leader   (2) Dynamic adopter   (3) Marginalized

Source:

UNDP, 2001, Human Development Report 2001.

LABOUR FORCE, ANNUAL GROWTH RATE, AND LABOUR-FORCE PARTICIPATION IN ECONOMIC ACTIVITY, BY ARAB COUNTRY/TERRITORY, 1997

	Labour force		Labour-force participation rate in economic activity (%)		
	Total (thousands)	Annual growth rate (%) 1980-1997	Males	Females	Both
Algeria	9416	4.0	46.9	16.7	32.0
Bahrain	260	3.8	62.5	20.6	44.6
Comoros	295	3.2	51.4	39.1	45.3
Djibouti	166	-	-	-	28.4
Egypt	23817	2.6	51.4	22.1	37.0
Iraq	5746	2.9	43.4	10.3	27.1
Jordan	1671	5.3	43.8	13.4	28.9
Kuwait	647	1.6	49.4	24.7	37.4
Lebanon	1068	2.1	49.6	19.1	34.0
Libyan Arab Jamahiriya*	1652	3.4	43.0	12.9	28.6
Mauritania	1100	2.3	52.1	39.9	46.0
Morocco	10748	2.6	51.0	27.1	39.1
Oman	645	3.9	42.9	8.6	26.9
Occupied Palestinian territory	635	5.5	-	-	20.1
Qatar	312	6.6	72.0	22.0	54.9
Saudi Arabia*	6355	4.9	50.3	10.4	32.6
Somalia	4411	2.2	49.4	37.1	43.2
Sudan	10945	2.8	55.7	22.7	39.2
Syrian Arab Republic	4559	3.7	44.5	16.2	30.5
Tunisia	3562	2.9	52.1	23.9	38.2
United Arab Emirates	1150	4.5	67.3	18.9	49.8
Yemen	5163	4.6	45.5	17.7	31.7
Arab region	94323				

* Native and expatriate labour.

Sources:

ILO,1998. World Employment Report 1998-1999: Employability in the Global Economy: How Training Matters, p. 218. Except for occupied Palestinian territoryand Djibouti from other sources.

OPEN UNEMPLOYMENT, BY ARAB COUNTRY/TERRITORY, LATEST AVAILABLE DATA

		Number of unemployed (age 15+)	Unemployment rate (%)	Sources and notes
Algeria	1995	-	29.9	- ILO, World Employment Report 2000, p. 298, French version.
	1997	2049000	26.4	
Bahrain	1997	6147	3.1	- Statistical Collection 1998, Bahrain, Central Bureau of Statistics
	April 2001	9670	-	- Declaration of the Labour Minister, Bahrain, 24\4\2001.
Comoros	-	-	-	
Djibouti	-	-	-	
Egypt	1996	1535000	8.7	- Final results of population census, 1996.
Iraq	-	-	-	
Jordan	1999	172080	14.4	- Annual Report of the Ministry of Labour, 1996.
Kuwait	1999	8917	7.1	- Major characteristics of population and labour force, 30/6/1999, Ministry of Planning.
Lebanon	1997	116058	8.5	- Labour force, 1997, Central Department of Statistics.
Libyan Arab Jamahiriya	1995	119532	11.2	- Statistical Collection of Arab countries, 1998, the Arab League.
Mauritania	-	-	-	
Morocco	1997	-	17.8	- ILO, World Employment Report 2000, p. 298, French version.
	1999	1456000	15.1	- Morocco, Ministry of Planning, Department of Statistics.
	End of 1999	1456000	14.5	- Ministry of Planning- Department of Statistics
Oman	1996	52510	17.2	- Labour force survey for 1996 carried out in December; results shown in 1999-Social statistics, Ministry of Economics.
Occupied Palestinian territory	1996	200000	51	- Palestinian Central Bureau of Statistics.
	1999	79000	11.8	- Abu El-Shokr (The bridges are closed).
Qatar	1997	6564	5.1	- General Census of Population and Houses, 1997, Planning Council.
Saudi Arabia	2001	128590	15.0	- (Among Saudi males) Saudi-American Bank Report, estimated number of unemployed out of labour force, 1996, with a growth rate of 3.3.
Somalia	-	-	-	
Sudan	1996	1250000	17.0	- Immigration and labour-force survey, Northern Sudan, Ministry of Labour.
Syrian Arab Republic	1998	393983	8.9	- Ministry of Labour, official report.
	1999	-	6.5	- Central Statistics Office, 1997.
Tunisia	1996 (18+)	180850	7.2	- ILO, Labour Statistical Yearbook 1999.
	1999 (14+)	490464	15.6	- The National Survey of Population and Employment 1999, the number of unemployed out of active people at 1999, estimated by 3144 (thousands).
United Arab Emirates	1995	335321	2.6	- UAE Annual Statistical Yearbook.
Yemen	1998	340999	8.2	- Statistical Yearbook 1999, Ministry of Planning and Development.

UNEMPLOYMENT AMONG YOUTH AGES 15 TO 24 YEARS, BY
SELECTED ARAB COUNTRY/TERRITORY, VARIOUS YEARS

	Youth unemployment rate (%)			Unemployed youth as share of total unemployed (%)		
	Males	Females	Both	Males	Females	Both
Algeria						
1990	46.2	14.4	38.7	65.0	78.0	66.0
1992	-	-	-	64.8	75.4	65.7
Bahrain						
1990	5.7	6.7	6.0	68.5	68.2	68.4
1995	11.9	13.5	12.6	77.6	71.1	75.4
1997	-	-	-	67.6	58.9	64.7
Egypt						
1990	17.1	43.4	26.4	57.9	66.3	62.5
1995	24.5	59.0	34.4	66.4	70.5	68.4
1998	-	-	-	63.1	59.9	61.5
Lebanon (1997)						
Aged 15-19	29.7	21.6	28.6	-	-	-
Aged 20-24	20.1	11.5	17.8	-	-	-
Morocco (Urban)						
1999	-	-	38.2	41.8	33.1	39.5
Occupied Palestinian territory						
1999	-	-	-	43.0	23.1	42.4
Qatar (1997)						
Citizens	-	-	-	44.2	45.4	44.6
Non-citizens	-	-	-	59.0	61.0	59.6
Syrian Arab Republic						
1998	-	-	-	73.7	71.3	73.2

Sources:

Same sources of unemployment rates by country and year (table 24). Except for Algeria, Bahrain, and Egypt (1990 and 1995): ILO,1999. "Key Indicators Labour Market". Geneva, p. 249.

REAL AND NOMINAL MANUFACTURING WAGES, BY SELECTED ARAB COUNTRIES AND REPUBLIC OF KOREA, 1991-
1996 (1990=100)

Country	1991		1992		1993		1994		1995		1996	
	Nominal	Real	Nominal	Real	Nominal	Real	Nominal	Real	Nominal	Real	Nominal	Real
Algeria*	-	-	100.0	100.0	124.6	102.5	139.0	86.8	162.7	79.1	191.6	77.4
Bahrain	98.1	97.2	90.8	90.3	84.6	82.0	83.7	80.8	-	-	-	-
Egypt	101.9	85.0	114.8	84.3	129.6	84.9	142.6	86.5	155.6	87.0	-	-
Jordan	100.0	92.4	103.5	92.0	106.7	91.9	112.2	93.2	114.6	93.0	-	-
Sudan	-	-	322.4	68.1	-	-	-	-	-	-	-	-
Republic of Korea	116.9	106.9	135.2	116.3	149.9	123.0	173.1	133.9	190.2	140.8	213.5	150.6

* (1992=100)

Source:

ILO, 1999, "Key Indicators of the Labour Market", Geneva, p. 399.

CONSTITUTIONS IN FORCE, BY ARAB COUNTRY/TERRITORY

	Constitutional document	Dates of basic documents and subsequent amendments
Algeria	-	1976, 1988, 1989, 2001
Bahrain	Charter of National Action	1973, 2001
Comoros		
Djibouti	-	-
Egypt	Constitution	1971, 1980
Iraq	Constitution	1990
Jordan	Constitution - National Charter	1952, 1992
Kuwait	Constitution	1962
Lebanon	Constitution	1926, 1996
Libyan Arab Jamahiriya	Declaration of the Establishment of the Authority of the People	1977
Mauritania	Constitution	1991, 1994
Morocco	Constitution	1972, 1992, 1996
Oman	Basic law	1996
Occupied Palestinian territory	-	-
Qatar	-	-
Saudi Arabia	Basic law	1992
Somalia	-	-
Sudan	-	-
Syrian Arab Republic	Constitution	1973
Tunisia	Constitution	1991
United Arab Emirates	-	-
Yemen	Constitution	1996

Source:

Web site: http://www.Constitution Finder.

VOTER PARTICIPATION, BY ARAB COUNTRY/TERRITORY

	Type of election	Date	Rate of participation (%)
Algeria	Presidential	1997	66.30
	Legislative	1999	60.25
Bahrain	Referendum on the National Charter	2001	90.30
Comoros	-		-
Djibouti	-		-
Egypt	People's Assembly	2000	27.50
Iraq	Legislative	2000	83.60
Jordan	Legislative	1989	63.20
	-	1993	68.30
	-	1997	45.45
Kuwait	Council of the Nation	1999	80.00
Lebanon	Legislative	1992	44.00
	-	1996	-
	-	2000	-
Libyan Arab Jamahiriya			-
Mauritania	Presidential	1997	65.60
	Legislative		
Morocco	Legislative	1993	63.70
	-	1997	58.30
Oman	Shura Council	1997	-
Occupied Palestinian territory	National Legislature	1996	90.00
Qatar	Local elections	1999	85.00
Saudi Arabia	-		-
Somalia	-		-
Sudan	Presidential, Legislative	2000	-
Syrian Arab Republic	Legislative	1998	77.80
	Presidential	2000	N.A.
Tunisia	Presidential	1999	89.70
	Legislative	1999	91.50
United Arab Emirates	-		-
Yemen	Legislative	1997	61.00
	Presidential	1999	66.00
	Local	2001	-

Source:

Arab Social Science Research (ASSR) web site.

MAJOR AND BANNED POLITICAL PARTIES, BY ARAB COUNTRY/TERRITORY

	Number of authorized parties	Number of political parties in the government,2000	Number of banned parties
Algeria	37	6	4
Egypt	16	1	10
Iraq	1	1	19
Jordan	36	Non-partisans	-
Lebanon	18	-	-
Libyan Arab Jamahiriya	-	-	10 Exiled groups
Mauritania	-	-	-
Morocco	22	7	1
Occupied Palestinian territory	6	1	-
Sudan	15	1	9 Clandestine groups
Syrian Arab Republic	6	1	6
Tunisia	7	1	9
Yemen	5	2	-

Source:

Banks, Arthur S. and Thomas C. Muller (eds.), Political Handbook of the World, CSA Publication, Binghamton, State University of New York, 1998.

30 POLITICAL PARTICIPATION

STATUS OF FREEDOM OF ASSOCIATIONS, BY ARAB COUNTRY/TERRITORY

	Number of civil societies (year)		Number of professional associations	Number of trade unions	Percentage of elected leaders*
Algeria	-		-	-	-
Bahrain	66	(1992)	10	-	-
Comoros	-		-	-	-
Djibouti	-		-	-	-
Egypt	13239	(1991)	23	23	93.6
Iraq	-		-	-	-
Jordan	587	(1992)	12	17	-
Kuwait	29	(1988)	16	-	-
Lebanon	1302	(1993)	-	-	66.7
Libyan Arab Jamahiriya	-		34	-	-
Mauritania	7	(1988)	-	-	93.4
Morocco	159	(1993)	-	-	-
Oman	16	(1989)	-	Not Auth.	-
Occupied Palestinian territory	444	(1992)	-	-	71.5
Qatar	3	(1988)	-	-	-
Saudi Arabia	125	(1992)	-	Not Auth.	-
Somalia	-		-	-	-
Sudan	262	(1991)	-	13	77.0
Syrian Arab Republic	628	(1992)	-	-	-
Tunisia	5186	(1993)	-	-	91.7
United Arab Emirates	89	(1992)	10	Not Auth.	-
Yemen	223	(1992)	-	-	-

* From a sample of 1,457 societies in 11 Arab countries/territory.

Sources:

Al-Baz, Shaheeda, 1997, Arab People's Organizations on the Eve of the Twenty-first

Century: Determinates of Their Present Reality and Future Prospects. Follow-up

Committee of the Congress of Arab People's Organizations (in Arabic), Cairo, p. 101. Except for a number of civil societies: Nafissa, S. and A. Kandil, 1994, Civil Societies in Egypt. Centre for Strategic and Political Studies of Al-Ahram (in Arabic), Cairo, p. 38

31 POLITICAL PARTICIPATION

ACCESSION TO MAJOR INTERNATIONAL HUMAN RIGHTS CONVENTIONS, BY ARAB COUNTRY/TERRITORY, 2000

	Convention on the Elimination of All Forms of Racial Discrimination	Convention on Civil and Political Rights	Convention on Economic, Social and Cultural Rights	Convention on the Elimination of All Forms of Discrimination against Women	Convention relating to the Status of Refugees	Convention on the Elimination of All Forms of Torture and Other Cruel, Inhuman or Degrading Treatment or Punishment	Convention on the Rights of the Child
Algeria	**	**	**	*	**	**	**
Bahrain	**					**	**
Comoros				**		**	
Djibouti					**		**
Egypt	**	**	**	**	**	**	**
Iraq	**	**	**	**			**
Jordan	**	**	**	**		**	**
Kuwait	**	**	**	**		**	**
Lebanon	**	**	**	**			**
Libyan Arab Jamahiriya	**	**	**	**		**	**
Mauritania	**						**
Morocco	**	**	**	**	**	**	**
Oman							**
Occupied Palestinian territory							
Qatar	**					**	**
Saudi Arabia	**		(**)¹			**	**
Somalia	**	**	**			**	
Sudan	**	**	**		**	*	**
Syrian Arab Republic	**	**	**				**
Tunisia	**	**	**	**	**	**	**
United ArabEmirates	**						**
Yemen	**	**	**	**	**	**	**

* Signature not yet followed by ratification.

** Member State

1 In September 2000, Saudi Arabia ratified the International Convention on the elimination of all forms of discrimination against women.

Sources:

UNDP, 2000, Human Development Report 2000. Except for convention on the refugees' status:

Amnesty International, 2000, Amnesty International Report 2000. London: Amnesty International Publications.

	Government expenditures (% of GDP)		Private investment rate (%)		Public investment rate (%)		Openness rate (%)		Inflation rate (%)	
	1972-84	1985-98	1960-84	1985-98	1960-84	1985-98	1960-84	1985-98	1960-84	1985-98
Algeria	-	-	29	20	12	10	58	45	8	17
Bahrain	33	33	-	-	-	-	219	189	9	0
Comoros	-	-	-	-	-	-	-	-	-	-
Djibouti	-	35	-	-	-	-	-	115	-	-
Egypt	49	36	12	11	13	12	51	51	9	14
Iraq	-	-	-	-	-	-	-	-	-	-
Jordan	-	-	19	18	17	10	121	125	10	6
Kuwait	35	66	-	-	-	-	100	98	7	3
Lebanon	-	34	-	-	-	-	-	92	-	-
Libyan Arab Jamahiriya	-	-	-	-	-	-	90	-	-	-
Mauritania	43	-	15	12	16	10	97	106	-	7
Morocco	33	30	12	12	11	10	46	56	7	5
Oman	-	-	-	-	-	-	97	85	-	-
Occupied Palestinian territory	-	-	-	-	-	-	-	-	5	3
Qatar	-	-	-	-	-	-	96	77	7	1
Saudi Arabia	-	-	-	-	-	-	-	-	-	-
Somalia	-	-	-	-	-	-	-	-	-	-
Sudan	-	-	10	10	5	3	31	15	14	72
Syrian Arab Republic	41	25	-	-	-	-	45	59	8	17
Tunisia	32	34	13	14	15	12	60	86	9	6
United Arab Emirates	-	-	-	-	-	-	107	118	-	-
Yemen	-	32	-	-	-	-	-	61	-	-
Hong Kong	-	-	-	-	-	-	-	-	-	6
Indonesia	20	18	15	21	8	8	12	21	99	11
Malaysia	27	27	18	22	11	12	55	65	4	3
Singapore	20	22	-	-	-	-	89	156	4	2
Republic of Korea	16	17	22	27	6	8	312	362	14	6
Thailand	17	16	20	29	7	8	42	76	6	5
Arab Countries	27	30	16	14	13	9	87	86	12	17
Mixed oil economies	-	-	29	20	12	10	58	45	8	17
Oil economies	34	49	-	-	-	-	118	114	7	2
Diversified economies	39	32	14	14	14	11	65	78	8	10
Primary exports economies	43	33	12	11	10	6	64	74	14	39
East Asia	20	20	19	24	8	9	102	136	25	5
Sub-Saharan Africa	26	30	10	11	10	9	64	70	14	20

Source:

World Bank, Global Development Network Growth Data.

	Percentage of coastal and sea navigable rivers(%)	Population density of 100 km around coastal and sea navigable rivers	% of temperate
Algeria	4	221	6.5
Bahrain	87	985	0
Comoros	-	-	-
Djibouti	95	8	0
Egypt	37	175	0
Iraq	1	178	1.9
Jordan	12	52	10.7
Kuwait	91	96	0
Lebanon	100	337	100.0
Libyan Arab Jamahiriya	10	28	1.4
Mauritania	7	14	0
Morocco	35	117	0.1
Oman	45	7	0
Occupied Palestinian territory	-	-	-
Qatar	96	63	0
Saudi Arabia	11	35	0
Somalia	-	-	-
Sudan	2	15	0
Syrian Arab Republic	12	338	37.5
Tunisia	46	97	0.1
United Arab Emirates	70	37	0
Yemen	37	53	0
Hong Kong	-	-	-
Indonesia	24	453	0
Malaysia	83	528	0
Singapore	76	77	0
Republic of Korea	89	6466	5.8
Thailand	27	170	0
Arab Countries	42	150	8.3
Mixed oil economies	3	200	4.2
Oil economies	59	179	0.2
Diversified economies	40	186	24.7
Primary exports economies	35	23	0
East Asia	60	1539	1.2
Sub-Saharan Africa	27	79	1.8

* Geographic Information System Data (GIS).

HDI, BY ARAB COUNTRY/TERRITORY AND SELECTED REGIONS, 1998

Country	HDI	Population (million)	Life expectancy (years)	Adult literacy rate (%)	Combined gross enrol-ment rate (%)	GDP (billion US$)	GDP per capita (PPP US$)
Algeria	0.68	28.9	69.2	65.5	69	47.3	4792
Bahrain	0.82	0.6	73.1	86.5	81	5.3	13111
Comoros	0.51	0.7	59.2	58.5	39	0.2	1398
Djibouti	0.45	0.6	50.8	62.3	21	0.5*	1266
Egypt	0.62	60.7	66.7	53.7	74	82.7	3041
Iraq	0.58	21.8	63.8	53.7	50	-	3197
Jordan	0.72	4.8	70.4	88.6	69	7.4	3347
Kuwait	0.84	2.3	76.1	80.9	58	25.2	25314
Lebanon	0.74	3.4	70.1	85.1	77	17.2	4326
Libyan Arab Jamahiriya	0.76	5.2	70.2	78.1	92	-	6697
Mauritania	0.45	2.5	53.9	41.2	42	1.0	1563
Morocco	0.59	28.8	67.0	47.1	50	35.5	3305
Oman	0.73	2.3	71.1	68.8	58	15.0	9960
Occupied Palestinian territory	-	-	-	-	-	-	-
Qatar	0.82	0.5	71.9	80.4	74	9.2*	20987
Saudi Arabia	0.75	20.7	71.7	75.2	57	128.9	10158
Somalia	-	-	-	-	-	-	-
Sudan	0.48	29.5	55.4	55.7	34	10.4	1394
Syrian Arab Republic	0.66	15.6	69.2	72.7	59	17.4	2892
Tunisia	0.70	9.3	69.8	68.7	72	20.0	5404
United Arab Emirates	0.81	2.8	75.0	74.6	70	47.2	17719
Yemen	0.45	17.1	58.5	44.1	49	4.3	719
Arab region	0.64	258.0	66.0	59.7	60	473.6	4140
Low HDI	0.42	49.7	50.9	48.8	37	197.0	994
Medium HDI	0.67	202.1	66.9	76.9	65	4779.8	3458
High HDI	0.91	6.2	77.0	98.5	90	23251.2	21799
South Asia	0.56	1364.5	63.0	54.3	52	670.5	2112
World	0.71	5819.8	66.9	78.8	64	28228.1	6526

* Data for 1997.

Sources:

UNDP, 2000, Human Development Report 2000. Except for population: League of Arab States, Arab Fund for Economic and Social Development, Arab Monetary Fund and OAPEC, 2000, "Unified Arab Economic Report, Cairo.

FREEDOM AND INSTITUTIONAL CONSTITUENTS OF WELL-BEING: STANDARDIZED INDICATORS*, BY ARAB COUNTRY/TERRITORY, 19971998

	Voice and accountability	Political instability	Government effectiveness	Regulatory burden	Rule of law	Graft
Algeria	-1.31	-2.42	-1.09	-1.17	-1.10	-0.88
Bahrain	-1.04	-0.08	0.24	0.75	0.67	-0.22
Comoros	0.06	-	-	-	-	-
Djibouti	-0.60	-	-	-0.52	-0.24	-
Egypt	-0.67	-0.07	-0.14	0.12	0.13	-0.27
Iraq	-1.75	-2.25	-1.88	-3.14	-1.84	-1.27
Jordan	0.15	-0.06	0.63	0.42	0.71	0.14
Kuwait	0.00	0.68	-0.06	-0.09	0.91	0.62
Lebanon	-0.40	-0.25	0.17	0.10	0.26	0.40
Libyan Arab Jamahiriya	-1.35	-1.18	-1.32	-2.38	-1.11	-0.88
Mauritania	-0.97	-	-	-0.85	-0.56	-
Morocco	-0.24	0.09	0.27	0.22	0.68	0.13
Oman	-0.57	0.91	0.90	0.31	1.08	0.48
Occupied Palestinian territory	-	-	-	-	-	-
Qatar	-0.78	1.38	0.48	0.33	1.27	0.57
Saudi Arabia	-1.10	0.24	-0.35	-0.15	0.49	-0.58
Somalia	-	-	-	-	-	-
Sudan	-1.50	-1.73	-1.70	-0.83	-1.35	-1.05
Syrian Arab Republic	-1.36	0.08	-1.18	-0.92	-0.29	-0.79
Tunisia	-0.59	0.66	0.63	0.43	0.65	0.02
United Arab Emirates	-0.55	0.83	0.14	0.30	0.77	-0.03
Yemen	-0.42	-1.47	-0.62	-0.52	-1.01	-0.85
Arab region	-0.75	-0.27	-0.29	-0.40	0.01	-0.26
Low HDI	-0.87	-1.60	-1.16	-0.68	-0.79	-0.95
Medium HDI	-0.76	-0.39	-0.31	-0.56	-0.03	-0.32
High HDI	-0.59	0.70	0.20	0.32	0.90	0.24

* These are standardized scores on the standardized normal distribution (the mean is zero and the standard deviation is unity).

Sources:

Indicators calculations based on data from: Kaufmann, D., A. Kraay and P. Zoido-Lobaton, 1999a; "Governance Matters"", Working Paper no. 2195, World Bank, Washington, D.C.; Kaufmann, D.,A. Kraay and P. Zoido-Lobaton, 1999b; ""Aggregating Governance Indicators", World Bank, Washington, D.C., mimeo.

RANKING OF 111 COUNTRIES ON HDI AND AHDI

	HDI ranking 1998	AHDI ranking	Education index, 1998	Internet hosts (per 1,000 peple), 1998	LE, 1998	Freedom scores, 1998	GEM, 1995	Carbon dioxide emissions per capita (million metric tons of carbon equivalent), 1996
Sweden	5	1	0.99	42.86	78.7	1.00	0.76	6.2
Switzerland	12	2	0.93	34.51	78.7	1.00	0.51	6.1
Canada	1	3	0.99	36.94	79.1	1.00	0.66	13.8
Netherlands	7	4	0.99	39.75	78.0	1.00	0.63	10.0
Norway	2	5	0.98	71.75	78.3	1.00	0.75	15.4
New Zealand	18	6	0.98	35.20	77.1	1.00	0.64	8.3
Finland	11	7	0.99	89.17	77.0	1.00	0.72	11.6
Australia	4	8	0.99	40.09	78.3	1.00	0.57	17.0
Austria	15	9	0.95	21.20	77.1	1.00	0.61	7.3
Denmark	13	10	0.97	56.29	75.7	1.00	0.68	10.8
United States	4	11	0.97	112.77	76.8	1.00	0.62	19.7
United Kingdom	9	12	0.99	24.59	77.3	0.98	0.48	9.5
Spain	19	13	0.96	7.79	78.1	0.98	0.45	5.9
France	11	15	0.97	8.57	78.2	0.98	0.43	6.2
Italy	18	15	0.93	6.71	78.3	0.98	0.59	7.1
Belgium	7	16	0.99	20.58	77.3	0.98	0.48	10.5
Ireland	16	17	0.96	15.17	76.6	1.00	0.47	9.8
Japan	8	18	0.94	13.34	80.0	0.98	0.44	9.3
Portugal	24	19	0.92	5.60	75.5	1.00	0.44	4.9
Barbados	25	20	0.91	0.16	76.5	1.00	0.55	3.2
Uruguay	31	21	0.91	4.68	74.1	0.98	0.36	1.8
Luxembourg	15	22	0.89	18.26	76.8	1.00	0.54	20.2
Costa Rica	35	23	0.85	0.85	76.2	0.98	0.47	1.4
Hungary	32	24	0.91	9.41	71.1	0.98	0.51	6.0
Malta	23	25	0.87	4.79	77.3	1.00	0.33	4.8
Bahamas	27	26	0.88	1.63	74.0	0.98	0.53	6.0
Belize	39	27	0.86	1.10	74.9	0.98	0.37	1.6
Cyprus	20	28	0.92	7.94	77.9	0.75	0.39	7.1
Greece	22	29	0.91	4.71	78.2	0.97	0.34	7.7
Poland	33	30	0.92	3.37	72.7	0.98	0.43	9.3
Chile	30	31	0.90	2.03	75.1	0.68	0.40	3.4
Argentina	28	32	0.91	1.84	73.1	0.67	0.42	3.7
Philippines	51	33	0.91	0.13	68.6	0.82	0.44	0.9
Bulgaria	42	34	0.90	1.23	71.3	0.82	0.48	6.5
Panama	40	35	0.85	0.27	73.8	0.82	0.43	2.5
Trinidad and Tobago	36	36	0.84	1.52	74.0	0.98	0.53	17.2
Dominican Republic	57	37	0.79	0.59	70.9	0.83	0.41	1.6
Republic of Korea	26	38	0.95	4.01	72.6	0.83	0.26	9.0
Mauritius	48	39	0.77	0.50	71.6	0.98	0.35	1.5
Colombia	47	40	0.85	0.44	70.7	0.65	0.44	1.8
Guyana	63	41	0.88	0.08	64.8	0.83	0.46	1.1
Fiji	45	42	0.88	0.27	72.9	0.52	0.31	1.0
Singapore	21	43	0.86	21.20	77.3	0.33	0.42	19.5
Romania	44	44	0.88	1.05	70.2	0.83	0.35	5.3
Mexico	37	45	0.84	1.18	72.3	0.65	0.40	3.7
Sri Lanka	55	46	0.83	0.03	73.3	0.65	0.29	0.4
Venezuela	44	47	0.84	0.34	72.6	0.82	0.39	6.5
El Salvador	66	48	0.73	0.14	69.4	0.82	0.40	0.7
Ecuador	59	49	0.85	0.13	69.7	0.82	0.38	2.1
Paraguay	53	50	0.84	0.22	69.8	0.52	0.34	0.7
Nicaragua	74	51	0.66	0.16	68.1	0.82	0.43	0.7
Thailand	50	52	0.84	0.34	68.9	0.82	0.37	3.5
Brazil	49	53	0.84	1.30	67.0	0.65	0.36	1.7
Peru	52	54	0.86	0.19	68.6	0.35	0.40	1.1
Cape Verde	67	55	0.75	0.00	69.2	0.98	0.38	0.3
Honduras	72	56	0.68	0.02	69.6	0.82	0.41	0.7
Solomon Islands	77	57	0.57	0.05	71.9	0.98	0.20	0.4
Cuba	38	58	0.89	0.01	75.8	0.00	0.52	2.8
Malaysia	42	59	0.79	2.16	72.2	0.33	0.38	5.8
Bolivia	73	60	0.80	0.08	61.8	0.97	0.34	1.3
Samoa (Western)	61	61	0.75	0.01	71.7	0.82	0.31	0.8
Botswana	78	62	0.74	0.42	46.2	0.83	0.41	1.4
Maldives	58	63	0.89	0.38	65.0	0.18	0.29	1.1
Guatemala	76	64	0.61	0.08	64.4	0.65	0.39	0.6

	HDI ranking 1998	AHDI ranking	Education index, 1998	Internet hosts (per 1,000 peple), 1998	LE, 1998	Freedom scores, 1998	GEM, 1995	Carbon dioxide emissions per capita (million metric tons of carbon equivalent), 1996
Swaziland	71	65	0.76	0.29	60.7	0.20	0.36	0.4
Suriname	46	66	0.89	0.00	70.3	0.65	0.35	4.9
Turkey	56	67	0.76	0.73	69.3	0.48	0.23	2.9
Jordan	60	68	0.82	0.06	70.4	0.48	0.23	2.5
Indonesia	69	69	0.79	0.07	65.6	0.20	0.36	1.2
Kuwait	29	70	0.73	3.44	76.1	0.35	0.24	25.3
Ghana	82	71	0.60	0.01	60.4	0.67	0.31	0.2
China	64	72	0.79	0.01	70.1	0.02	0.47	2.8
Lebanon	54	73	0.82	0.74	70.1	0.18	0.21	4.6
United Arab Emirates	34	74	0.73	7.61	75.0	0.18	0.24	36.3
Nepal	91	75	0.46	0.01	57.8	0.65	0.32	0.1
Zimbabwe	84	76	0.81	0.08	43.5	0.35	0.40	1.6
Papua New Guinea	85	77	0.54	0.03	58.3	0.82	0.23	0.6
Benin	101	78	0.40	0.00	53.5	0.83	0.27	0.1
Morocco	79	79	0.48	0.07	67.0	0.35	0.27	1.0
India	81	80	0.55	0.01	62.9	0.82	0.23	1.1
Mozambique	107	81	0.37	0.01	43.8	0.65	0.35	0.1
Bangladesh	93	83	0.39	0.00	58.6	0.80	0.29	0.2
Malawi	104	83	0.64	0.00	39.5	0.82	0.26	0.1
Zambia	99	84	0.67	0.03	40.5	0.35	0.27	0.3
Comoros	88	85	0.52	0.01	59.2	0.35	0.16	0.1
Mali	105	86	0.34	0.00	53.7	0.67	0.24	0.0
Haiti	96	87	0.40	0.00	54.0	0.48	0.35	0.2
Guinea Bissau	108	88	0.36	0.01	44.9	0.64	0.33	0.2
Senegal	100	89	0.36	0.02	52.7	0.50	0.27	0.4
Pakistan	87	90	0.44	0.02	64.4	0.48	0.15	0.7
Burkina Faso	111	91	0.22	0.02	44.7	0.35	0.28	0.1
Egypt	75	92	0.60	0.04	66.7	0.17	0.24	1.5
Tunisia	65	93	0.70	0.00	69.8	0.18	0.25	1.8
Togo	92	94	0.57	0.03	49.0	0.18	0.18	0.2
Cameroon	86	95	0.64	0.00	54.5	0.03	0.34	0.3
Central African Republic	106	96	0.38	0.00	44.8	0.65	0.21	0.1
Algeria	68	97	0.67	0.00	69.2	0.18	0.27	3.3
Gambia	103	98	0.37	0.01	47.4	0.03	0.32	0.2
Djibouti	95	99	0.49	0.01	50.8	0.33	0.13	0.6
Islamic Republic of Iran	63	101	0.73	0.00	69.5	0.17	0.24	3.8
Ethiopia	110	101	0.33	0.00	43.4	0.50	0.21	0.0
Equatorial Guinea	84	102	0.76	0.00	50.4	0.00	0.25	0.4
Syrian Arab Republic	70	103	0.68	0.00	69.2	0.00	0.29	3.1
Burundi	109	104	0.38	0.00	42.7	0.02	0.34	0.0
Sudan	90	105	0.48	0.00	55.4	0.00	0.22	0.1
Côte d'Ivoire	99	106	0.43	0.02	46.9	0.20	0.16	0.9
Nigeria	97	107	0.55	0.00	50.1	0.20	0.20	0.7
Mauritania	94	108	0.41	0.01	53.9	0.18	0.16	1.3
Angola	102	109	0.36	0.00	47.0	0.17	0.28	0.4
Iraq	80	110	0.52	0.00	63.8	0.00	0.39	4.4
Congo	89	111	0.74	0.00	48.9	0.03	0.21	1.9

GDP PER CAPITA, BY ARAB COUNTRY/TERRITORY, 1999

	GDP per capita	HDI category (high/medium/low)
	(PPP US$)	
Bahrain	13688	High
Kuwait	-	High
United Arab Emirates	18162	High
Qatar	-	High
Libyan Arab Jamahiriya	-	Medium
Lebanon	4705	Medium
Saudi Arabia	10815	Medium
Oman	-	Medium
Jordan	3955	Medium
Tunisia	5957	Medium
Syrian Arab Republic	4454	Medium
Algeria	5063	Medium
Egypt	3420	Medium
Morocco	3419	Medium
Comoros	1429	Medium
Yemen	806	Low
Djibouti	-	Low
Sudan	-	Low
Iraq	-	-
Occupied Palestinian territory	-	-
Somalia	-	-

Sources:
UNDP, 2000, Human Development Report 2000. Except for GEM:
UNDP, 1995, Human Development Report 1995; freedom
scores: Freedom House, 1999. ""Annual Survey of Freedom,
Country scores 1972-73 to 1998-99"". Freedom House web site,
visited on 11 February 1999; and Arabic human development
indicator (AHDI): Report team calculations.